WHAT IS THE FUT
OF SOCIAL WO

Edited by
Michael Lavalette

With a foreword by
Peter Dowd

P

First published in Great Britain in 2019 by

Policy Press
University of Bristol
1-9 Old Park Hill
Bristol
BS2 8BB
UK
t: +44 (0)117 954 5940
pp-info@bristol.ac.uk
www.policypress.co.uk

North America office:
Policy Press
c/o The University of Chicago Press
1427 East 60th Street
Chicago, IL 60637, USA
t: +1 773 702 7700
f: +1 773-702-9756
sales@press.uchicago.edu
www.press.uchicago.edu

British Library Cataloguing in Publication Data
A catalogue record for this book is available from the British Library

Library of Congress Cataloging-in-Publication Data
A catalog record for this book has been requested

978-1-4473-4081-2 hardback
978-1-4473-4082-9 paperback
987-1-4473-4083-6 ePub
978-1-4473-4097-3 ePDF

Cover design by Andrew Corbett
Front cover image: Alamy
Printed and bound in Great Britain by CMP, Poole
Policy Press uses environmentally responsible print partners

Contents

List of figures and tables

Figures

Tables

Notes on contributors

Peter Beresford OBE is Professor of Citizen Participation at the University of Essex and Emeritus Professor of Social Policy at Brunel University London. He is a long-term user/survivor of mental health services and co-chair of Shaping Our Lives, the independent UK disabled people's and service users' organisation (www. shapingourlives. org.uk/). He has a long-standing interest in issues of participation as researcher, writer, campaigner, educator and service user. He is author of *A Straight-Talking Introduction to Being a Mental Health Service User* (PCCS Books, 2010) and his latest book is *Madness, Violence, and Power: A Critical Collection* (University of Toronto Press, 2019, co-edited with Andrea Daley and Lucy Costa).

Brid Featherstone qualified as a social worker in the early 1980s and worked in the areas of juvenile justice and generic social work as a practitioner and manager. Since 1992 she has been involved in higher education as a lecturer and researcher. She has been involved in a number of international research projects on gender issues in child welfare and was a member of the team on the project Fathers Matter, a six-year research programme on fathers' engagement with social work and social care services. With Kate Morris and Sue White she has written the influential and widely discussed book, *Re-imagining Child Protection: Towards Humane Social Work with Families* (Policy Press).

Iain Ferguson has worked in social work education from the early 1990s; before that he worked for many years as a community worker and social worker in a range of different settings in the west of Scotland. These included area teams, a lone parent groupwork project and a psychiatric hospital, where he qualified as a Mental Health Officer. He is a founder member of the Social Work Action Network and a founding editor of *Critical and Radical Social Work: An International Journal*. His most recent books are *Politics of the Mind: Marxism and Mental Distress* (Bookmarks, 2017) and (with Michael Lavalette and Vasilios Ioakimidis) *Global Social Work in Political Context* (Policy Press, 2017). He retired from the University of the West of Scotland in 2014.

John Harris is Emeritus Professor at the University of Warwick and works at Coventry University. Before becoming an academic, he worked for 15 years in local authority social work, where he was secretary of the shop stewards committee and, for the last five years, a district manager. One of his interests has been the changing nature of social work under neoliberalism, in the UK and elsewhere, an interest that has been pursued in publications such as *The Social Work Business* Routledge, 2003) and *Modernising Social Work: Critical Considerations* (Policy Press, 2009). He is the co-editor (with Vicky White) of the *Oxford Dictionary of Social Work and Social Care* (2nd edn, 2018).

Chris Jones was born in 1951 in England. He is very much a child of the British welfare state that was put into place between 1946 and 1950. One of the most tangible benefits was free education, which included his years in state schools and then into higher education. It also gave him a career in teaching and research, latterly as Professor of Social Work at Liverpool University, which he terminated in 2006 when he moved to Samos, a Greek island in the eastern Aegean close to the Turkish coast. On Samos, he continues to work with Tony Novak and a new collaborator, Sofiane Ait Chalalet. Together they work with refugees and write to share their experiences on their blog, Samos Chronicles.

Michael Lavalette is Professor in Social Work and Head of the School of Social Sciences at Liverpool Hope University. He was a founding member of the Social Work Action Network and is co-editor of *Critical and Radical Social Work: An International Journal*. He has written and edited a total of 17 books and numerous academic papers. His most recent books are (with Steve Cunningham) *Schools Out! The Hidden History of School Student Strikes* (Bookmarks, 2016) and (with Iain Ferguson and Vasilios Ioakimidis) *Global Social Work in Political Context* (Policy Press, 2017). He is Editor-in-Chief of the journal *Critical and Radical Social Work*, published by Policy Press.

Mark Lymbery is an Honorary Associate Professor in Social Work at the University of Nottingham. He has published numerous books and articles that focus on the practice of social work, especially with older people and adults. Particularly pertinent in respect of this is a recent book (written with Karen Postle), *The Social Work Role in Transforming Adult Social Care: Perpetuating a Distorted Vision?* (Policy Press, 2015).

Gurnam Singh is currently Principal in Social Work at Coventry University and Visiting Professor of Social Work at the University of Chester. Prior to entering academia in 1993, he worked as a professional social worker and community activist. He completed his PhD from the University of Warwick in 2004 on anti-racist social work. Gurnam has developed an extensive academic profile over the past 25 years. He has presented over 100 papers at national and international conferences, many as an invited keynote speaker, and contributed as single or joint author to over 50 books, articles, research reports and blogs.

Jan Walmsley is an independent researcher and teacher, with the honorary title of Visiting Chair History of Learning Disabilities at the Open University. She is best known for work in two linked areas: inclusive research with people with learning disabilities and the history of learning disability. While working at the Open University in the 1990s, she founded the Social History of Learning Disability Research Group to pioneer inclusive approaches to rediscovering the history of learning disabilities, drawing on the memories and reflections of people with learning disabilities, families and people who worked in the system. The Research Group celebrated its 21st birthday in 2015, and continues to flourish, holding inclusive conferences every year.

Editor's acknowledgements

I would like to take this opportunity to thank all the contributors to this book. Unusually, I required two things from them: deliver a talk in Liverpool to local social workers and write up the talk into a suitable chapter. Each delivered their talk with great aplomb – and their manuscript on time!

At Policy Press Isobel Bainton and Shannon Kneis were both incredibly helpful and supportive in making sure the book got into its final form.

I'd also like to thank my colleagues in the social work section at Liverpool Hope University. They embraced the idea for a series of 'distinguished lectures' by eminent social work professors and helped to ensure each event was well attended by staff, local practitioners, social work students and by service users. In my time at Liverpool Hope (an unbelievably quick ten years) they have worked to establish our programmes in the area and develop programmes and research agendas which are shaped by a commitment to a more egalitarian and radical social work practice.

At the end of 2018, my close friend and comrade for many, many years, Iain Ferguson, retired from the leadership of the Social Work Action Network, and from a more active role on the journal *Critical and Radical Social Work*. We have written together about social policy and social work for close to 25 years – and have done so while involving ourselves in a range of social movement networks, groups, marches and activities. Although he will continue to write and research in the area of 'mental health' and social work, I want to take this opportunity to thank him for his friendship and intellectual endeavour!

Foreword

Peter Dowd
Member of Parliament for Bootle
Shadow Chief Secretary to the Treasury

The great reforming Labour Government of 1945 set out to address the 'five giants' – the five great social problems – that had been a blight on British society in the interwar years: unemployment, ill-health, poor education, bad housing and poverty. It tackled these problems head-on by setting up the post-war welfare state. The result was a dramatic improvement in the lives of ordinary people: better education, better standard of living, better housing and health care, secure employment and, as a result, improved life expectancy, healthier lives and more time and money to spend on consumer goods. The result, to quote Conservative Prime Minister Harold Macmillan, was that we had 'never had it so good'!

The social work profession was always a central part of the developing welfare state. After the Kilbrandon and Seebohm Reports social work and social service departments became integral parts of the welfare system – with social workers as key state employees, hired to help people navigate their way through the system, and help and support them as they decided to bring about change to their lives.

The vision of 1945 – of an integrated welfare system, geared to meet the needs of 'the many, not the few' – has, however, been under concerted attack over the best part of forty years. Ideas of 'marketisation', consumerism, privatisation and individualism have been used to erode the commitment to a welfare system that can be accessed as a right of citizenship.

This timely book looks at the impact of this process on social work. Each of the authors is a well-known, leading social work academic. Each has turned their attention to what has happened to social work (broadly understood to include the service, the profession and the people who use services). Each tells a tale of huge potential, of the strengths that social work brings to help and support people at times of difficulty and change. But each also traces how this potential has been made more difficult to fulfil and the task more challenging by a combination of government interference, privatisation of the welfare state and austerity. The book could be depressing: a litany of government failure and its impact on people's lives. Yet each author has provided a few answers to the difficult question: what is to be done? Each offers short, medium and longer-term solutions to the problems social work and social work service users face.

Before I became an MP I worked in health and social care for over 35 years. I am a qualified social worker and have worked in some of the poorest parts of Liverpool. I firmly believe that social work, at its best, is a powerful force for change and for good.

As a former practitioner, I recognise intimately many of the issues the authors cover here. I was always aware of the important role social workers played in helping, supporting and guiding people through our welfare system and supporting people as they tried to bring about change to their lives. But I was always aware of the societal barriers that hindered people at points of crisis and conflict in their lives.

The writers gathered here call out for social work to be taken seriously; for social workers – in practice and in the academy – to be listened to; for the voices of service users to be included in debates about the future of welfare delivery; of the urgent need to, once again, see welfare services as a fundamental social right of citizenship.

The chapters in this book, taken together, challenge politicians: how can we save and promote an engaged social work that works 'for the many'?

Introduction: what is the future of social work?

Michael Lavalette

This volume brings together a number of the UK's most eminent social work professors to ask: *what is the future of social work?* Social work is regularly deemed to be 'in crisis' but after four decades of neoliberalism and ten years of austerity what is left of social work? Or at least, what is left of the dream that the social work profession, adequately funded, could provide a range of ways of working that supported individuals, families and communities during times of trouble? What happened to the expectation that the social work profession could guide people through the intricacies of the welfare and benefit systems offering empathy, hope and (financial) support when vulnerable people made the decision that they wanted to bring about change in their lives? What happened to the dream that social work could be a profession that stood shoulder to shoulder with some of the poorest and most marginalised people in our society and was prepared to 'speak truth to power', so that the voices of the marginalised could be heard, their perspectives and 'knowledge from experience' considered? Are these aspirations still relevant in the twenty-first century? Or have the years of neoliberalism, managerialism and welfare service retrenchment undermined the profession – increasingly turning it into 'a job', reduced to a series of 'skills' that can be undertaken by almost anyone, that implement government policies, often in ways that damage those we work with?

These questions shape the contributions to this volume. The book developed out of a series of distinguished lectures held at Liverpool Hope University in academic year 2016/17. Thanks to Policy Press we knew the lectures would become book chapters, so each lecture included time for reflection and contributions from the floor, with the intention that those would be filtered into the final chapters.

First a brief note about the contributors. Each has been involved in the social work field for a considerable number of years. They draw on both their practice and their academic experience – as long-term social work academic leaders within UK social work. Each is well known in the field, each has an established reputation and each is recognised for the rigour of their research and analysis.

For the early chapters (Featherstone, Lymbery, Ferguson) the lectures and the book chapters were asked to do three things: to consider 'how we got here', to reflect on what are the contemporary problems in their field, and, finally, to consider 'what is to be done'.

By asking each author to think about 'How we got here' the intention was to develop a brief overview of their area of specialism – child protection (Featherstone), adult social work (Lymbery), or mental health (Ferguson). The contemporary situation required them to look at the impact of welfare cuts, austerity, changes to social work practice and their impact on service users. Finally, they were asked to turn to the question 'what is to be done?', prompting them to consider both immediate and longer term solutions to crisis in their area.

The next three chapters (Walmsley, Beresford, Singh), deal less with areas of service provision than with service user groups, with each author asked to consider the lessons that social work needs to embrace from practise in the fields of learning disabilities (Walmsley), service user engagement (Beresford) and anti-racist social work (Singh). The argument was simple. Whatever is 'to be done' must consider the needs, perspectives and knowledge bases of carers, service users and those committed to all manner of anti-oppressive working.

The final two chapters look at vital issues facing social work today. First Harris develops his work assessing the social work labour process. If social work is to maintain its 'professional status' and not simply become a welfare processing 'job' then what happens on the social work frontline is crucial. In the 1970s, in the wake of the Seebohm report, social work offices were often termed 'Seebohm factories', suggesting that social work was increasingly like a 'job' or factory. Harris argues this was always an exaggeration, but he suggests today's social work labour process is undergoing rapid processes of transformation (breaking down of tasks, control over the work process, managerialism, managerial control embodied in IT systems and so on) which sociologist Harry Braverman highlighted as being part of the 'the degradation of work' in the twentieth century. In other words, recent transformations are making social work, less 'professional' and more 'job-like'.

Finally, Chris Jones reflects on his recent work experiences supporting refugees on Samos. It leads him to consider what are the key aspects of a humane social work – and this poses the question about how we can demand that 'humane work' becomes embedded in all our practice. A concluding chapter tries to draw some of the lessons together and assert what a progressive, contemporary social work could look like.

1

Austerity and the context of social work today

Michael Lavalette

Introduction: social work in crisis

A recurrent theme over the last 40 years, broadly covering the move away from 'classic' welfare statism to the neoliberal period in British politics, has been the perceived 'crisis in social work'. At times this has been focused on a claim that the profession is too concerned with 'political correctness', rather than carrying out statutory state duties (Philpot 2000). Occasionally, it is deemed to be a 'failing profession' because of its perceived role (whether central or marginal) in a case involving the death of a child (Corby 2005). While, at times, politicians generate the crisis by attacking social work as an 'easy target', often alongside an attack on welfare recipients (especially benefit recipients), to play to their support base (SWAN 2013).

Of course, in the debates generated around each of these examples, there may be elements or aspects of social work theory or practice that we can reflect upon, learn from and improve. We do not need to be defensive. We should be much more assertive about what we do right and open to the idea that we can improve some aspects of our activities. But this notwithstanding, the impression is that social work is always in some form of crisis situation – and, at heart, this opens up questions about the nature and viability of what we might term 'the social work project' (the possibility of an actively engaged profession, committed to working alongside, and in support of, individuals and communities striving to bring change to their lives and environment).

At present this sense of crisis is more entrenched than ever. Ten years of austerity and 30 years of significant welfare transformation (if we date this from the 1987 Conservative Manifesto commitment to introduce internal markets into health and social care via what would become the NHS and Community Care Act 1990) have made life far more difficult for social work service users, reduced the scope for practitioners to intervene in meaningful ways to support vulnerable people, embedded market forms of delivery onto the 'social work business' and, as a consequence, opened up significant debate over the nature and task of contemporary social work.

This book is a contribution to the debate over the future of social work – and this chapter starts by outlining some of the 'macro' issues confronting contemporary social work in the UK. In no small measure this context is one that is shaped by austerity. So this chapter asks 'Is austerity inevitable?' and then looks at how it has shaped British society and how it has transformed our welfare system.

I start, however, by asking whether the austerity crisis is, in fact, a UK-wide crisis, or something peculiar, or more acute, within England (and, to a lesser extent, Wales). It is sometimes suggested that the situation in Scotland, post-devolution, is significantly different to that operating in the rest of the UK (rUK). Recently Smith and Cree (2018: 1) have argued: 'Scotland and England are going in different political and, arguably, social and cultural directions and social welfare is one arena in which these divergent agendas are played out.' So the first issue I address is the extent to which austerity is impacting differently on the differing component parts of the UK.

A crisis in England?

One response to the crisis in social work and welfare is to see this as a peculiarly English (or English and Welsh) problem, but not one that is UK-wide because of the impact of devolution in Scotland (see Cree 2018). Scotland has always had a separate and distinct legal and education system, but in September 1997 people in Scotland voted for devolution. The Scotland Act (1998) led to the creation of the Scottish Parliament that has sat since 1999. The Scotland Act 'reserved' powers for the UK Parliament, but this allowed the Scottish Parliament to make law in other, non-reserved, areas. The Scotland Act has been amended in various ways since 1998, most notably with the Scotland Act (2012) and the Scotland Act (2016). These latter two pieces of legislation have strengthened the position of the Scottish Parliament over issues of taxation and welfare, in particular. The non-reserved areas include, among others, health, abortion, Scots law, local government, policing, prison services, housing and related benefits, and social work. The government has some (limited) tax raising powers (BBC 2016), but some social work related areas, such as social security, are 'reserved'.

These changes have certainly introduced greater variation across the UK welfare system than was previously the case (Smith and Cree

4

2018). It is noticeable, for example, that in some popular areas of welfare delivery the system in Scotland is significantly more generous than is the case south of the border. In Scotland prescriptions are free, university students don't pay fees, and 'free personal care' is available for anyone over the age of 65 who has been assessed by the local authority as needing it (and this covers services such as assistance with personal hygiene, food and diet, mobility). Even before devolution, the creation of separate NHS trusts and foundation trusts were resisted in Scotland, as was GP fundholding and its subsequent variations. Post-devolution, the NHS in Scotland looks increasingly different to its counterpart in England, as it puts an emphasis on integrated health and social care (rather than market provision of services) as the solution to meeting patient needs (Hudson 2012). More specifically, in social work, BA Social Work education and training courses are four years in Scotland (like all honours degrees) and three years in England; probation remains a key part of social work in Scotland, but has almost disappeared in England; adult social care is significantly different, and child protection, via the Children's Panel System, has always been different. Though there is social work specialisation in Scotland, there is still an emphasis on genericism, while in England there is a greater shift towards specialisation both on training courses (on university courses and also via Step-Up, Frontline and Think Ahead) and in practice.

The differences are significant, but it would be wrong to suggest that devolution has brought about a break with either austerity or the main government drivers towards welfare restructuring and opening up public services to private providers. For example, free personal social care for over 65s is a legal right, but local authorities have met this requirement by cutting deeper into other areas of social and public spending (Bell 2018). In Scotland various Private Finance Initiative (PFI) projects (primarily to fund hospital, school and road building programmes) have produced dividends for private investors in excess of £430m over the last decade (Borland 2018) and though the Scottish government has stopped any new PFI agreements under the 'Scottish Futures Trust' (SFT), the 'Non-Profit Distributing model' still ties government projects to for-profit providers. Indeed contracts awarded under the SFT have been heavily criticised for their secrecy and the fact that 'private lenders were given unduly generous deals'. Looking at 42 recent deals for projects including secondary schools, GP surgeries, a blood transfusion service HQ and three motorway upgrades, Carrell (2017) notes that 'Their construction cost a total of £2.6bn but over their lifetime the projects will cost £7.6bn due to maintenance contracts lasting from 25–30 years, management fees and interest of up to 11.3% on borrowing.'

It is not just in its relationship with the market, and for-profit providers of public services, that Scotland remains similar to rUK. In Scotland, levels of poverty remain entrenched. Almost one in four children (230,000) are officially recognised as living in poverty, causes being a mixture of low wages, underemployment, worklessness and inadequate social security benefits (CPAG in Scotland 2018). Inequality is also growing in Scotland. According to a study carried out by Oxfam (2017),

> [the] richest 10% of the Scottish population live in households with a net income of more than £912 per week. In contrast, the equivalent figure for the poorest 10% is less than £240. The figure is above £2,608 per week for the richest 1%. ... Wealth inequality in Scotland is even starker. The ... wealthiest 10% own 9.4 times more household wealth than the bottom 40% put together.

At the end of 2018, there were trade union disputes in teaching and social care in Scotland, marked by both strikes and demonstrations against the impact of austerity imposed by the national UK government and the Scottish Parliament. Interestingly, the SNP council in Glasgow threatened legal action against the local government workers' union Unison for the use of 'illegal' pickets during the dispute, emphasising their willingness to use 'anti-union' legislation introduced by the Conservative government in London (Carrell 2018).

In devolved Scotland, the Scottish Parliament, and the SNP administration that has governed either in coalition or on its own since 2007, has often spoken out about the impact of austerity, but it has failed to significantly counter its impacts and consequences. Scotland, it would seem, is not the social democratic haven it is sometimes portrayed as! As Smith and Cree (2018: 2) note:

> Scotland is hardly a land of milk and honey; political ambitions are curtailed not only by 'austerity' measures, but also by what might be identified as an innate conservatism on the part of government – there is no real challenge to dominant neo-liberal or managerial paradigms.

The conclusion is, perhaps, that there are significant, and growing, differences between Scotland and rUK in terms of welfare provisions.

Nevertheless, they continue to face similar economic problems, have politicians who posit similar solutions to those problems and in both Scotland and rUK the politics of austerity continue to impact on services, workers and people in dramatic ways.

A crisis of austerity?

Much of the framing for contemporary debates on social work relate to the impact of austerity on workers, services and service users. It's necessary to unpick some of the debates around the 'politics of austerity'.

On 15 September 2008 the Wall Street investment bank Lehman Brothers crashed. It was a stark example of the financial crisis that had been developing, especially in the US, since 2007 as more and more banks discovered they could not balance their books. The roots of the banking crisis were in the US housing market, where soft loans had been offered to poor working families to enable them to buy homes (or perhaps more accurately, get mortgages on homes they were never likely to own). As those mortgage holders struggled to pay off their mortgage debts, repossessions increased and the 'bad debt' was passed on and up the financial system through the activities of banks, financial institutions and hedge funds. The bad debt in the system produced a credit crunch, as banks stopped lending to each other.

By 2008 the credit crunch had turned into a full-blown economic crash, spreading from the financial system to the main centres of manufacturing, production and service delivery. It marked the deepest recession experienced in the UK, and much of the western world, since the Second World War (Harman 2009). Indeed, Roberts (2016) argues that the recession of 2007/08 can now be identified as the start of a 'long depression', one of three great depressions that have marked modern capitalism (and hence are different in length and intensity from capitalism's regular and recurring slumps and recessions). These three great depressions were in 1873–1897, 1929–1939 and now the depression that started in 2008 which, as yet, shows no end point.

In 2008, as panic set in, governments across the globe poured resources into the banks and key manufacturing sectors (like the car industry) in the hope of stopping the unfolding crisis. As a result government debts ballooned. At its peak the UK government provided support for the UK banking and finance sector of £1,162bn (NAO 2018). The 'quantitative easing' that governments initiated did not stop the recession, but it did produce a government debt crisis, which governments across the globe responded to by adopting the politics of 'austerity': a commitment to rapid reduction of government spending to reduce both deficit and debt.

The government debt crisis is rooted in the actions of politicians to support and bail out failing banks and industry, not in the costs of welfare delivery or public spending. However, in country after country it was claimed that the credit crunch had revealed a system of overgenerous social and public spending. It was claimed that governments had to introduce economic and social policies that reduced the 'structural deficit' and tackled debt; and in these circumstance 'there is no alternative' to welfare retrenchment: the restructuring of welfare and public services to reduce reliance on government spending. This approach was followed by the Labour government under Gordon Brown (2007–2010), the Conservative-Lib Dem coalition under David Cameron (2010–2015), and the Conservative governments of Cameron (2015–2016) and Theresa May (2016–present).

From 2007 to the present, each of the governments/parties has told us the debt was unsustainable, needed to be repaid quickly and the main mechanism to do this was by reducing government net borrowing (the deficit).

Government debt and deficit are not the same thing. Debt is how much a government owes banks, other countries and various other lenders. Those debts have sometimes been in place for many years. The UK government, for example, is still paying off debts accrued during the First World War and only finally paid off debts to the US and Canadian governments from Second World War loans at the end of 2006 (BBC 2006). Government deficit is how much a government has to borrow to cover its spending commitments; it covers the gap between its spending compared to how much money it is bringing in (via taxation, for example). Each year in which a government runs a deficit, it adds to its net debt. So debt and deficit are linked, but are not the same. For ten years governments in the UK have cut spending to reduce the deficit.

> In the financial year ending March 2018, the UK general government deficit was £40.7 billion, equivalent to 2.0% of gross domestic product (GDP). This … was the lowest since the financial year ending March 2002 when it was 0.4%. (ONS 2018b)

Figure 1.1 shows the UK government deficit (as a percentage of GDP) from 1995 and the decline in the deficit since 2010. After ten years

Figure 1.1: UK general government net borrowing ('deficit') as a percentage of GDP, 1995–2018

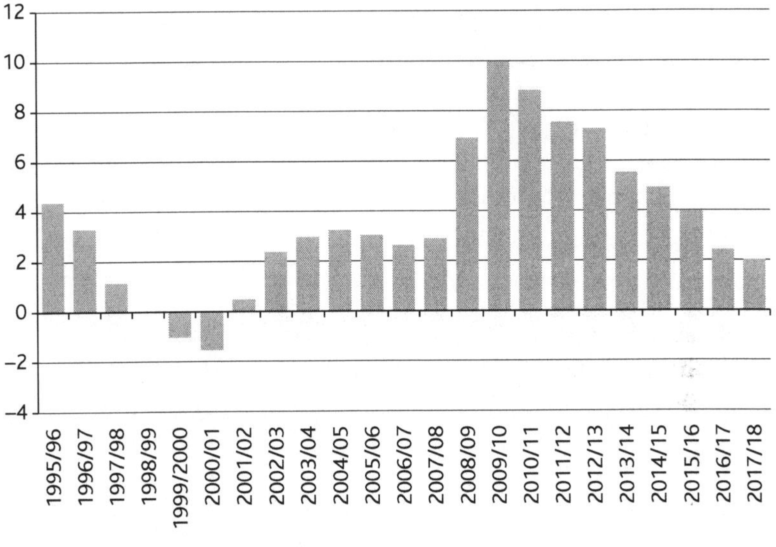

Source: ONS 2018b

of hard austerity, however, the UK government is still running an annual deficit.

Reducing the deficit has been the main policy goal of UK governments since 2010. But there are lots of ways to do it.

From 2010 UK governments focused on cutting public spending, especially those areas related to welfare spending. According to the House of Commons library, it is estimated that 'by 2021, £37bn less will be spent on working-age social security compared with 2010':

> just under half the total savings will come from the freezing of most working-age benefit levels since 2016 ... Some of the most striking cuts are in disability benefits – personal independence payments (PIP) and employment and support allowance (ESA) – which together will have shrunk by nearly £5bn, or by 10%, since the start of the decade. ... Other cuts include: tax credits (£4.6bn), universal credit (£3.6bn), child benefit (£3.4bn), disability benefits (£2.8bn), ESA and incapacity benefit (£2bn) and housing benefit (£2.3bn). (Butler 2018)

To cut the deficit, successive governments have launched cuts year after year in public sector funding. These have led to reduced local authority spending on public services (Asthana 2017), have severely cut welfare benefit spending (Ryan 2017), and have reduced resources in the housing, health and educational spheres (IFS 2015) – in turn leading to work intensification for public sector workers (Ellis 2017) – and led to a significant tightening in living standards (Wright and Case 2017). The direct impact of austerity can be seen in recent work done by Fitzpatrick and colleagues (2018) for the Joseph Rowntree Foundation, which found that about 1.25 million people in the UK are currently living in destitution where they are unable to buy the essentials needed to eat, remain warm and ensure personal hygiene. It is the politics of austerity that has led to the appalling institutionalisation of food banks within the UK welfare state (Garthwaite 2016). Harrop and Reed (2015) estimate that 2 million more children in England will be living in poverty by 2030 if current policy trajectories remain the same. By choosing to make cuts in these areas of public spending, UK governments have significantly increased 'social harm' (Cooper and Whyte 2017).

There were (and are) alternatives. For example, it would have been possible for the government to reduce the deficit by cutting spending in other areas. For example, they could have protected welfare spending and made cuts to defence budgets; the UK has the fifth largest defence budget in the world (BBC 2018) and, in addition, in 2016 it committed itself to renewal of the Trident nuclear missile programme at an estimated cost of £205bn over the next 30 years (MacAskill 2016).

Alternatively, it could reduce the deficit by increasing its revenues. There are a number of ways of doing this. For example, the government could invest to create good quality 'green jobs', hence reducing welfare payments to people formally out of work and increasing the tax take from the direct tax and National Insurance payments of those with the new jobs in this sector (CCC 2014). In addition, it could address the problem of tax avoidance. It is estimated that the UK loses about £2.2bn each year through tax avoidance (Buchan 2017). And income could be increased by raising corporation taxes – which have been cut from 28 per cent to 17 per cent in the last ten years (Tax Justice UK 2018).

There are potentially lots of ways of reducing government deficit. The key thing for us to note is that the cuts that have taken place are not inevitable, but the result of political choice. And, of course, for social workers these choices have made the lives of service users much harder, increased poverty and a range of social problems, threatened services to the most vulnerable – and cut the resources available to practitioners to support people in need.

The government's failure (in its terms) to eradicate the deficit means that it continues to add to the national debt – the national debt is greater today than it was when 'austerity' started.

How great a problem is the 'debt crisis'?

In 2007/08 the banking crisis led to the UK government pouring vast sums into the banking sector to 'stabilise' the system. As a consequence UK government debt increased dramatically. In 2010, the incoming coalition government's Chancellor of the Exchequer, George Osborne, argued that the debt was so severe that urgent measures were necessary to bring it down within one government term of office (five years), the justification for the harsh austerity programme initiated by the Conservative-Lib Dem coalition.

One of the problems facing laypeople when discussing the debt is the scale of the sums involved – in many ways they are beyond our comprehension. We may have some concept of a hundred pounds (some item of clothing, perhaps), a thousand pounds (a new racing bicycle, for example), or even several hundred thousand pounds (a new house) but conceptualising a million, a billion or a trillion pounds is much more difficult. The numbers seem immense. And because of the bank bailout in 2010 the figures were increasing fast. In 2005 the UK National Debt was less that £0.5 trillion. After the banking and financial crisis the National Debt increased rapidly and went over £1 trillion in 2011. In June 2018, UK public sector net debt was £1.78 trillion, equivalent to over 85% of GDP (ONS 2018a). Table 1.1 traces the growth of UK government debt, both in absolute figures (in billions) and as a percentage of GDP.

The scale of the figures was highlighted in the press and media, and by politicians, who argued that urgent measures were needed to tackle the UK debt crisis. In some ways this produced what Naomi Klein (2008) calls a 'social shock'. Klein's work is based on the aftermath of 'environmental' disasters (like the flooding of New Orleans in 2005, or the South Asian Tsunami at the end of 2004). Here she argued that 'shocked' societies, suffering from the trauma of the disaster they had been through, were increasingly vulnerable to hawkish representatives of private corporations who saw the disaster as an opportunity to privatise swathes of public services and make huge profits out of these suffering societies (Klein 2008). Here I'm suggesting that the scale of the debt crisis, the speed at which it developed and how it was reported, produced a similar situation in Britain: given the scale of the debt crisis, and in the absence of alternative narratives, the notion

Table 1.1: UK debt, 2010–2018

Financial year	Debt (£bn)	Debt as % of GDP
2010/11	1,214.5	75.6
2011/12	1,349.7	81.8
2012/13	1,425.6	83.3
2013/14	1,522.5	85.5
2014/15	1,604.0	86.5
2015/16	1,652.0	86.4
2016/17	1,720.0	86.5
2017/18	1,763.8	85.8

Source: ONS (2018b)

that we had to make cuts and introduce 'austerity measures' to deal with the debt gained traction. It also created a situation where private, for-profit organisations increasingly moved to take up contracts within the public sector, effectively privatising large sections of the welfare state (Dorling 2018).

But let's look at the debt in a little more detail.

Although the absolute figures are significant, in fact, like all debt, they are only significant if they cannot be paid off. In a sense it's like an individual's mortgage. Some of us will qualify for a mortgage of £100,000, some will be able to get a mortgage for £200,000: the determining element, for the bank or lending company, will be how much we earn – how much we earn, compared to how much we want to borrow. This is called the earnings to debt ratio. In terms of national economies the key is how much the debt is, compared to how much the country 'earns' (what the debt is as a proportion of its GDP). The second line of data in Table 1.1 outlines this as the amount of UK debt as a percentage of UK GDP (our 'debt to earnings ratio').

Looking at debt as a percentage of GDP gives us a way of comparing debt across countries. Table 1.2 presents the debt (as a percentage of GDP) in a number of countries.

As Table 1.2 indicates, while the debt in the UK may be high, it is not significantly different to that in many of its trading partners, and presently UK debt sits just below the average for the euro area.

Going back to Table 1.1, there are three things to note. First, the rising level of debt (remember in 2005 the figure was less than half the 2010 figure). Second, the debt as a percentage of GDP. Here it is worth noting that the 'Maastricht protocol' and the EU Stability and Growth Pact (the agreed EU figure for manageable debt in its economic models) is that debt should be below 60% of GDP and that this point was

Table 1.2: Debt (as % of GDP) various countries (end of 2017)

Country	Debt as % of GDP
Japan	253
Greece	178.6
Italy	131.8
Portugal	125.7
US	105.4
Spain	98.3
France	97
Canada	89.6
Euro area	86.7
Brasil	74
India	68.7
Germany	64.1
Australia	41.9

Source: Trading Economics (2018)

breached in March 2010, when it was 69.6% of GDP (ONS 2018b). The 'Maastricht protocol', however, is an arbitrary figure, produced by economists and politicians committed to a particular, market-driven vision of how the market economy 'should' work (and it's worth noting that it is a mark currently being breeched by Greece, Italy, Spain, Portugal, France, the average for the euro zone, and even Germany!). Third, despite the claims of austerity boosters in the Conservative-Lib Dem coalition in 2010 and within the Conservative party since, the austerity measures taken over the last ten years have not reduced the debt – the debt has increased, despite austerity.

The figures for 2018 in Table 1.1 also draw our attention to something else. Here the debt (in absolute figures) has gone up, but as a percentage of GDP it has reduced slightly. This is because GDP has grown. And this reminds us that there are always alternative ways to tackle the debt/deficit crisis. Promoting economic growth and creating jobs, for example, will reduce spending on welfare benefits and increase government revenues through the tax take, thereby reducing the deficit and paying off some of the debt.

These arguments become more pertinent when we take a longer look at the UK debt burden. Governments always work with a debt burden of some description. In Britain, debts from various wars and imperial adventures are still being repaid; there is nothing that says we need to repay debts in the space of one, or two, government terms of office. Figure 1.2 presents a long-term picture of UK government debt from the start of the twentieth century (as a percentage of GDP).

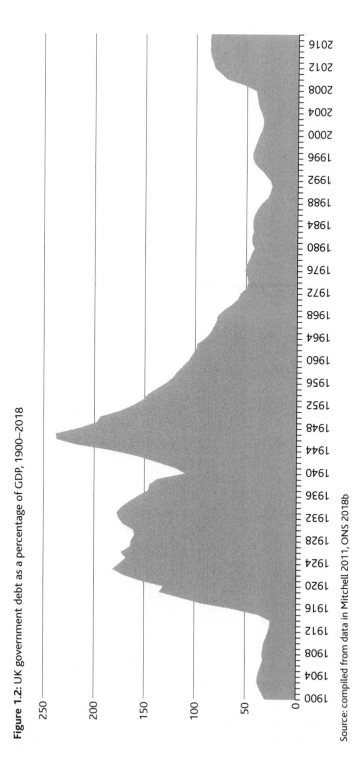

Figure 1.2: UK government debt as a percentage of GDP, 1900–2018

Source: compiled from data in Mitchell 2011, ONS 2018b

14

The data in Figure 1.2 tells us that, at the start of the twentieth century, the National Debt was 30% of GDP. It went above 150% in the First World War and stayed high in the inter-war years. Debt breached 200% during the Second World War (it peaked at around 270% of GDP just after the end of the war), it then declined to 50% of GDP by the 1970s, dipping to 25% by 1990. The National Debt began a rapid increase in the aftermath of the worldwide financial crisis of 2008. Today it is 85.8% of GDP (OBR 2013; ONS 2018b).

The interesting thing, for those of us involved in social policy and social work, is that the period when the post-war welfare state was created coincides with the period when debt as a percentage of GDP was well over 200%. Despite high levels of debt, the NHS was founded (via the National Health Service Act 1946), the poor law abolished (via the National Assistance Act 1948) and 'cradle to grave' national insurance established (the National Insurance Act 1946). In addition, a rapid house building programme was launched and a range of public utilities (gas, water, electricity) and key sectors of the economy (rail and mines, for example) were nationalised. Again this emphasises that government debt does not, inevitably, require cuts to public spending. The mantra of the last ten years, that 'there is no alternative', is simply not true; there are alternatives, alternatives that look to protect the vulnerable, to create jobs and tackle inequality, for example. 'Austerity', and within this the notion that public services need to be cut, is a political choice made by the governing political parties.

A crisis shared?

The second great mantra of the UK governments since 2010 (especially under former Chancellor George Osborne) is that the austerity pain will be shared by all and that we are 'all in it together' (Cowburn 2015). Despite the claims, the reality of austerity is quite different. It has reinforced inequalities and established Britain as a place where the rich get richer and the poor get poorer. For those at the bottom, Oxfam (2013) summarises the picture nicely:

> Economic stagnation, the rising cost of living, cuts to social security and public services, falling incomes, and rising unemployment have combined to create a deeply damaging situation in which millions are struggling to make ends meet. Just one example among many is the unprecedented rise in the need for emergency food aid, with at least half a million people using food banks each year.

Currently over one-fifth of the UK population (14 million people) are classified as poor (JRF 2017) and in 2017 1.5 million people, including 365,000 children, were destitute at some point, meaning they were unable to access basics like heating, housing or food (Fitzpatrick et al 2018).

Many of the poor are in work. Figure 1.3 traces median earnings since 2000. Over this period there have been four distinct periods. Between 2000 and 2002 median earnings grew at 2.2% a year; between 2002 and 2009 at 1.0%; they fell 1.8% per year between 2009 and 2014; and grew at 1.5% a year between 2014 and 2017 (Cribb and Johnson 2018). Commenting on these figures, Kollewe (2018) notes that for those in work, 'annual wages [are] still £760 lower [in 2018] than they were a decade ago', while Cribb and Johnson (2018) note that for 'those in the 20s or 30s, median earnings in 2017 were 5% and 7% lower than in 2008'.

These 'median figures' hide the levels of in-work poverty. The Resolution Foundation notes that:

> in 2017 … 18 per cent of employees earned less than two-thirds of the median hourly wage [the low pay threshold], equivalent to 4.9 million people. 14 per cent of men and 22 per cent of women fell below this threshold … 23 per cent of employees were paid less than the voluntary Living Wage. (D'Arcy 2018: 5)

Figure 1.3: UK real median hourly earnings, 2000–2017

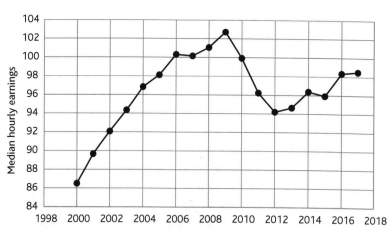

Source: ONS (Annual Survey of Hours and Earnings)

The crisis of in-work poverty led the TUC general secretary, Frances O'Grady, to argue that:

> UK workers suffered one of the worst pay squeezes in the world after the financial crash. And with food prices and household bills shooting up again, another living standards crisis is a real danger. (Osborne 2017)

After ten years of austerity the majority of us, in real terms, are worse off – and that's before you take account of declining and deteriorating public services.

Yet, in sharp contrast, over the last ten years the wealth of billionaires has risen on average by 13% per year, six times faster than the wages of ordinary workers (Alejo Vázquez Pimentel et al 2018): 4 January 2019 was dubbed 'Fat Cat Friday' – the fourth day of the year marks the point when the average UK CEO has earned, for that year, the equivalent of a worker's average annual salary. As Jones (2018a) notes:

> Top executives now earn 133 times more than the average worker; in 1998, the ratio was 47. The salary of the average FTSE chief executive is the same as that of 386 Britons on minimum wage combined.

Since 1989, the *Sunday Times* has produced a 'Rich List' that estimates the wealth of the 1,000 wealthiest people in the UK. These are almost certainly an underestimation of their wealth; their use of tax havens and offshore accounts makes it very difficult to estimate their actual wealth. Nevertheless the release of the *Sunday Times* data is greeted with great aplomb and covered in much of the print and television media as a celebration of the 'wealth creators' in our midst.

Figure 1.4 shows a quite remarkable growth in wealth of the 1,000 wealthiest people, the 'take-off' occurring in the early 2000s as a result of various deregulating pieces of legislation introduced under the New Labour governments of Blair and Brown. The figure shows a clear dip in wealth that coincided with the crisis of 2008, but the fabulously rich had recovered their wealth by 2012 and it has grown phenomenally, year-on-year, since then. The figure from May 2018, £745bn, was up £87bn from the £658bn figure of May 2017. As the Equality Trust point out, the wealth owned by the richest 1,000 people is already more than that of the poorest 40% of households put together and the gap is growing (Equality Trust 2018).

Figure 1.4: Combined wealth of the 1,000 richest people in the UK, 1997–2018

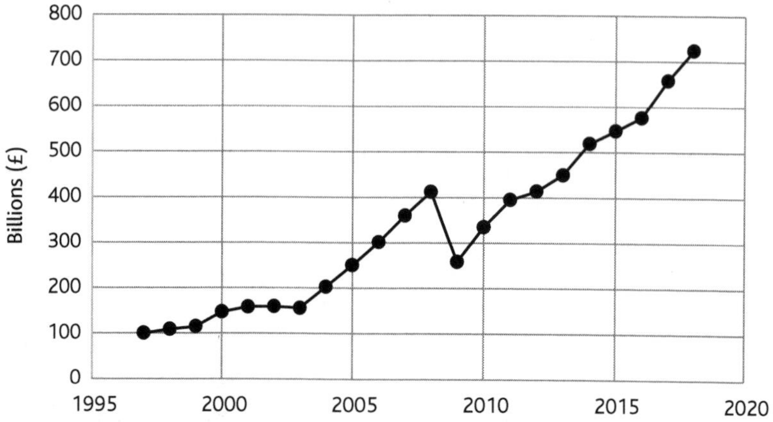

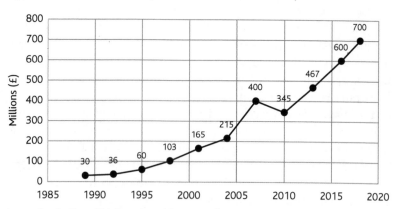

Source: *Sunday Times Rich List*, 1997–2018

To emphasise the rapid and exponential growth in wealth it is worth considering one aspect of the Rich List highlighted by *Sunday Times* editor Andrew McCall. Looking back over the 30 editions of the Rich List, he notes that when the List started in 1989, you needed £30m to enter the 'Top 200'; today you need £700m (McCall 2018). Figure 1.5 plots the rise in the 'minimum' entry point to the 'Top 200'.

It is worth putting these figures alongside some of the data for welfare spending. According to the Office for Budget Responsibility (OBR 2018) in 2016/17 the total UK public sector spend (for defence, roads, welfare, education, health and so on) was £771bn, slightly more than the wealth of the 1,000 richest people in the UK at £745bn! Of this

Figure 1.5: Minimum wealth needed to be included in the 'Top 200'

Source: *Sunday Times Rich List*, adapted from McCall 2018

total public sector spend, £217bn went to various aspects of welfare, £92bn went on state pensions (so we could take the equivalent of total welfare spending off the 1,000 wealthiest people, leaving them with 'only' £528bn between them – slightly more (£1bn) than what they had in 2015 when their combined wealth was £527bn. If we break it down further, the total spend on disability benefits was £22bn, family tax credits was £23bn, housing benefits was £25bn and Jobseekers Allowance was £2bn. These benefits have been targeted, identified as part of the problem of an 'overgenerous' welfare state, yet their combined total payment (£72bn) is less than the increase in wealth experienced by the UK's fabulously wealthy over the year from 2017 to 2018 (£87bn).

It comes as no shock, therefore, to realise that the austerity decade has increased inequality levels in the UK, with the UK now the most unequal society in Europe (Dorling 2018). The conclusion is clear: the costs of austerity have not been shared equally, we are not 'all in it together'; the austerity choices made by the Conservative and Conservative-Lib Dem coalition governments have increased inequality and deepened poverty and hardship for many families (both in and out of work).

A crisis of welfare transformation

As we have moved through the discussion, we have noted the impact of austerity on service users and social work practitioners – something that the following chapters will cover in greater detail. But there is one further 'macro-level' impact we must address. Naomi Klein's argument is that during periods of 'social shock' the representatives of capital (corporations, bankers and financiers, politicians and government bureaucrats) exploit public disorientation to transfer public resources and services to the ownership or control of private interests. In a much-cited example of Klein's thesis, soon after the financial crisis broke out in 2008, Rahm Emmanuel, an adviser to Barack Obama, argued in an interview that: 'You never want a serious crisis to go to waste. And what I mean by that is an opportunity to do things you think you could not do before' (Emmanuel, cited in North 2009).

In a similar manner, in 2013, then Prime Minister David Cameron told the Lord Mayor's Banquet that what his government was aiming to introduce was the 'permanent disassembling of the state' (Watt 2013a). Cameron went on:

> We are sticking to the task. But that doesn't just mean making difficult decisions on public spending. It also means

something more profound. It means building a leaner, more efficient state. We need to do more with less. Not just now, but permanently. (Watt 2013a)

The sheer scale of the various UK governments' assault on welfare indicates that what is involved here is something much more fundamental than simply 'deficit reduction'. Rather, the austerity crisis has been used as a cover to make structural and strategic changes that would be more difficult to push through in 'normal' times, the aim of which are to change significantly the whole basis of the post-war welfare settlement. In Kimber's (2011) words, 'To force the market even deeper into society, increase privatisation, weaken workers' collective strength, and make the welfare state serve capital rather than fulfil any of the needs of the majority' The 'transformation' of welfare under the cover of austerity was behind a range of changes – from student loans, to the Bedroom Tax – the aim of which was to transfer responsibilities away from the state and onto individuals.

But transformation was also about opening up services to for-profit providers. The transformation can be seen in the care sector, for example, where Hudson (2018) suggests:

> In 1979, 64% of residential and nursing home beds were still provided by local authorities or the NHS; by 2012 it was 6%. In the case of domiciliary care, 95% was directly provided by local authorities as late as 1993; by 2012 it was just 11%.

Ray Jones (2018b) has carefully traced these transforming pressures within social service departments and in regard to children's services in particular. As he notes:

> The government has been clear about its ambition to reduce public services and to create the opportunities for private companies to receive public funding. … It may have been thought that, as for the rest of the world, child protection was a step too far. Not for this government. (Jones 2015)

Jones lists some of the companies attending an Education Department briefing for potential tendering companies for children's services. It included G4S – who have several contracts across public service networks but also the building and engineering companies, Mouchel and Amey and the accountancy and taxation services company KPMG.

And the goal of welfare transformation opened up more and more areas of service delivery (for example, prisons, probation, police, forensic science services, the health service, benefits assessments and schools) to the multi-billion pound 'public services industry' – with companies like Capita, G4S, Serco, ATOS and Pinder making vast profits from services.

Of course the transformation of the 'welfare state' started before the crisis of 2008. During the 1980s and 1990s under the Conservatives, and under New Labour at the start of the twenty-first century, the market has been promoted as the key element in the 'modernisation' of the welfare state. But the austerity 'shock' has been used to deepen these transformative processes – to try and bring about Cameron's 'permanent change'.

In 2011 Gosling undertook an important study for local government union Unison, looking at the long-term consequences of the moves towards privatisation and marketisation. Gosling suggested that the on-going transformation of welfare services had led to the significant growth of a 'public services industry' that generates massive profits for a narrow group of giant companies. Gosling's (2011) key findings were that:

- Key players in the 'public services industry' are banks, infrastructure funds, private equity houses, consultancy firms, multinational corporations, 'third sector' enterprises, and a new breed of 'multi-service' firms focused on winning government contracts.
- Private sector providers – including many operated by private equity houses focused on short-term financial returns – now dominate much of the social care 'marketplace'.
- Private equity investors have had a core role in transferring public sector assets into commercial activities.
- Private equity tends to be a short-term holder of assets, seeking fast returns on investments. This encourages sometimes repeated transfers of ownership, undermining service continuity.

But Gosling also noted that, while some companies have been successful, others have been failures and when these companies fail public bodies have to pick up the pieces and meet the additional costs.

The failures of care home providers Southern Cross and Four Dimensions and of general provider, and PFI specialist, Carillion emphasise the point: increasingly we are privatising services to allow profits to be generated for a relatively small number of providers while socialising any risk associated with their activities by the state acting as guarantor, stepping in when they fail.

What is the future of social work?

Over the chapters that follow, we look at the impact of austerity and welfare transformation on a range of social work areas. We do so in the shared belief that things can, and should, be done differently and better. Social work is an activity that can bring real, fundamental change to people's lives. Social workers – properly resourced and with appropriate discretionary powers to act to support people in need – are, overwhelmingly, value-driven, hard-working professionals who can, and do, act to meet human need and protect human rights. But social workers, and the social work profession, cannot fulfil these lofty ambitions in the face of austerity and welfare retrenchment. This opening chapter has set out to make one fundamental argument: austerity is a political choice, followed over the last ten years by governments that have consciously stood by as inequality has grown and the majority of people's lives have got harder. We were told by the coalition government in 2010 that 'there is no alternative' – there was and there is. We were told, by then Chancellor George Osborne, that 'we were all in it together' – we weren't! And, under the cover of austerity, the government has used the crisis as an opportunity, a business opportunity, to break up and privatise services and transfer responsibility to meet needs from a collective state provision onto an individual responsibility – one that the vast majority struggle to meet.

Collectively, the authors in this volume remain committed to the value of social work, but good social work needs an end to austerity, to privatisation and marketisation. It's time to put people first, to put people before profit and to create a welfare system that values service users and workers together.

2

Contemporary developments in child protection in England: reform or reaction?

Brid Featherstone

Introduction

This chapter argues that a dangerous disconnect has become increasingly apparent since 2010 in England allowing successive governments to claim they are improving child protection while simultaneously promoting and implementing policies that increase the numbers of children living in poverty, reduce the support services available to them, and reinforce the inequalities that limit their potential.

Key developments in the current policy climate will be discussed, locating these in a historical canvas; and alternative understandings drawing from research on the relationship between poverty, inequality and the harms children and their families suffer will be provided. The chapter will explore why a social model of 'child protection' is needed, outline its main features, and address how it might offer progressive possibilities for families and those who work with them as well as wider society.

Contemporary visions

We want every child in the country, whatever their background, whatever their age, whatever their ethnicity or gender, to have the opportunity to fulfil their potential. Children's social care services have an essential role to play – whether by keeping children safe from harm, finding the best possible care when children cannot live at home, or creating the conditions that enable children to thrive and achieve. To make that happen, it is essential that everybody working within children's social care has the knowledge and skills to do their jobs well, and the organisational leadership and culture to support and challenge them to keep improving. (DfE 2016: 3)

In 2016 the Department for Education (DfE) articulated its vision for child protection, identifying activity in relation to three areas: people and leadership; practice and systems; governance and accountability. It highlighted initiatives to bring the 'best' people into the profession, give them the 'right' knowledge and skills and develop leaders equipped to nurture practice excellence. It stressed the importance of creating the right environment for excellent practice and innovation to flourish, using data to show strengths and weaknesses in the system, and developing innovative organisational models with the potential to radically improve services.

At the heart of the vision is practice, practice that is focused on getting families to change through equipping workers with methodologies such as motivational interviewing and systemic family therapies. However, as Bywaters (2017) notes, commenting on the statistics on looked-after children in 2016–2017, there are gaps in what the DfE is concerned to address and explore. While funding has indeed been made available to research innovations in practice methodologies and system change, there has been a puzzling lack of interest in investigating the range of factors that may be impacting on why children become looked after and what might be needed to support their safe care at home.

Bywaters (2017) points out that in 2010, 64,400 children were being looked after; now that number has increased to over 72,000. This increase has been accompanied by a reduction in overall spending on Children's Services. Indeed, an analysis of local authority expenditure returns shows a total reduction in expenditure per child on services of 14% between 2010 and 2015, with the most deprived third of local authorities being cut by 21% compared to 7% in the least deprived areas (Bywaters et al 2018).

But where is the government-commissioned research into whether the consequent reduction in early help and family support has impacted upon the rise in the numbers of children coming into care?

There is a continuing disconnect at the heart of government policy which these figures reflect and which is receiving insufficient attention. At the same time as the increase in numbers coming into care with all the financial and human costs involved, we continue to see policies that increase the numbers of families living in poverty, with all the consequences in terms of access to housing, food and other necessities of life (ADCS 2017). Yet there is no government-commissioned research into whether there is a relationship between these issues.

Moreover, despite the concerns expressed by DfE about improving data, there is a really big limitation that is not the subject of government action: data is only collected on children but not on their parents' social and economic circumstances. As Bywaters (2017) asks, how can we not know the most basic details about parents' ages, their marital status, or their health or educational backgrounds? He notes that it is incomprehensible that data is not collected about parents' circumstances - their income, housing or debt levels, for example - even though research suggests that these are key social determinants of good enough childhoods.

How have we got here?

The modern child protection system emerged from a concern to stop babies dying or being 'battered' by parents who were considered to be suffering from a lack of empathic mothering in their own lives. Poverty, poor housing and other social issues were screened out as holding helpful explanatory value (Parton 1985). From those early beginnings, rooted in concern for those who were powerless and voiceless and compassion for their emotionally deprived parents, the system has expanded enormously in terms of remit, research base, influence and power. The constructions of children and parents have changed too; children now have rights and parents have responsibilities (Dartington 2012). Moreover, the focus on parents has morphed into an increasingly punitive enterprise as part of a move from the Keynesianism of the 1960s through the decades as neoliberalism tightened its grip (see Featherstone et al 2018).

This story, honed in the 1960s, has proved remarkably enduring with its emphasis on the actions of individual parents/carers and its focus on the intra-familial as the key focus of professional attention. Thus today the key elements appear as follows:

- The harms children and young people need protecting from are normally located within individual families and are caused by acts of omission or commission by adult caretakers.
- Poverty is often denied as a risk factor in child maltreatment as it is argued that not all poor people harm their children.
- Parents and adult carers are often offered a limited range of subject positions by professionals with little evidence of partnership working.

- When they ask for help, evidence of need too often morphs into evidence of risk.
- 'Interventions' are framed as concerned with protecting children in individual families by identifying what distinguishes this family from others in similar circumstances rather than by identifying common challenges to good parenting such as the physical environment, economic circumstances, debt and poor housing.
- The categorisations that are employed, such as the 'toxic trio' (referring to domestic abuse, substance misuse and mental health problems), do not locate human behaviours in terms of their social determinants.
- Developing procedures, expert risk assessment and multi-agency working are promoted as central to protecting children (see Featherstone et al 2018).

The following sections explore the evidence that suggests this story poses serious ethical and human rights concerns with its individualising gaze and its conversion of need to risk.

Dealing with the poor or giving them a poor deal?

The work of Loic Wacquant (2010) has proved helpful in seeking to conceptualise what is happening to the poorest children and their families in our society. Wacquant's work demonstrates that, far from retreating under neoliberalism, the state has actually been reconstructed and re-engineered. He outlines the development of a 'centaur state' (see also Parton 2014). The centaur state presents a 'comely and caring visage towards the middle and upper classes, and a fearsome and frowning mug towards the lower class' (Wacquant 2010: 217). In this new model, the state has retreated from a number of areas, most notably the regulation of the market, but for the urban poor the scope and extent of state regulation has increased:

> While it embraces laissez-faire at the top, releasing constraints on capital and expanding the life chances of the holders of economic and cultural capital, it is anything but laissez-faire at the bottom. Indeed, when it comes to handling the social turbulence generated by deregulation and to impressing the discipline of precarious labour, the new Leviathan reveals itself to be fiercely interventionist, bossy and pricey. The soft touch of libertarian proclivities favouring the upper class gives way to the hard edge of authoritarian oversight,

as it endeavours to direct, nay, dictate the behaviour of the
lower class. (Wacquant 2010: 214)

This analysis can help to locate some of the empirical findings around
how child protection systems operate that have emerged in recent
times. For example, there has been a steady increase in the numbers
of families experiencing investigations for suspected abuse in the last
decades, the majority of which do not appear to uncover actual abuse
and/or result in help being offered to families. This is a trend across
a range of Anglophone countries, but if we focus on England we see
that investigations increased by 79.4% in the period from 2009/2010
to 2014/2015 (Bilson and Martin 2016). Did this reflect increases in
actual abuse? While the numbers on child protection plans did rise,
this rise of 40.5% fell far below those actually investigated.

This 'investigative turn' is impacting disproportionately on the
poorest children and their families. Bilson, Featherstone and Martin
(2017) estimated the proportion of children born between 1 April 2009
and 31 March 2010 who had reached various stages of involvement in
children's services before their fifth birthday from areas in the tenth
decile of deprivation. They estimated that 14 children (45%) would
have been referred to children's social care, six suspected of abuse
or neglect and three children formally investigated while two would
have been placed on a child protection plan and one in care. This
estimate is focused on the 10% most deprived communities and only
covers children until the age of five. There is no data on lifetime
involvement or even more deprived communities. This is important
since over half of all referrals and investigations concern children over
the age of five and if the gradient of deprivation rises within the
bottom 10% then a very high proportion indeed of children from
these communities will be involved in the child protection system.
Thus, for a significant amount of deprived children, it is conceivable
their first encounter with the state (apart from universal health services
which are increasingly under pressure and being hollowed out) is via
a Section 47 investigation. At the other end of the scale for children
in the least deprived 10%, a similar class might include just one child
who had been in need or referred to children's social care.

The contribution of deprivation to the rise in care appears to be
denied or dismissed by key constituencies with a clear preference for
focusing on the individual behaviour of parents and of local authorities,
as Bywaters and colleagues (2018) outline in detail. For example, in
relation to the former, Mr Gove, the former Minister for Education,
captured the policy zeitgeist:

In too many cases, social work training involves idealistic students being told that the individuals with whom they will work have been disempowered by society. They will be encouraged to see these individuals as victims of social injustice whose fate is overwhelmingly decreed by the economic forces and inherent inequalities which scar our society. This analysis is, sadly, as widespread as it is pernicious. It robs individuals of the power of agency and breaks the link between an individual's actions and the consequences. It risks explaining away substance abuse, domestic violence and personal irresponsibility, rather than doing away with them. (Gove 2013)

In relation to the performance of local authorities, Michael Wilshaw, then Chief Inspector of Ofsted, wrote in his final annual report on children's services, referring to the those local authorities judged inadequate that:

These weaknesses can be overcome through grit and determination and with good leaders, who make the work easier to do well. Our inspectors have seen this across the country and we now know that: inadequacy is not a function of size, deprivation or funding, but of the quality of leadership and management. (Ofsted 2016: 5)

A discourse has emerged focused on individual responsibility and targeted at improving particular practices within families and local authorities. This is a highly voluntarist project that denies or obscures the evidence highlighting the social determinants of many of the difficulties that are to be found in families and dealt with by local authorities. For example, there is a robust body of evidence that child welfare interventions (such as becoming looked after or subject to child protection plans) increase with each level of deprivation in areas (see Bywaters et al 2018). At its starkest, this means that across England, children in the most deprived 10% of small neighbourhoods are over ten times more likely to be 'looked after' in care (LAC) or on a child protection plan (CPP) than children in the least deprived neighbourhoods.

Hood and colleagues (2016) have linked the national datasets for all children in need and child protection services in England. The study aimed to examine variations and patterns of response in local authorities to demand for child welfare services in their area. One hundred and fifty-two local authority census returns and other statistical indicators covering up to a 13-year period were combined into a single dataset. Statistical analysis was undertaken to explore the characteristics of demand, workload and workforce, trends over time and variations between local authorities. The results showed that the overall system has become increasingly geared towards protective interventions, especially since the death of Peter Connolly. Deprivation levels continue to be the key driver of referrals and other categories of demand, and are strongly associated with variations in service response, particularly in the initial stages of referral and assessment.

As yet, the questions this body of research raises have not received the level of serious interrogation they merit. A key question surely concerns why interventions are focused on the poor. This is particularly puzzling in a context where there seems to be a widespread denial of the relationship between poverty and child maltreatment in policy maker, manager and practitioner accounts (see Featherstone et al 2018). Thus, we have a very odd set of circumstances. Practitioners, managers and policy makers deny the relevance or salience of the relationship. Yet their practice is focused predominantly on those who are poor. If poverty is not relevant why is there a focus by agencies on the poor and, moreover, should there be? Why isn't the work more distributed across populations? Why are managers and practitioners engaged in investigating poor children at the same time as arguing that poverty has no relevance to their work? What are the ethical and human rights issues here?

However, we know from multiple empirical studies that poverty is indeed relevant to child maltreatment in all sorts of complex ways and is implicated in, and reinforces, a range of inequalities, including those arising from class, race and gender relations. An international evidence review (Bywaters et al 2016) of the relationship suggests the need to think about the role of poverty in a dynamic and multifaceted way. It argues that socioeconomic circumstances can be both a direct and/or indirect contributory causal factor of child abuse and neglect. The direct effects occur when a parent is not able to adequately feed, shelter or clothe their children or keep them warm. The growth of benefits sanctions, the 'bedroom tax', the welfare cap and the cutting of emergency hardship payments means a growing number of families are unable to meet these primary needs at some point.

The indirect effects of income are essentially the impact of inadequate employment and its associated features such as poor housing, unsafe environments, low self-esteem and family stress. The interactions of low income with factors such as poor physical and mental health, disability, substance use and violence are key. If you have a substance habit but are well off, it is very unlikely children will become looked after because there are other means of achieving good enough parenting, and ways of convincing children's services that you can do a good enough job. If you are poor this is much more difficult. Just as with depression, poverty is not a necessary or sufficient cause, but poverty makes depression much more likely and much more difficult to manage successfully (Bywaters et al 2016; Marmot et al 2010).

There is other evidence from the inequalities literature that is also of relevance and that requires the making of links that are not being made currently. For example, the differences between areas in terms of child removals maps onto differences in life expectancy rates, as illustrated in this example: John in Blackpool is many times more likely to live away from his family in care than James, his counterpart, in Wokingham. Moreover, male life expectancy at birth in Blackpool is 74.7 and 81.8 in Wokingham (ONS 2016b). Thus, if present trends continue, John will die before James and is statistically more likely to experience the death of his father, Warren, earlier than James. Currently, the bodies of evidence for such statements do not engage with each other as the removal of children has not been considered within an inequalities frame but rather understood within a defiantly individualising one. Warren's life chances are more likely to be understood within a health inequalities frame when engaged with as an individual man; however, as a parent, he is often only explicable within a risk frame.

As Gillies and colleagues (2017: 169) argue, an alternative to the actuarial preoccupation, with its obsessive assessment and management of personal risk, is to adopt a much broader concept of social harm as a framework for understanding and tackling social ills. Writers from within this perspective include Dorling and colleagues (2008) and Pemberton (2016):

> The approach that we have sought may encompass the detrimental activities of local and national states and of corporations upon the welfare of individuals, whether this be lack of wholesome food, inadequate housing or heating, low income, exposure to various forms of danger, violations of basic human rights, and victimisation to various forms of crime. Of course, when we speak of people's welfare, we refer not (simply) to an atomised individual, or to men and women and their families, the social units who often experience harm. For it is clear that various forms of harms are not distributed randomly, but fall upon people of

different social classes, genders, degrees of physical ability, racial and ethnic groups, different ages, sexual preferences, and so on. (Dorling et al 2008: 14)

As Gillies and colleagues (2017: 169) argue, rather than attempting to calculate individual risk, social harm theorists identify collective responses to personal injuries. This approach enables a much wider investigation of precipitating factors and accountability, as well as an appreciation of the consequences of governments failing to act to address deprivation or corporate exploitation. A social harms lens reveals that the most pervasive and intractable social injuries derive from the pursuit of particular political and policy directions rather than intentional actions or personal deficits.

Pemberton (2016) examines comparative rates of homicide, suicide, obesity, road traffic injuries, poverty, financial insecurity, long working hours, youth unemployment, social isolation, as well as infant mortality across 31 countries. This analysis demonstrates how different policy regimes affect, for better or worse, these particular issues. Pemberton outlines how nation states can be categorised in relation to the harm reduction strategies they pursue. He then assesses the variance of statistical indicators of these harms across the different regimes. His analysis demonstrates that regimes that are characterised by highly individualised societies with weak collective responsibility for others, a minimal welfare safety net, and heavily privatised and means-tested social services are associated with the highest levels of social harm. In contrast, social democratic regimes were found to be the least harmful. Pemberton identified three aspects of social democracies that appear to reduce the incidence of social harm. First, social solidarity is evident in the form of low levels of inequality and high levels of empathy towards others. Second, the dominant approaches separate the worth of human beings from their ability to accumulate wealth and thus provide generous universal welfare provision. Finally, the exploitation of workers is reduced through enforcing employment rights and supporting union membership.

A literature on inequality complements this social harms perspective. The work of epidemiologists Wilkinson and Pickett (2009) has opened up possibilities for challenging the disembedding of practices, such as substance abuse by individuals, from their social determinants. This work remains seriously underexplored in the child protection research and practice literature. Wilkinson and Pickett have collected internationally comparable data on health and a range of social problems: mental illness including drug and alcohol addiction, life expectancy and infant mortality, obesity, children's educational performance, teenage births, homicides, imprisonment rates and social mobility. Their findings suggest that there is a *very strong* link between ill health, social problems and inequality. Differences in average income between whole populations or countries do not seem to matter once a certain level is reached, but differences *within* those populations or countries matter greatly. The amount of income inequality in a country is crucial. Wilkinson and Pickett (2009) note findings from the data that levels of trust between members of the public are lower in countries where income differences are larger. For example, people trust each other most in the Scandinavian countries and the Netherlands, and least in very unequal countries.

Wilkinson and Pickett (2009) argue that inequality *within* a society 'gets under the skin' of individuals, leaving them feeling unvalued and inferior. They explore writings on shame to argue: 'Shame and its opposite, pride, are rooted in the processes through which we internalize how we imagine others see us' (Wilkinson and Pickett 2009: 41). Greater inequality heightens anxieties because it increases the importance of social status, thus social position becomes a key feature of a person's identity in an unequal society.

Peacock and colleagues (2014) use findings from a qualitative psycho-social study employing biographical-narrative interviews with women in Salford (England) to understand experiences of inequality. They did indeed find evidence for the sorts of damage resulting from inequality as posited by Wilkinson and Pickett. However, in addition to these, the most striking finding was the repeated articulation of a discourse that they termed 'no legitimate dependency'. Dependency of almost any sort, whether on others or the state, was disavowed and responsibility was assumed by the self or was 'othered' in various ways.

A 'no legitimate dependency' discourse, they propose, is a partial (and problematic) internalisation of neoliberal discourses that become unquestioned at the individual level. They speculate that these sorts of discourses in conjunction with the hollowing out of resources lead to increasing stress and strain and account in part for the damage that occurs in an unequal society.

This particular analysis is of vital importance, I would suggest, as a discourse of 'no legitimate dependency' is actively produced and reproduced at its harshest in child protection encounters. The issue of who is responsible for what is at the heart of practices. Moreover, as Peacock and colleagues (2014) note, the individualised language of therapy can be readily co-opted into discourses emphasising individual responsibility and agency, but at the cost of being unable to embrace social or collective solutions to everyday problems. In that way, they are congruent with the 'no legitimate dependency' discourse.

Their analysis highlights how practices mesh with the understandings particularly of women to reinforce feelings of shame and impede those that illuminate. Shaming and blaming experiences in child protection are apparent and require considerable resources to counter and reframe.

This is very evident in the area of domestic abuse, with differing implications for men and women. In England, the recognition that domestic abuse is a child protection issue, the legislative manifestation being the Adoption and Children Act 2002, has had mixed but often problematic impacts. While drawing attention to the harms that children can suffer as a result of the abuse between adults and, indeed, the coincidence often of abuse to women and children, the implications for mothers especially can be problematic. They can be judged as failing to protect and become invisible in terms of their own needs as women. There can be unrealistic pressures placed upon them to keep children away from violent men (men they are themselves afraid of): 75% of child protection plans now are made in relation to emotional abuse or neglect, with domestic abuse strongly implicated in both (Jutte et al 2015). Research suggests mothers can experience child protection services as blaming and punitive in such contexts (Featherstone et al 2014).

As Featherstone and colleagues (2018) argue, practice in child protection can be confusing and inconsistent. For example, women who are experiencing domestic abuse are often treated as risks to their children, with a focus on signing agreements to leave the men and/or ensuring the children have no contact. As individuals, they carry responsibility for protection – they alone are responsible, with scant attention paid to the economic, social and psychological challenges of mothering alone. The men who abuse them also receive an individualised response that instructs them to leave this particular family and have no contact. This, of course, means that they are often moving from one family to another, causing untold damage and trauma. However, if they do access a perpetrators' programme – and this by no means at all certain, given resource issues – they may receive a reductive social approach where their individual life stories are subsumed within a universalising narrative of men's desire to have power and control.

Overall, there has been a fragmented and siloed approach to families in a context where there is a great deal of fear and distrust of child protection services. There have been few services to support families who wish to stay together, with a consequent focus on separation and rupture. All these issues are now subject to scrutiny and critique and the consequent development of new practice initiatives.

However, a key area that requires further attention and has, to date, not received this concerns the role of poverty in domestic abuse. Nixon and Humphreys (2010: 164) argue that the traditional feminist message that domestic violence is widespread, victimises women and occurs across all classes and cultures is in need of reworking. They note that in this process, attention to an evidence base that is constantly changing and being updated is critical, as is engagement with a body of work on intersectionality, with its focus on the interlocking patterns of gender, race, ethnicity, class, disability and sexuality.

Sokoloff and Dupont (2005: 40) argued that both an intersectionalities perspective and a social structural perspective were needed in order to provide women from diverse backgrounds with the kinds of personal and social change required for safety and growth at the individual and communal levels. They contended that a 'traditional' feminist approach stressing the equal vulnerability of all women of all classes, ethnicities and cultures to violence was highly problematic and obscured complexity and the structural causes of violence.

Since then, the evidence has indeed made clear that while it might be correct to say that domestic violence occurs across all classes and cultures it is not correct to say there is equal vulnerability across all classes and cultures (Nixon and Humphreys 2010). A review for the Joseph Rowntree Foundation by Fahmy, Williamson and Pantazis (2015) concludes that there is a host of evidence showing vulnerability to domestic violence and abuse to be associated with low income, economic strain and benefit receipt. The mechanisms linking these are not well understood but the most common relate to the effects of financial strain on relationship stress and quality and issues arising from men's inability to fulfil the male breadwinner role.

Nixon and Humphreys (2010) suggest that the increased vulnerability to domestic violence of ethnic minority women that is found in the research evidence from a range of countries is most likely related to poverty and income, noting the evidence that ethnic minority families are likely to be poorer than white families.

These analyses on the differing vulnerabilities of women to domestic violence by implication raise issues about the differences between men who are violent and the factors in men's abuse. The relationship between poverty, masculinity and domestic abuse is underexplored. However, the recognition that poverty is a factor in domestic abuse and, as previously suggested, is linked to men's perceptions of the breadwinner role suggests how vital it is to understand and engage with social constructions of masculinity.

Overall, given the extensive evidence that has emerged of the focus by child welfare and protection systems on deprived populations, the levels of domestic abuse found in families subject to child protection processes are to be expected and add fuel to concerns about the invisibility of poverty in contemporary child protection policies and practices. Moreover, the Joseph Rowntree Foundation review, among other research, found that a range of system interventions can either trap women in abusive relationships or be a driver of their vulnerability to poverty post-separation. This reinforces the need to critically interrogate the implications of system interactions including child protection systems.

Currently, as indicated, there are innovations in terms of practices although many remain focused on separation and rupture (Ofsted 2017). Interestingly, while Ofsted notes the importance of practices that move beyond a reactive protective focus to stress prevention and repair, their individualising gaze means they can offer no strategies in relation to these.

Another way?

A number of authors have turned to writings on the social model to explore alternatives to a model that pays little attention to the social determinants of the harms that manifest in individual families (Featherstone et al 2016, 2018). The social model of disability emerged out of activism by physically disabled people in the 1970s. The term was coined by Oliver (1983) and it captured the idea that disabled people were not disadvantaged by physical impairments but by the barriers to well-being that result from social inequalities and the negative attitudes of other people. Over the subsequent decades, the idea of a social model has been extended to learning disability, mental health, end of life care and dementia.

The social model is a starting point for challenging the biomedical perspective on disability and the focus on individual 'deficits' that this perspective entails. In simple terms, the model shows how people are 'disabled' by the barriers placed in their way by society rather than by individual features of their bodies or selves more generally. What the social model does *not* do is provide an adequate explanation for why barriers come into existence in the first place. It is not, by itself, as its earliest protagonists recognised, 'an explanation, definition or theory' (Finkelstein 2001: 6).

In arguing for a social model for 'child protection' it is not being suggested that the social model of *disability* should be extended to encompass this domain (see Featherstone et al 2018). It is, however, suggested that the key conceptual shift that such a model involves is central. This means moving away from a sole focus on the individual or individual family and applying therapeutic or quasi-therapeutic methodologies to effect change in family behaviours and functioning.

It requires a focus on the economic, social and cultural barriers faced by individuals and their families and the socio-relational nature of the pressures they face. It also involves articulating the need for very different policies and practices to those promoted currently. It requires a focus on social harms and how these shape and are profoundly imbricated in risks that manifest themselves at the individual level.

So what could a social model for supporting families and protecting children look like? A social model acknowledges that what is defined as child abuse is socially constructed and historically changing. Based upon research into the social determinants of so many 'family troubles', a social model recognises that structural inequalities, including poverty, sexism and racism, impact in interrelated ways on people's lives. An individual's agency is recognised but so are the constraints of interlocking structural factors. This approach challenges the child protection narrative that what parents do or do not do is due to rational choices.

It would demand a different frame and practices by all concerned: policy makers, managers and practitioners and many other different community actors. For example, across the UK, Fairness or Equality Commissions have been set up to work with communities on tackling and reducing inequality at local levels (NEF 2015). These have mobilised politicians alongside a wide variety of actors to conduct audits on pay, housing, education and so on and could be revised to include work on indicators we see as contributing directly to inequalities for children in terms of being able to live safely and flourish within their families of origin and communities.

Crucially, practitioners would foster family and community engagement in order to build upon the strengths and capacities for care that exist and counter 'us' and 'them' discourses. Here the work of Kimbrough-Melton and Melton (2015) offers pointers where outreach workers worked within communities to strengthen their capacities to notice when families were struggling and to care by offering support whether of a material or social type. In turn families supported others as they started to cope better. The parent advocacy projects in New York described by Tobis (2013) offer inspiring examples of parents who had children removed from their care as a result often of drug addiction working within the system to reform how it worked with families and to support parents in similar situations to keep their children safe. The practices that were developed placed an emphasis on helping families through the provision of a wide range of services and support and led to significant reductions in the number of children in foster care. Parents with experience of the child welfare system were involved in the design and delivery of services, for example as parent advocates working alongside families; and linking with other rights-based organisations to advocate for broader social reforms to address structural inequalities (Tobis 2013).

The compatibility of the Capability Approach (CA) (Sen 1983, 1999) and the social model of disability has been explored by Burchardt (2010). The CA starts from a position of asking: what do this child and this family need in order to flourish and how can we ensure their human rights are promoted? (Gupta et al 2014). A person's capabilities represent the effective freedom of an individual to choose between different functioning combinations and between different kinds of life that the person may value and has reason to value. The relational aspects of an individual's well-being are stressed in terms of interpersonal relationships and community and wider social structures. There are close connections between adequate social opportunities and how individuals can shape their own lives and help each other (Sen 1999).

In terms of the social work relationship, this approach would recognise the power of professionals to promote strengths and enhance capabilities, but also to diminish and destroy (including the power to 'shame').

Conclusion

Over 30 years ago Dingwall and colleagues (1983: 244) wrote these wise words:

> [C]hild protection raises complex moral and political issues which have no one right technical solution. Practitioners are asked to solve problems everyday that philosophers have argued about the last two thousand years ... Moral evaluations can and must be made if children's lives and wellbeing are to be secured. What matters is that we should not disguise this and pretend it is all a matter of finding better checklists or new models of psychopathology −

technical fixes when the proper decision is a decision about what constitutes a good society.

It is vital that we place complex moral and political issues back at the heart of policy and practice and that we challenge contemporary policy and practice disconnects. Improving the protection of children must place improving the economic and social circumstances of their families at its heart. A social model is premised upon this recognition and could provide an important rallying call in a climate where individualised notions of risk and responsibility act to reinforce the already oppressive circumstances of marginalised populations.

3

The slow death of social work with older people?

Mark Lymbery

Introduction

It is clearly understood that social work with older people is one of the least well-developed areas of the profession (Milne et al 2014). While there have been times when it has been positively promoted (for example around the implementation of community care in 1993), more common has been an impression of neglect. This has two consequences. First, and arguably most important, the quality of practice may well have been affected. Second, and this is at least partly as a result of the first point, it has long been an area of social work that is less favoured by students in training (Quinn 2000). Certainly, from my own experiences as a social work educator, there were few students who wished to get into this area of practice.

Of course, this actuality tends to undercut the essential premise of the chapter: in reality, there has never been a 'golden age' for social work with older people, from which the current period represents a fundamental retreat. However, even in relatively recent times, there was an expansion in social work with older people, combined with a growth in the scope of academic material which focused upon it (see, for example, Lymbery 2005 and 2014a; Ray et al 2015; Richards et al 2014). Despite this, there have been many practical changes which have led inexorably to a diminution of its role, a number of which are detailed in subsequent sections. It is therefore hard to see how social work with older people can be recovered. Nevertheless, there are in fact a number of steps that would help with this, and the final section highlights what these are.

Before then the chapter starts by outlining the various 'requirements' for social work involvement with older people. (By 'requirements', I mean the range of factors that present compelling reasons for the allocation of social workers to this group. It is of course fascinating that the existence of these 'requirements' has not heralded a massive increase in the presence of social workers with older people. I call them 'requirements' simply because they should bring about such a growth!) The chapter also briefly considers the history of social work with older people, commenting on its relatively slow development and low status. It analyses the employment patterns of social workers with older people, focusing particularly on the core role for local authorities in this. From this it discusses the various alternative locations for social workers, considering both the practical and conceptual advantages of each. The chapter concludes by outlining the various obstacles that stand in the way of a wider involvement of social workers with older people, and the steps that can be taken to overcome them. I will argue that, although there are many issues that require a fundamental realignment within society, there remain a number of factors that are within the existing compass of social workers; as a result, it is far from an entirely gloomy outlook.

It is important to clarify my position on this subject at the start of the chapter. I have been actively engaged in social work directly affecting older people since 1990, first in the general development of policy for adult social care, then in the more specific position of helping to educate new entrants into the social work profession. It has been a core preoccupation throughout my entire academic career, and I have published over 50 papers that bear on the subject. At least partly as a consequence, I have drawn more on my own previous work than I have sought out countervailing views. This is perhaps the inevitable consequence of arguing a 'line' that has been consistent over the past two decades. I have also taken the view that it is best for the reader – in a book of this nature – to be given a single perspective. As a result, it is also important to include a reminder for the curious reader that there is much other material out there which is worthy of consideration (see, as a starting point, Milne et al 2014); much of this literature may well take a different view.

Is social work necessary for older people?

Underpinning the title of this section is a more wide-ranging critical question: is social work necessary for anybody? If so, what circumstances call it into being? Perhaps because of my background, I sometimes find it too easy to assume that its place in the world is guaranteed and unchanging. However, it is important to remember that the shape of social work that we have come to understand in the UK is both nationally and temporally defined (McDonald et al

2003). Therefore, we can assume little or no permanence in the way in which we conceptualise the social work task for any person or group. Taking the national context into account, my view is simply that a social worker intervenes where there are problems in the relationship between an individual and the wider environment. As I have argued in more detail elsewhere (Lymbery 2005), there are a number of issues that might indicate that an older person would benefit from the involvement of a social worker. While some of these could affect all members of the population, others are given particular force by an individual's chronological age. While much of what a social worker actually does involves putting people in touch with a range of services, there is more to the social work role than simply being an intermediary, a view I will expand on later.

1. It is undoubtedly the case that the onset of physical illness, an increase in the level of physical disability or frailty, is likely to promote the involvement of social care services. While these issues can affect any individual, they become increasingly common with age, potentially compromising the ability of each person to carry out the tasks of daily living. Given the increase in the population of older people, both overall and as a proportion of the total (ONS 2016a and ONS 2016b), this is an obvious and pressing problem. Such people are simply more likely to require the intervention of a social worker, particularly in more serious cases.

2. The involvement of a social worker would become almost certain where there are significant levels of cognitive impairment through dementia, depression or other causes. In all such cases, which again are particularly likely to affect older people, it is almost certain that a social worker would prove essential. In addition, the scale of this problem is huge and growing. While there were approximately 850,000 people with dementia in 2015, it is estimated that this figure will increase to over 2 million by 2051 (Alzheimer's Society 2014). It is clear that the financial burden falls largely on people with dementia and their families, alongside social care services and health services.

3. Largely because of the impact of increasing physical and mental frailty, the needs of carers have become particularly important. Rather than simply seeing them as a resource, they should be recognised as people with a variety of needs, which can often be complex and profound. The ability of a social worker to identify these needs and hold them in balance with the needs of the frail older person is therefore potentially significant.

4. The notions of transition and change are critical for any older person, and characterise the points at which they enter crises that call for a professional response. A good example of this is the point of discharge from hospital when support is often required but can be difficult to organise – and which represents a serious problem within the health and social care system (Lymbery 2006). More generally, change characterises many of the events of old age, whether involving the effects of physical or psychological illness. While social workers should never underestimate the effect of such issues for the individual, they must also be wary about assuming that there will be a standard emotional response to them.

5. Although the experience of bereavement and loss is inevitable for all, at some point it is particularly typical of the experiences of older people. This can create a need for social workers to engage in the inner psychological workings of individuals; as I have previously observed (Lymbery 2005), social work has historically engaged relatively seldom with such concerns – particularly with older people – even though their potential impact is critical. There has been an assumption that complex problems can be resolved simply; the effect of this is to flatten their complexity and thereby to assume that a practical response would be adequate.

6. Responding to the abuse of older people and their consequent need for protection has become a major part of a social worker's tasks in recent years, following a series of events that highlighted the need to focus on this aspect of practice (Ash 2013). As a consequence, social workers have an increasingly vital role in ensuring that older people are able to live safely, in managing the investigation processes in cases where their safety is threatened, and in ensuring that their autonomy is maintained.

7. Finally, social workers need to be reminded of their essential commitment to challenging and confronting injustice (Lymbery and Postle 2015), which has arguably become magnified due to the inequities highlighted by government policies. In particular, social workers have a duty to point out the ageism that disfigures society, alongside the other forms of injustice experienced by older people.

Broadly similar lists have been produced by influential bodies in relation to the social work role in personalisation a few years ago (ADASS/ DH/SFC/BASW/SCA 2010; SCIE 2010). In addition, a collection of esteemed social work academics have made largely similar arguments (see Milne et al 2014, and a range of papers drawn from this research: Ray et al 2015; Richards et al 2014). In summary, then, it can be seen that older people may have the same sorts of need as other groups in the population, as well as a number of issues that directly relate to their age. However, the most telling argument in favour of the continuance of professional social work with older people rests with the totality of what a social worker can contribute rather than in its individual elements. Overall, therefore, it is my contention that the case for social work involvement is unarguable, a perception that is given urgency by the reality that older people are also the fastest growing group in society (ONS 2016b). The 'requirements' will therefore increase, and it is vital to ensure that they are responded to properly. However, as the following section makes explicit, social work with older people is one of the least well developed areas of professional activity. It is important to understand why this has come to pass and to chart the consequences that derive from it.

A brief history of social work with older people

Throughout social work's history, there has been more attention paid to all other areas of practice than social work with older people (Lymbery 2005). It has consistently been an unpopular area with prospective practitioners, with proportionately fewer students on qualifying courses expressing interest in and enthusiasm for this aspect of practice (Lymbery 2014a), particularly in comparison to work with children and families. Research has confirmed that this is true internationally, not just in the UK (Hughes and Heycox 2006). Three specific reasons have been advanced for this position:

- It is a reflection of the low status of older people in society.
- The perceived simplicity and straightforwardness of the practice that is needed for older people.
- A rejection of the emotional challenges of the work, particularly given the necessary engagement with service users' mortality. (Quinn 2000)

In policy and practice there has been an assumption that the various complex emotional needs of older people can be 'resolved' by the application of administratively focused actions: this response has served to confirm the low status of social work with older people, as potential practitioners are led to see the work as both essentially straightforward and lacking in professional satisfaction for the practitioner (Lymbery 2005). The reasons for this are simple: the priority in many social care systems has been to manage increasingly tight budgets rather than to work with older people to develop their lives positively. Arguably this was the primary reason for the establishment of community care policies in 1993 (Lymbery 2005), and has certainly affected policy since. Consequently, social work practice has been tightly circumscribed and experienced as limited in relation both to its complexity and in the level of satisfaction it affords (Lymbery 2005). This has led to a focus on the 'surface' of life events, rather than an appropriate examination of their 'depth' – a point which Howe (1996) presciently argued was critical to understanding the way in which social work has been conceptualised in general terms: it applies particularly clearly to social work with older people.

A cursory glance at the way social work with older people has been developed through history confirms this general analysis (Wilson et al 2011, Chapter 4). In social work's early years, practice with older people was not presumed to need a professional qualification. Many people of my generation can recall 'generic' teams where all the work relating to older people was delegated to an unqualified social work assistant, and revolved around the provision of residential care, on the basis that such work was unproblematic (Lymbery 2005). While this appeared to change with the introduction of community care, a policy that vastly increased the numbers of qualified social workers, their role remained largely administrative, focusing on enabling local authorities to meet their budgetary targets (Lymbery 2005).

Although the establishment of personalisation as the guiding philosophy underpinning social care was accompanied by a recognition that older people do have complex needs (Lymbery 2014b), the development of a viable social work role has been hampered by the simultaneous need for local authorities to cut their services to meet the stringent demands of austerity (Lymbery 2014c). This has further curtailed the development of the social work role in relation to older people. The following section will examine the impact of austerity in more detail as this is a key determinant of the place of social work for older people, before the chapter moves on to consider the range of alternatives that exist for the employment of social workers.

The impact of austerity

The origins of austerity are in the financial crash of 2008/09, where the dramatic worsening of public finances was the direct consequence of a massive failure of the banks (Taylor-Gooby 2012) – not, as has subsequently been the government mantra, because of the overspending of the previous Labour administration (Lymbery and Postle 2015). Due to this mistaken belief, buttressed by an ideological favouring of the 'small state' (Toynbee and Walker 2017), the government has crafted its policies based on the overwhelming presumed need to reduce public spending. Despite the fact that the only clear beneficiaries of austerity are financial speculators (Konzelmann 2014), governments across the Western world have pursued such policies with avidity. This has created a specific problem in relation to the evident and growing levels of inequality in society, particularly in relation to widening social divisions (Konzelmann 2014). All of this is despite the evidence for the success of austerity to be equivocal at best; indeed, some academics see it as a 'dangerous idea' (Blyth 2013), largely because it engenders social inequality.

Further exploring the issue of social division, Duffy (2013) has passionately argued that the impact of the cuts has been significantly worse for disabled people than for any other segment of society. While many older people have been somewhat insulated from the worst effects of these cuts – due to the 'triple lock' on old age pensions – the poorest among them are dependent on local government to fund their care, and there is little doubt that austerity has had a major impact on local government:

> Councils argue that a combination of increasing demographic pressures, which they can manage down no further, and rising costs, which have been held down for too long, added to the fact that they have been relentless in implementing the efficiency approaches that they believe to be possible locally, means that it is unlikely that councils can continue to make cuts of this scale without putting services for vulnerable people at risk. (LGA 2014: 7; see also Duffy 2013)

The financial consequences of this are exacerbated by the demographic changes that have affected society, to which reference was made earlier. In particular, there has been growth not just in the numbers of older people in the population, which will increase substantially as the century wears on (Lymbery 2014a), but also in the numbers of the 'oldest old' (ONS 2016b). In turn this needs to be viewed in the context of the overall budgetary settlement for local authorities, which also provides the base for almost all the social workers operating in this area of activity.

Despite the increase in numbers of those who require their services, local authorities were required to accommodate a reduction of 51%

in their budgets by 2014/15 (IFS 2015); in addition, those authorities which are categorised as the most deprived have been forced to accept the largest burden of cuts (Hastings et al 2015; Innes and Tetlow 2015). Since adult social care is the single largest area of expenditure for local government (Burchardt et al 2016), this reduction in finances is extremely problematic. This is compounded by the fact that there is no effective protection of social care budgets, despite the attempt to safeguard this area of expenditure with the 'adult social care precept' (Burchardt et al 2016), which has been proved to be little more than a deception. As a result, most councils that provide social care are having to rationalise their provision (for a good example of this, see Nottinghamshire County Council 2014, which notes the connection between rising demand for services and an unprecedented reduction in the council's income).

It is worth exploring this illusory shield a little further. It consists of two elements: (1) an additional 2% that could be levied on council tax for the specific use of adult social care, and (2) the creation of the Better Care Fund – a pooled budget to support the integration of health and social care, which would amount to an additional £1.5bn by 2020. However, when examined in more detail, this protection is not all that it seems. Even with this extra money that would be available until 2020, there would still be an overall reduction in local authorities' resource base of 7%, coming as it does on top of substantial previous cuts. In addition, the Better Care Fund income would only come in any significant sense from 2018/19, meaning that it will have little effect on the immediate shortfall (Glasby 2017). Finally, the 'adult social care precept' will benefit the authorities which raise a higher proportion of their income through council tax: it will therefore do little for those areas of highest deprivation and therefore greatest need, all of which raise smaller amounts through council tax (Schraer 2015); these have been, as I have previously noted, disproportionately affected by the stringent financial regime that has dominated since 2010.

The implications of this for the employment of social workers in the context of adult social care will be addressed in a future section. At this stage it is important to note that, for adult social care in general and social workers in particular, the position is further compromised by the fact that two major external reforms are also being worked through – personalisation on the one hand, and the Care Act 2014 on the other (see Lymbery 2010 and 2014c; Slasberg and Beresford 2014 for a critical examination of each theme). The combined effect of this is that adult social care has been dominated by a toxic combination of cuts and 'reform'. Budgetary considerations have compromised both; they have vitiated the more progressive visions of personalisation (Lymbery 2014b; Lymbery and Postle 2015), and the impact of the Care Act has been materially weakened by the contradiction between the user-focused rhetoric governing its introduction and the resource-driven reality of its implementation (Slasberg and Beresford 2014).

The gap between rhetoric and reality is a core characteristic in both local government's implementation of personalisation and the provisions of the Care Act. (Indeed, I have previously argued that the conflict between ideals and realities is characteristic of social work more generally; Lymbery and Butler 2004.) West (2013) has noted how the official language of personalisation has focused almost entirely on its transformational possibilities, and ignored the harsh financial realities that underpin it, thereby encouraging councils to pursue what can best be termed 'fantasy' objectives (Lymbery and Postle 2015). Slasberg and Beresford (2017) have also identified how rhetoric has influenced local authorities in their implementation of the Care Act, in particular the adherence to the strengths-based practice that they suggest underpins it. They note how numerous authorities have compared the presumed benefits of strengths-based practice with the sterility of the preceding care management system. (A similar point could be made in relation to personalisation.) However, as they note, there is no attempt to grapple with a key conundrum regarding the very existence of care management:

> why have councils opted to employ a system that is so dysfunctional and so antithetical to the stated values and skills base of the dominant professional group, and why have practitioners been so compliant in delivering it? (Slasberg and Beresford 2017: 271)

Nowhere does it appear to be recognised that the effectiveness of care management systems was materially affected by the limited resources that were available to implement them even when they were first introduced. This failure to grasp economic realities will also obstruct the implementation of personalisation, as I have noted. In addition, the problematic economic climate has affected the capacity of local authorities to employ qualified social workers – and there seems little reason to believe that the future will be more positive.

As the political fallout from the Grenfell Tower fire in June 2017 illustrates, there appears to be a growing recognition that there is a connection between the systematic underfunding of local government and its ability to maintain its range of services, let alone improve them. There is certainly a strong thread in academic literature that is critical of austerity (see, for example, Blyth 2013). Whether this has meaningful consequences for the continuation of austerity remains to be seen; as the result of the 2017 General Election may also serve to confirm, there is now a belief in some quarters that austerity has run its course. However, this is more the focus of debate than of actuality. The harsh financial climate persists, and it is difficult to imagine that the Conservative government will radically reshape its economic thinking.

Future trends in the provision of services for older people

Any examination of these themes from the perspective of social work must grapple with two points:

- the specific history of social work in the UK;
- the relationship between social work and other professional groups in the provision of services.

On the first point, it is critical to remind ourselves that social work in Britain has always been 'state-mediated', where the state 'intervenes in the relationship between practitioner and client in order to define needs and/or the manner in which such needs are catered for' (Johnson 1972: 77). The role of the state highlights the difference between social work and other professional groups working in similar areas, such as medicine or the law. This is not the same as in other parts of the world, where social work has a more independent status (McDonald et al 2003). In the UK this mediation has been carried out through local government, where social work has predominantly been located for much of its history. As a result, the role and status of local authorities has a material impact on the profession. There are four key implications of this.

1. It has been suggested that the location of social work within local government has provided it with what Larson (1977: 184) has termed a 'protective institutional barrier'.
2. It has been also been strongly argued that this created an environment where practitioners were subjected to increasing levels of control from their managers and politicians (Lymbery 2014b).
3. In part because of the inability of social workers to define and control the nature and circumstances of their own practice,

there are inequities between the power and status of the various professions providing services for older people (Lymbery 2006).

4. Because local government has been so severely affected by austerity, social workers practice in conditions where their very existence is at threat.

As my wording implies, the first point was considered to be a strength for social work as it appeared to provide a level of certainty and security. The rise of managerialist thinking in social work (Lymbery 2004) challenged this orthodoxy as the insights of practitioners were given little value in comparison to managers, who were able to use their power and status to define more clearly and in a limited way the activities of social workers (Lymbery 2014b).

While the limited experience of self-government within social work has emphasised the difference between it and other long-established professions, the disproportionate impact of austerity on local government has also had a major effect upon social work. This is as true for work with children and young people as it is for work with adults (Ferguson and Lavalette 2013); however, my focus in this chapter is specifically on work with older people. The problems brought about by austerity have limited the opportunity to respond positively to the needs of this group. This is compounded by an awkward reality, as highlighted in a previous section: that adult social care is by far the single largest area of expenditure within local government (Duffy 2013) and hence has been hardest hit by the burdens of austerity. This has had a particular impact on the employment of social workers, as they are relatively costly members of the workforce.

If this makes it more difficult to secure a social work role in relation to services for older people, the problems are compounded when one considers the third point: the inequality of status and esteem between social workers and other professional groups – notably doctors (Lymbery 2006). This is particularly significant given the rhetorical power given to such terms as 'integration'. In recent years a call for greater integration has been a watchword in adult social care (Carey 2018), with little proper analysis of what it means, how to bring it about or even whether it is a good thing. One clear point is that it stands as another 'warmly persuasive word' (Williams 1975), of a type to have littered adult social care in recent times (Lymbery and Postle 2015). This has particular force politically, where greater integration is widely promised as a key component of improving health and social care services.

It is worth subjecting the claim that greater integration will dramatically improve the quality of care to greater scrutiny than has often been the case. As Carey (2016: 6) has pointed out: 'Despite rhetorical arguments in favour of integrated care, empirical evidence to support claims of more efficacious and efficient care remains in relatively short supply.' In other words, what appears to be self-evidently a good thing has more complex and nuanced outcomes in practice. This relative lack of clear and unequivocal evidence that demonstrates the effectiveness of integration is compounded by a plethora of other divisions that ought to argue caution. For example, there is a clear lack of a parity of esteem among the professional groups that compromises the ability of social workers to argue for a uniquely 'social' way of perceiving the problems of older people (Lymbery 2006). As a result, there has been a narrow focus on health and medical needs for older people, leading to what has been termed a 're-medicalisation' of later life (Means 2007). The collective impact of this affects both the quality of life for older people and the status and authority of a social work perspective.

The other critical point that is rarely considered when the presumed benefits of integration are discussed concerns the funding basis of health and social care. Whereas health care has proudly been sold to the public on the basis that it is free at the point of use, the fact that social care potentially attracts a charge has been less widely understood (Lymbery 2006). The implications of this were made clear during the General Election campaign of 2017, when the fact that cancer care would be free was compared to the fact that dementia care (as an example of expenditure that was labelled as social care) would potentially attract a substantial charge, leading to allegations that the Conservative party was planning a so-called 'dementia tax'. That the manifesto commitment was rapidly disowned testifies both to the sloppy thinking of a Conservative party that thought the election was already won and the intractable nature of the problem (Hughes 2017).

That this was 'news' highlights the limited understanding that exists about the boundaries between health and social care as this dispute – although dramatic in its scope and timing – is far from isolated, nor has it been recently discovered. Indeed many years ago Jane Lewis (2001) identified that the differential funding arrangements for health and social care were the source of what she termed the 'hidden policy conflict' between health and social care agencies. The upshot of this, as she identified, has been an unacknowledged battle between them to define certain conditions as the financial responsibility of the other agency – a fight that she was clear was being won by health care agencies, on the basis that they were more able to define problems as being 'social care' and hence attracting a charge (Lewis 2001). A key implication of this, therefore, is the fact that individuals and their families are required to contribute more where their problems are defined as being 'social care' – such as dementia. The estimate that the financial burden of dementia largely falls on people with dementia and their families (Alzheimer's Society 2014) strongly supports this contention.

Taken together, these issues imply that the location of social workers is unsettled, particularly when we consider the place of social work within local government, its funding base and the wider concerns about the integration of health and social care. However, there is a conceptual case to be made that social workers would be best able to represent the perspectives of service users were they to be located independently. While it is worth considering the potential for social workers to be employed outside health and social care agencies, in the voluntary or private sectors, it is hard to be optimistic about either for largely practical reasons. If we take the two settings separately, there are numerous close connections between many voluntary agencies concerned with social welfare and social workers. However, despite this, there are relatively few social workers employed by them. In addition, because many not-for-profit organisations are funded by local government, they have faced stringent cuts to their finances, rendering their very existence problematic (Allcock Tyler 2016). While it has also been suggested that social workers can contribute usefully to a variety of private organisations (Macias 2014), this is not typically in the sorts of setting that are needed to provide for the needs of older people. Indeed, the prospect of private agencies getting more involved in the provision of social care – an example being Virgin Care, which was approved to run adult care services in Bath and North East Somerset from April 2017 (McNicoll 2016) – will make many social workers deeply uncomfortable, as the collision between profit motives and care is highly problematic.

While policies of personalisation carry the potential of increasing the employment of qualified social workers in a diversity of settings, the failure to ensure that such policies are adequately funded militates against this coming to pass (Lymbery and Postle 2015). Consequently, despite there being a clear conceptual advantage that would argue for the location of social workers outside the state, there are compelling practical reasons that militate against such an outcome.

What can be done?

The final substantive section is the most difficult to conceptualise: it would be easy to think that it was impossible for social workers to act to reverse what can seem like an inevitable decline in the value of social work with older people. However, a counsel of despair would be neither the appropriate nor the correct response to the current difficult set of circumstances. Any analysis that does not provide practitioners with the capacity to respond proactively to the problems which they will encounter is an irrelevance to social workers in general (Wilson et al 2011). Indeed, it is possible to develop alternative directions for social work as a whole (Ferguson and Lavalette 2013). However, one should not underestimate the complexity of this: it depends both on a sophisticated understanding of the circumstances that confront social workers in their daily practice and of the wider potential of social work to provide an effective response to the specific circumstance of individuals and groups.

Some of the complexity that attends this can be gathered through an analysis of the nature of social work. In the view of Ife (1997), there are four quadrants which characterise different orientations to social work practice (see Figure 3.1).

As the preceding sections have made clear, in the recent past, social work practice with older people has been practised from a market orientation; in addition there has been a managerialist domination of practice, in thrall to the dominant philosophies that have governed social welfare (Lymbery 2004 and 2005; Lymbery and Postle 2015). As a result, practice that derives from broadly humanist approaches to practice – professional and community alike – have been less favoured. What I suggest is needed at this juncture is careful attention given to the 'roads less travelled' within social work. This means a continual search to reconcile different aspects of social work's past (Lymbery 2013), with practitioners working at a variety of levels, according to the nature of the problem being addressed. These issues – and potential ways to address them – are listed here.

1. **Combating austerity.** As the preceding pages have made abundantly clear, the pernicious grip of austerity has had particular consequences, particularly for people with disabilities and local government. While there are indications that the social consensus that has supported austerity may be breaking down – the percentage of votes cast for an avowedly anti-austerity Labour party in the 2017 General Election being a case in point – there is considerable ground to travel to make this a reality. The first step is to ensure that the funding for social care is sufficient: one of the key consequences of austerity – as I have shown – is that there has been a growing gap between the funding settlement for

Figure 3.1: Competing discourses of human services

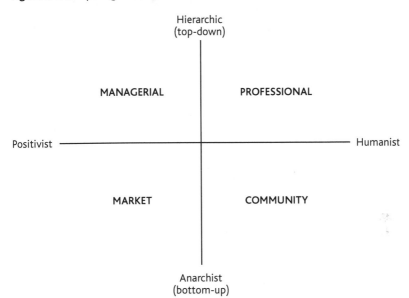

Source: Ife 1997: 47, Wilson et al 2011: 80

social care and what is actually needed. This has long been the case; it was noted in a much happier financial climate (Wanless 2006), and the gap between what is needed and what is provided has widened since. Much of the work to combat longstanding austerity will require a general political engagement rather than action that is specific to qualified social workers. However, it fits with a commitment to social justice that should characterise all social work (Beresford 2011).

2. **Making the case for social work with older people.** While the intellectual case for this has frequently been made (see, for example, Milne et al 2014), it is inevitably a more expensive option for local authorities to employ a greater proportion of qualified social workers than is currently the case. Given the financial pressures besetting local government, it is at least understandable that they should seek to save money in whatever fashion they can. It is therefore important to trumpet the added value that qualified and experienced social workers can contribute. It is also important to emphasise that such activity should not simply be focused on people where there are already defined problems, or limited to prescribed areas of activity such as safeguarding. The ability of a skilled social worker to identify a range of issues that have not previously been considered must be strongly valued (Lymbery and

Postle 2015). This is particularly clear in relation to assessment. Under community care, reductionist and procedural models dominated (Smale et al 2000); by contrast, the ideal that assessment should be constructed as an exchange of expertise between the service user and professional social worker has much to commend it (Lymbery and Postle 2015), but requires a skilled professional to put it into effect.

3. **Values.** While rhetoric about social work values is often high-flown and imprecise, it is reasonable to insist that a creative application of a values-based framework should underpin a social worker's practice (Postle 2007). Indeed, it is possible to argue that social work's value base is a key determinant of good quality practice for older people (Lymbery and Postle 2015). As Bisman (2004) has argued, the knowledge and skills used by social workers are relatively meaningless without a framework of values within which to place them. As far as work with older people is concerned, the principal – but far from the only – consideration must be combating ageism. After all, the very fact that older people receive a lower quality service than other groups is surely an example of ageism in action.

4. **Quality of practice.** In the final analysis we should not expect organisations and people who make difficult funding decisions to employ social workers unless the value that they add is clearly visible. In this sense, the quality of a social worker's practice is critical: the key reason to employ any costly practitioner is because the value of their practice is recognisably an improvement on others. Too often this has simply not been evident. Of particular importance will be the social worker's ability to reconcile the different parts of social work's history (Lymbery 2013). In particular, the ability of a social worker to establish a productive working relationship with the service user is critical.

In summary, the most telling argument in favour of the continuance of professional social work with older people rests with the totality of what a social worker can contribute rather than in its individual elements. There are three broad discourses within social work – transformational, therapeutic and social order (Payne 2006; see also Lymbery 2008). At different times in the history of social work one or other of these traditions has been particularly powerful. In recent times, the need for social workers to enable stringent budgetary targets to be met has predominated (Lymbery 2008), thereby placing practice firmly in the social order discourse. Indeed, I would not seek to argue that this is unimportant; however, I am convinced that other perspectives are equally vital.

For example, if we take the four issues noted earlier, it is clear that social work's transformational orientation is necessary to ensure that proper attention is given to the need to combat austerity. It is clear that this requires a broader conception of what social work is than simply a key contributor to social order. It is surely true that the response to the needs of older people as a cohort needs to transcend the limitations of a case by case approach: if it does not, there is little chance that their status as a group will improve. In addition, if we accept the point that social workers do have a role in combating austerity, this can apply equally to challenging the existing consensus that has brought austerity into being, highlighting the damaging effects of policy on vulnerable people – a task for which social workers are well qualified – and helping to lay out alternative patterns of service. In addition, a structural understanding of society is needed in order to be effective in tackling such debilitating social problems as ageism.

At the same time, in order to enable older people to feel themselves to be well served by social workers it is important to flag up the central nature of the relationship within social work, which is closest to the therapeutic discourse as outlined by Payne (2006). While I am not advocating that a social worker should be, or aspire to be, a therapist, it remains important to be aware that the skills of a social worker must encompass the capacity to develop a close and trusting relationship with a service user, as this serves as the medium through which positive changes can be brought about.

Rather than seeing the three core traditions within social work as existing in opposition to each other, a good social worker with older people should strive to bring them together. No one element is inherently more important than any of the others, yet without a single ingredient the totality of practice will be markedly less sophisticated. A social worker must therefore be capable not only of doing all the various aspects of their role, but also to integrate them into a whole. The pressing challenge for social work with older people therefore is first to recognise this and then to create the environment where such integration becomes possible. As I have argued throughout this chapter, this is a difficult but not impossible task.

Conclusion

If we return to the title of the chapter, there is little doubt that recent times have presented a profound challenge for social work with older people. While there is a good basis for assuming that social workers should be actively involved in the lives of many older people, this has not always been the case. Despite a growing recognition of the complexities of older people's lives, this position shows few signs of changing.

In order to challenge this it is important for social workers to act both individually through their organisations and collectively as part of other bodies that have the interests of social work and people who use social work services at their heart. In my view it is vital for all social workers to join and be active in the British Association of Social Workers (BASW), as this is the primary organisation that represents the professional interests of the profession. In addition, social workers should give serious thought to becoming active members of the Social Work Action Network (SWAN), as a body with a vital campaigning role for a wider version of social work. There is little doubt that it is possible for social workers to achieve more acting collectively than individually.

4

Mental health social work:
the dog that hasn't barked

Iain Ferguson

Introduction

More than 60 years have now passed since the publication in the USA of *The Sane Society* by Marxist psychoanalyst Erich Fromm (1955/2001). Fromm's main argument in that book was that in promoting the idea that the road to happiness and fulfilment lay in consumerism, in persuading people to conform to a very narrow conception of 'the good life', and in encouraging people to deny their real needs and feelings, American society in the 1950s was actually creating mental ill-health. Far from being a 'sane society', it was in fact an 'insane society'. Consumer capitalism, Fromm argued, was making people ill.

The book struck a massive chord and within weeks of its publication was fifth in the *New York Times* bestseller list. Since that time, it has sold more than 3 million copies.

Following Fromm, the central argument of this chapter will be that the world in which we live today – the world of neoliberal global capitalism – is also creating mental ill-health on an industrial scale. Three examples will illustrate the point. Firstly, according to the World Health Organisation, depression now affects over 300 million people worldwide and is the leading cause of disability in the world (WHO 2017). As George Brown and Tirril Harris argued some 40 years ago in their classic study of depression in women, while sadness, unhappiness and grief are inevitable in all societies, the same is not true of clinical depression (Brown and Harris 1978/2011). Rather, depression on this scale tells us something about the nature of the society we live in.

Then there is the current epidemic of loneliness. Neoliberalism, the ideology that preaches individualism and claims that 'there is no such thing as society', has contributed to a situation where loneliness and social isolation are having a devastating effect on the lives and health of both young and old people. According to research conducted by Age UK in 2014, for example, more than 80,000 people aged 65 and over living in Scotland said they always or often felt lonely (Davidson and Rossall 2014). Across the UK the figure was more than a million. Loneliness in itself of course is not the same as mental ill-health and there can be definite mental health benefits to solitude. However, chronic or persistent loneliness not only contributes to anxiety and paranoia but has been shown to have definite physical effects, equivalent to smoking 15 cigarettes a day.

Finally, there is the impact on mental health of the current war on the poor, graphically portrayed in director Ken Loach's award-winning film I, Daniel Blake. Loach's film highlights the extreme pressure that so-called welfare reform, backed up by brutal sanctions, is placing on the physical and mental health of millions of poor and disabled people. It is scarcely surprising then that demand for mental health services in England has risen by a staggering 20% over the last five years at a time when mental health service budgets were cut by 8% in real terms (McNicoll 2015). Research has also shown that the introduction of fit-to-work tests for sick and disabled people have coincided with 590 'additional' suicides, 279,000 cases of mental illness and 725,000 more prescriptions for antidepressants (Cooper 2015).

In this chapter, I want to suggest that these findings should have considerable implications for mental health social work. For if we choose to use the language of 'evidence-informed practice', there is now a huge body of evidence which shows that the causes of mental ill-health are overwhelmingly social, rather than biological or genetic. That does not mean that our brains do not react to changes in our material situation or to negative experiences, particularly of trauma – of course they do. Nor does it mean that some people may not be more predisposed to mental ill-health than others. But what is clear is that it is primarily the things that happen to us in our lives, rather than what happens in our genes or our brains, that underlie mental health or distress. As the leading neurologist Steven Rose has argued:

> Consider the world-wide epidemic of depression identified by the World Health Organisation (WHO) as the major health hazard of this century, in the moderation – though scarcely cure – of which vast tonnages of psychotropic drugs are manufactured and consumed each year. Prozac is the best known ... Questions of why this dramatic rise

in the diagnosis of depression is occurring are rarely asked – perhaps for fear it should reveal a malaise not in the individual but in the social and psychic order. Instead the emphasis is overwhelmingly on what is going on within a person's brain and body. (Rose 2005: 5–6)

So if social rather than biomedical factors are the main causes of mental ill-health, one might assume that a profession called 'social work' – the clue is in the name – should be making an important contribution towards the alleviation of that distress. Sadly that is far from being the case. As Terry Bamford has observed in his recent history of the profession, social work has been marginalised in most areas of mental health work (Bamford 2015). The key strategy paper for England and Wales, for example, *No Health without Mental Health*, published in 2011, contains not a single reference to social work, despite lots of references to the key role of social factors in causing mental ill-health (Department of Health 2011). Nor does Scotland fare much better. The recently published ten-year mental health strategy contains two mentions of social work, one a reference in a footnote to the 1968 Social Work (Scotland) Act, the other a passing reference to the statutory work of Mental Health Officers (the Scottish equivalent of Approved Mental Health Practitioners) (Scottish Government 2017).

Social work has not always been marginalised in this way. At one time mental health social workers were perceived as making an important contribution to mental health services. The central part of this chapter will address some of the reasons for this marginalisation of social work within mental health and the profession's relative silence in the face of the current crisis – why, in other words, like the dog in Conan Doyle's short story, the social work dog hasn't barked.

The final part of the chapter will pose the question 'what is to be done?' If social work as a profession still retains some potential to make a contribution both to the understanding of mental ill-health and also to relieving the emotional misery it frequently produces, then how can we begin to move from our present position of marginalisation towards becoming a stronger voice within mental health policy debate and discussion?

On the margins: social work and mental health

In answering the question of why social work isn't playing a more central role within mental health services, I want to suggest four main reasons.

Dominance of the biomedical model

The first is the continuing dominance of the biomedical model of mental ill-health. There are two main aspects to that dominance. Firstly, there is organisational dominance. In contrast to social work and social care, NHS psychiatric services are universal services. While that universalism has been severely undermined by neoliberal policies of austerity and privatisation in recent years, they have in general been better protected than the mental health services provided by local authorities or the voluntary sector (which in reality are often funded by local authorities). That dominance is likely to be reinforced by the integration of health and social care services currently taking place both in Scotland and in England and Wales.

Secondly, there is the ideological/cultural dominance of the biomedical model. It is a model based on three main assumptions: firstly, that mental illness can be described in terms of discrete categories; secondly, that mental illnesses, particularly conditions such as schizophrenia or bipolar illness, have an organic basis; thirdly, that these conditions are primarily amenable to medical interventions, particularly pharmacological interventions.

All three of these assumptions have been the object of a powerful critique in recent years coming mainly from a new critical psychology and psychiatry. Like the anti-psychiatry of the 1970s, this body of work challenges some of the basic tenets of biomedical psychiatry but on the basis primarily of empirical scientific research. Some flavour of this critique can be gained from the following quote from one of its leading proponents, Richard Bentall:

> A wide range of evidence suggests that our current system of diagnostic classification has led psychiatry down a path that is no more scientific than astrology. Like star signs psychiatric classifications are widely believed to tell us something about ourselves, to explain our behaviour and personality, and to predict what will happen to us in the future. Like star signs diagnoses fail on … all of these counts. (Bentall 2004: 195)

The central contention of this discourse is that despite the millions that have been spent over decades searching for an organic basis for mental disorders, whether in the form of chemical imbalances or genetic markers for conditions such as schizophrenia or bipolar illness, we are no nearer finding any such evidence. The reason, in a nutshell, is that we are looking in the wrong place. As Read and Sanders argue:

> If there is a common message it is perhaps that we aren't born with the problems we have as adults, they aren't somehow inherently and inevitably built into our brains; they come from our interactions with other people, especially, but not exclusively, early on in life. (Read and Sanders 2010: 124)

Despite this body of evidence, however, the biomedical model shows no sign of disappearing. One reason is that it can seem to make sense of people's experiences. Mental distress, whether its takes the form of frightening moods, suicidal thoughts, hearing voices or struggling with food, is precisely that: distress. We do not feel 'ourselves'. So despite the stigma that labels like schizophrenia can carry, seeing it as an illness with a name can sometimes seem helpful to the person experiencing it (and their families), in terms of giving a sense of control and also as a passport to services.

More important, however, is that viewing mental distress as an illness plays an important ideological function in individualising distress and diverting attention from the social reasons why people become unwell. Not surprisingly, then, it is a model that tends to be promoted by governments which wish to obscure any connection between poverty, inequality and oppression on the one hand and mental distress on the other.

Thirdly, and crucially, constructing mental distress as illness is hugely profitable. The profits of the big drug companies are higher than any other sector of industry – including the banks – while nearly all psychiatric research is now pharmaceutically financed – more than 90% in the UK. That is one reason for the creation of hundreds of new categories of mental illness over the past four decades. To quote Stephen and Hilary Rose:

> This rise in the medicalization of everyday distress consequent on job loss, bereavement, divorce and the many other adversities of daily life has continued unabated [and is] ... a process facilitated by the close relationship between the American Psychiatric Association, health insurance and the pharmaceutical industry. The underlying practical and theoretical problem, which remains to the present day, though cheerfully ignored by psychopharmacologists

and many biological psychiatrists, is how to relate the classifications of the DSM which are essentially phenomenological, based on listening to and observing the patient, to the assumed neurochemical causes. There were – and still are – no neurochemical markers to match against the DSM diagnoses. (Rose and Rose 2016: 23–24)

So the first factor that has contributed to the marginalisation of social work within mental health services is the continuing dominance of the biomedical model.

Neglect of social determinants literature

Next there is the failure of the social work profession to make more creative use of research findings concerning the role of social factors in causing mental distress. Here, I will refer to three areas of findings which in principle could be more effectively deployed by social workers.

Firstly there is inequality. As Wilkinson and Pickett demonstrated in *The Spirit Level*, levels of mental ill-health, as well as a whole range of other social problems such as violence, obesity and how much people feel they can trust each other, are much worse in societies with bigger income differences between rich and poor (Wilkinson and Pickett 2010). This is not just about the material effects. It has more to do with feelings of superiority and inferiority, feelings of being devalued, disrespected, looked down on, being at the bottom of the pile. The UK is the third most unequal country in Europe so perhaps it's not surprising we also see such high levels of mental ill-health.

Secondly, there is the impact of trauma on mental health. There is now substantial evidence demonstrating a link between different forms of child abuse and mental health problems in later life. A review of 59 studies of the most severely disturbed psychiatric patients found that 64% of the women and 59% of the men had been physically or sexually abused as children (cited in Read and Sanders 2010: 85). Other types of traumatic experience, whether in childhood or in later life, has also been shown to result in mental health problems, with research showing links to bullying, rape and violence in adulthood, and war trauma (with the label 'post-traumatic stress disorder' having originated out of the experience of Vietnam War veterans). In a study of homeless people in Glasgow who were labelled as having a personality disorder, one psychiatrist commented:

'I would go as far as to say that I can't think of any patients I've seen in the last two and a half years of the homeless population who described what you might call a normal upbringing. And I'm not exaggerating, I really can't think of anyone.' (Cited in Ferguson et al 2005b: 21)

Thirdly, there are the effects on mental health of different forms of oppression, such as racism and sexism. Research by University of Manchester academics, for example, has revealed for the first time how harmful repeated racial discrimination can be on mental and physical health, an especially relevant finding given current levels of Islamophobia across Europe and the US (Wallace et al 2016).

In respect of sexual oppression, the 2014 Adult Psychiatric Morbidity survey found that more women in the UK aged from 16 to 24 are experiencing mental health problems than ever before. 'Young women have become a key high risk group', the report concluded (NHS Digital 2016). Psychological distress is now so common that one in four in that age group have harmed themselves at some point. One factor contributing to this is the impact of social media. According to journalist Rhiannon Lucy Coslett, girls and young women routinely alter the photos they post to make themselves look smoother and slimmer. Some phones, using their 'beauty' settings, apparently can do it for you without asking. As George Monbiot (2016) has commented: 'Is it any wonder, in these lonely inner worlds, in which touching has been replaced by retouching, that young women are drowning in mental distress?'

There is scope in each of these areas to imaginatively develop the kind of individual, group, community responses and political responses (as well as drawing on social pedagogy approaches) which were a feature of social work practice at different times and places in the past (and still are in some parts of the world). In reality, however, the shrinking of social work practice to assessment and care management in the UK following the implementation of the 1990 NHS and Community Care Act means that such responses have largely disappeared from the social work canon or have been contracted out to health promotion professionals or the voluntary sector.

Neoliberalism and social work

The third factor contributing to the marginalisation of social work within mental health provision is the deliberate transformation of social work resulting from the creation of what John Harris called 'the social work business' in the early 1990s (Harris 2003). While it would be wrong to suggest that there was ever a 'golden age' of social work practice, the period of the late 1960s and the early 1970s did see an increased awareness among many social workers of the impact of poverty on the lives of their clients and the need for less individualised, more collective approaches such as groupwork and community development.

By contrast, as previously noted, the introduction of the market into social care in the early 1990s has meant that not only are social workers much less likely to draw on these approaches but there is also much less scope for the forms of therapeutic casework that had previously been common, especially in psychiatric social work. And the experience of social workers throughout the UK suggests that the current personalisation agenda, based on giving people individual budgets to buy their own care, far from opening up the great new era for social work which its advocates promised, means that adult care social workers are now more involved than ever in assessing risk and rationing services, based on tighter and tighter eligibility criteria, rather than working in preventative or creative ways (Beresford 2014).

Supporters of the purchaser/provider split argued it would lead to greater choice as a result of the increased role that would be played by the voluntary and private sector in the provision of services, including mental health services. And given the limitations of the NHS psychiatric services on offer, some of the new services that were developed in the 1990s did seem to offer more user-centred ways of responding to mental distress. Research into mental health service user involvement in Scotland in the mid-1990s, for example, found several examples of projects employing a social model of mental health, with service users playing a central role (Ferguson 1999; McPhail 2008). My own perception as a social work tutor in this period was also that larger numbers of social work graduates were opting to work in voluntary sector organisations, often for lower pay, in the hope that they could do 'real social work' there.

More than two decades on, however, the limitations of the market as a means of providing mental health services are increasingly obvious.

Firstly, the voluntary sector has changed massively during this period. Many large national organisations which were previously active campaigning organisations are now service providers, dependent on winning contracts from local or national government. Not surprisingly, that means that few are now willing to speak out, let alone campaign against, government policy. The experience of the homelessness charity Shelter following the Grenfell Tower tragedy in London in 2017 highlights the point. According to reports, there was considerable disquiet within the organisation over its apparently muted response to the tragedy. One possible reason for that response became clear when it emerged that Shelter's chairman Sir Derek Myers was a former chief executive of Kensington and Chelsea council, which owns Grenfell Tower, while trustee Tony Rice was chairman of Xerxes Equity, the sole shareholder in Omnis Exteriors – the company that sold the cladding used in the tower, the flammable properties of which contributed to the deaths of over 80 tenants. Both resigned soon after (Butler and Foster 2017).

Secondly, a key rationale for the introduction of a mixed economy of care was precisely to drive down welfare costs. And as both academics and trade unions in the voluntary sector have argued, the past two decades in the voluntary sector have seen 'a race to the bottom' in terms of wages and conditions (Cunningham 2008). In addition, following the election of the coalition government in 2010, and despite David Cameron's (now long forgotten) Big Society rhetoric, the voluntary sector has been one of the biggest casualties of the cuts that have taken place since then (UNISON 2014).

Mental health under pressure: cuts and austerity

That brings us to the fourth factor that has led to the marginalisation of mental health social work – namely cuts and the loss of resources, especially resources in the community since the implementation of austerity policies from 2010 onwards. When the role of Mental Health Officer was created by statute in the 1980s, the rationale for that role was that these would be the professionals who have a knowledge of what resources existed in the community and would be able to come up with alternatives to hospital care. The reality is, however, that not only did these roles quickly become overly legalistic and shaped by psychiatric perspectives but also the disappearance in recent years of many community-based mental health resources means that such alternatives are now few and far between. Instead, Approved Mental Health Officers in England now find themselves chasing fewer and fewer hospital beds across the country (Gilburt 2015) while the other face of reduced community support is an increase in the use of coercion in the form of both community treatment orders and electroconvulsive therapy (ECT) (Burns 2014).

What is to be done?

How, then, do we begin to challenge this marginalisation of social work? Four possibilities suggest themselves. Firstly, in terms of the knowledge base, as previously noted, there is now a very considerable body of theory and research stretching from trauma theory to Wilkinson and Pickett's (2010) work on the impact of inequality on mental health which highlights the role of biographical and social factors in the production of mental distress. The two key concepts that emerge from this work and are particularly relevant to us as social workers are *context* and *life experiences*. Read and Saunders in *The Causes of Mental Health Problems* sum up the core finding of that body of knowledge as being:

> Problems in mental health are more often than not the result of complex events in the environments in which we live and our reactions to them. These reactions can also be influenced by our biology or the way we have learned to think and feel. (Read and Sanders 2010: x)

In other words, many of the thoughts, feelings and behaviours that people identify as mental illness are a response to difficult life experiences, whether that be past life experiences such as abuse or neglect, being bullied or feeling undervalued or a response to current contexts of racism, work-related stress, loneliness or the effects of inequality. That social model of mental health needs to be at the heart of every qualifying social work programmes' teaching on mental health – and not just for students whose placements are in mental health settings or practitioners who are training to become Approved Mental Health Practitioners (AMPHs). In a recent paper in the *British Journal of Social Work* McCusker and Jackson refer to 'the universality of mental distress'. As one of the students whom they interviewed about practice placement commented:

> 'From my experience it [mental health] is one of the few areas of social work that is involved in all specialisms and affects people from every age group, background and ethnicity. Every placement I was on during the course involved mental health issues, although I did not have a mental health placement.' (McCusker and Jackson 2016: 1660)

People do not live their lives in boxes with children in one corner, older people in another and people with mental health problems in another. Hence the limitations of qualifying programmes like the Think Ahead programme in England which treat mental health social work as a specialism (https://thinkahead.org). Instead, an understanding of mental health and of the impact of mental distress should be at the core of all generic practice.

Secondly, we need to be more assertive about the social work role in mental health. For all its current limitations, to a greater extent than other mental health professions social work is underpinned by an awareness of the impact of structural factors such as racism and sexism on people's mental health and quality of life as well as an understanding of the need to take service users' experience seriously and involve them in decisions about their own lives. In their research, McCusker and Jackson found that what they call 'transformative social work practice' rested on three elements:

> [F]irst, a relationship-based approach, central to which was genuine interest in and drive to get to know the service user; second, a holistic approach to assessment that explored the potential impact of wider structural/situational factors on people's circumstances; third, persistence in the face of the many personal, cultural and organisational barriers encountered. (McCusker and Jackson 2016: 1661)

Thirdly, we need to develop new critical understandings of individualism and collectivism. The dominant policy agendas in mental health and in adult social care more generally such as personalisation and recovery approaches sound very progressive – all about people having more choice and control. In reality, however, unless supports in the form of good services are in place, then we are creating a false idea of independence which is setting people up to fail. There is a very dark side to a neoliberal model of independence which preaches that if you don't stand on your own two feet, you will be punished, whether that be through benefit sanctions, psycho-compulsion in the form of cognitive behavioural therapy (CBT) coaching or detention in the community. By contrast, the definition of independence proposed by the Independent Living Movement is clear that without good services and supports, real independence will remain an illusion:

> Independent living means all disabled people having the same freedom, choice, dignity and control as other citizens at home, at work and in the community. *It does not necessarily mean living by yourself or fending for yourself. It means rights to*

practical assistance and support to participate in society and live an ordinary life. (Emphasis added; http://www.ilis.co.uk/independent-living)

Finally, we need to continue to develop the kind of radical campaigning activities and collective forums for discussion that the Social Work Action Network has tried to promote, with some success, in recent years. Central to that process is the dual task of building alliances with other radical mental health professionals such as Psychologists against Austerity and service user organisations such as Recovery in the Bin while at the same time carving out a clear and distinctive role for a new radical mental health social work. SWAN's Charter for Mental Health is a good example of what that dual strategy looks like in practice (Weinstein 2014). This is a challenging agenda but not an impossible one. Recent political developments in the UK and elsewhere suggest that the tide may finally be turning against the individualist neoliberal deluge which has done so much damage to society, to relationships and to our collective mental health over more than three decades. Social workers need to ensure that they are part of that hopeful movement for change.

5

Learning disabilities and social work

Jan Walmsley

Introduction

Despite considerable policy and legislative changes over the past century, society continues to exclude, neglect and frequently damage people with learning disabilities. Hence the need for families to advocate on behalf of their relatives. How might social work respond?

At the time this chapter was written an initiative from the English government was launched to pilot a named social worker for people with learning disabilities (SCIE 2017). The fact that such an initiative was perceived to be needed in 2017 is, at first sight, quite astounding. As I will demonstrate in this chapter there is overwhelming evidence from families dating over the past 50 years that they want a trusted person to support them both in navigating around the services they may require, and in managing the emotions and stresses associated with bringing up and supporting a family member with learning disabilities. There is also evidence, almost as convincing, that having that trusted person can avert a crisis when family carers become ill. But, with few exceptions, families have looked in vain for such an individual.

The Named Social Worker initiative was directed at individuals at risk of hospital admission or admission to an Assessment and Treatment Unit, not families. This continues a trend that was noted as long ago as 1996 by researchers Burke and Signo (1996: 109): 'Many professionals consider that their work is with the person with disabilities, independent of their family … this could worsen family functioning because the whole family needs support and counselling'.

Although unfashionable, I tend to agree that attention to the whole family, particularly when the person in question lives with them, is vital. For that reason, in this chapter I draw extensively on the experiences of the families of people with learning disabilities and the work of local voluntary groups representing families. I use this to consider what role social work has played, and might play, in their lives. Much of this data comes from research conducted over a long period by the Open University's Social History of Learning Disability Research Group[1] (Rolph 2002; Rolph et al 2005; Tilley 2006; Walmsley 2000) of which the author is a founder member. The chapter's scope stretches back to the mid twentieth century, as that was the period when collective parent advocacy began to take shape, and social work to respond.

Why family testimony

As previously noted, it has been the practice of many professionals to regard the person with learning disabilities as their client, with families as, at best a distraction, at worst a barrier to independence and adulthood (see Walmsley et al 2017). In this chapter, I made a conscious decision to consider the role of social work in relation to learning disabilities through the eyes of families. This is because families have been the most consistent individuals in the lives of most people with learning disabilities (Walmsley et al 2017). In the twenty-first, as in the twentieth and earlier centuries, families act as the first and last resort for care. The majority of people with learning disabilities live with family (Foundation for People with Learning Disabilities 2012). Even at the height of institutionalisation, in 1969, more than 50% of people with learning disabilities lived outside institutions, most with family (Shennan 1980; Walmsley 2000). Historically families have had to fight for support and resources (Rolph et al 2005) and this has changed little over time (Rolph et al 2005; Walmsley et al 2017).

Recent literature on families caring for adults with learning disabilities demonstrates clear continuities with the past. Firstly, families do not trust the state to provide safe, consistent care for their relatives. Many describe a lack of confidence in current and future service provision, particularly what will happen when parents die (Fitzroy 2015).

In an interview conducted in 2013, a parent surprised the interviewer with this response to the question

> 'What do you see as the future for your children, Cath?'
> 'Well, we want to bury them.'
> (Unpublished interview with parent aged 60, 2013)

In saying this she echoed views of families over time. From Gerald Sanctuary's 1984 book *After I'm Gone What Will Happen to My Handicapped Child?* to the Report by Fitzroy (2015) entitled *Who Will Care After I'm Gone: An Insight into Pressures Facing Parents of*

People with Learning Disabilities families have worried that without their oversight, their relatives will come to harm and distress. At the very least, families report problematic relationships with professionals, and difficulty in getting the family's knowledge of the person taken into account (Heslop et al 2013); HealthWatch Oxfordshire 2014). Social work responses are not always reassuring.

Two contemporary examples illustrate this. The first comes from a blog published in late 2016. It was written by a woman who had cared for a slightly younger woman with severe learning difficulties for many years, but whose health was failing. She had hoped that the woman she cared for could go to live in the place where she had had respite, and where she had appeared to be content. Instead, a new social worker visited her and asked: 'If we give you more support, could she continue to live at home?' She replied that now it was too late. 'Years of struggling had ruined my health and I told him so.' His response: 'Care Providers will bid for her. She'll be put out to tender and we'll see what offers come in. We usually take the lowest' (Daly 2016).

The second example, also from a blog, is by a mother seeking help to manage her son's behaviour, which had become increasingly violent and unpredictable:

> Yesterday, I raged enough at the emergency social care guy to get the duty psychiatrist to call me. This is the *learning disability* team psychiatrist. We had an astonishing exchange that went on for nearly 20 minutes. He kept insisting that, if anything happened this weekend, we had to call the out of hours GP who would give us a prescription for LB. He would email the other psych, who had discharged him, and tell her what had happened for Monday. I tried to explain that when LB goes off on one, he goes off on one and there ain't really a convenient space to call the GP, collect a prescription and find a nearby chemist. He didn't get it. LB ain't his patient. He ain't seen him. He can't do anything else. (Ryan 2013)

The upshot, a month or so later, was that the young man was admitted to The Slade, an NHS Short Term Assessment and Treatment Centre in Oxford. He was 18 and he died there, two months later, from neglect. The failure to provide support to his family in this case had fatal consequences. His name was Connor Sparrowhawk, and his mother, blog author Sara Ryan, has been seeking proper accountability for his death ever since (Ryan 2017).

In the chapter, I will show that these two modern examples are illustrative of how social work has been with people with learning disabilities since the 1930s – but that things can be different.

The evolution of social work and people with learning disabilities

This section does not purport to be a comprehensive history of social work with people with learning disabilities. Readers interested in this are advised to turn to Duncan Mitchell and John Welshman's chapter 'In the Shadow of the Poor Law: Workforce Issues' published in my book (with John Welshman) *Community Care in Perspective* (2006). Rather, it seeks to set some of the enduring problems of social work with people with learning disabilities into historical context.

The predecessors of social workers in learning disability in the period before the Second World War were mostly volunteers, recruited and trained by the Central Association for Mental Welfare, a voluntary organisation which worked in partnership with national and local statutory authorities (Thomson 1998; Walmsley et al 1999). Their main functions were to 'ascertain' (identify) 'defectives', and, once they were certified as 'defective' by two doctors, to supervise those people who had not been admitted to institutions, mostly those living with families.

This is an extract from the quarterly report made by the Bedfordshire Voluntary Visitor to the Mental Deficiency Committee on her supervisory visits in 1936:

> She helps her mother a good deal with the work of the house.
>
> A dear little mite and most attractive.
>
> Very grateful to the Committee for the provision of extra tuition.
>
> This little lad is very frail, although I understand he is being offered cod liver oil and malt ... the house is a poor one but I think the parents do their best. George is a nice little lad and one who would benefit from training. Would the committee wish that I should suggest it to the parents? (Report of Voluntary Visitor to Bedfordshire Mental Deficiency Committee 1936)

The first three extracts are benign, even helpful – note the reference to money for extra tuition which the Visitor had requested from the Committee in a previous report. But the last is an instance of the iron fist in the velvet glove. Following this report, George was removed to the local 'colony', Bromham House, ostensibly for 'training'. He remained there for over 30 years, and told his story to my colleague Dorothy Atkinson in the 1990s (Atkinson 1993).

During the 1930s local authorities began to appoint salaried staff to replace the volunteers from the Central Association for Mental Welfare (CAMW) to ascertain and supervise 'defectives'. In Northamptonshire, for example, after criticism from the Board of Control, the government agency responsible for mental deficiency, that their 'ascertainment'[2] rates were low, and a report which claimed that over 1,000 undetected defectives were abroad in the county and reproducing at an alarming rate, a female Mental Welfare Social Worker was appointed in 1936, at a salary of £250 per annum.[3] The ascertainment rates rapidly increased thereafter.

The pre-war, predominantly female volunteer workforce was, after the Second World War, replaced by salaried Mental Welfare Officers (MWOs). These were often former Poor Law Relieving Officers, mostly male (Mitchell and Welshman 2006; Rolph et al 2003). In Bedfordshire in 1949 there were five Mental Welfare Officers - three were former Poor Law Relieving Officers - one to every 59,744 of the population. There were then 427 'defectives' under community care in the county (French 1971). By 1966, there were still only eight MWOs dealing with both mental health and learning disability, although the numbers on the books were continually growing (Rolph 2005b: 61).

These MWOs had enormous caseloads. Technically those 'defectives' living outside institutions should be visited every quarter, but MWOs also had the often more glamorous task of managing emergency mental health cases, which inevitably took precedence (Rolph et al 2003), and former MWO Cecil French, when interviewed by the author in 1991, acknowledged that in Bedfordshire they managed only one or at best two visits a year (Walmsley 1995).

In both the pre- and post-war workforce there were also Duly Authorised Officers, a role whose origins lay in the Poor Law – Officers 'duly authorised' under the 1890 Lunacy Act to commit pauper lunatics to asylums. The principal duties of the Duly Authorised Officer in the 1940s were little different. They were essentially to authorise people to be taken into an institution, or placed in guardianship, take someone neglected to a 'place of safety', take action where the person 'is not under proper care and control and there are no relatives or friends who intend to take proceedings for a reception order', and to take a person of 'unsound mind' to a hospital for the 'public safety or welfare of the person' (Matthews c. 1948: 40-41). This essentially custodial role, I would argue, has set the tone for social work with people with learning disabilities ever since.

Learning disability has always been low in the priorities of social work, with other client groups invariably taking precedence. This has been a long enduring phenomenon. Writing in 1975, shortly after social work had become 'generic', under the control of local authorities, researcher Kathleen Jones had this to say about Local Authority Social Work:

> Mental health social work has been one of the major casualties in social service reorganisation [in 1970]. Systems of care which had been quite highly developed in some places have been destroyed and as yet there is little to take their place. But even where Mental Health Services were well developed before ... 1970, they tended to concentrate on specific areas ...: child guidance and the urgent problems of the adult mentally ill absorbed much of their energies ... Even fewer have ever seen the provision of care for the adult mentally handicapped as an important part of their work. (Jones 1975: 179–180)

Jones' solution was a specialist profession for 'the mentally handicapped', a call echoed by Peggy Jay in her Report on Mental Handicap Nursing published in 1979. It never happened. Instead the profession has continued to prioritise what was then called child guidance and the urgent problems of people with severe mental health problems, and to turn attention to learning disability only when a crisis breaks, or where an individual's or public safety appears to be at risk – 'safeguarding' in modern parlance. Remarkably little has changed.

Family views of social work and social services

I undertook the research for this section by consulting my library, built up over many years, of personal accounts and research reports where family members comment upon their experience of social workers and social services. It is far from comprehensive, but I promise you that I did not start my reading with the intention of finding criticism of social workers. Nevertheless, according to my reading of this literature, with few exceptions family experiences of the services offered by

MWOs in the 1960s and 1970s, and in later decades by social workers were negative. The challenge was to find anything, any examples, of proactive and positive support.

Former Mental Welfare Officers themselves acknowledged the shortcomings in oral histories, recorded in the late 1990s. Russell Reeve worked in Norfolk. He remembered: "'We did very little work with people with learning disabilities in those days. We kept a register but we were run off our feet and the mentally handicapped sadly were on the back boiler'" (Rolph et al 2003: 345). "'You had nothing to offer'", recalled Trevor Last (Suffolk). "'All you had to offer was that you would see them again in 3 or 6 months time. There was nothing'" (Rolph et al 2003: 346).

Don Hardy, father of Margaret, born 1949, agreed:

'A MWO visited to help Margaret. She gave Margaret a toy to help her use her fingers. "What a marvellous idea." She said "I will visit again in a fortnight". We next saw her 11 months later. She was useless.' (Rolph 2005a: 41–42)

Michael Bayley's research in Sheffield in the late 1960s showed that few families were satisfied with MWOs, although, as the quotation indicates, social workers came even lower in their esteem.

Second, the mental welfare officer: he came off rather worse than the family doctor – only 10 (of 54) mothers thought he helped and 27 believed that he was of little or no assistance. Third, social workers: they were also criticized because of loss of contact and the unrelated advice given. Punctuality was often lacking. (Bayley 1973: 37)

In family accounts there are several recurrent themes. The following quotation points to two of them: rapid changes in personnel, and responding only in an emergency:

'I was really kind of leaving it to the social worker, but the social worker has left his job now, and we've never been contacted by anyone else. There's such a big caseload that if everything's going right for a while you are taken off the books until things go wrong again.' (Atkinson 2005: 141)

A group of mothers of adults with learning disabilities in Devon recorded their experience of different professions in an article published in 1989 (MacLachlan et al 1989). The theme of their account is that they received very little help from anyone once their children moved into adulthood, but social workers were particularly low in their estimation:

> 'We feel that we receive scant help from community nurses and social workers, social workers coming rather lower in our estimation than community nurses ... We have all gone for long periods without help from anyone; and if someone is allotted the support provided is not maintained for any length of time, so no feelings of trust can be established.' (McLachlan et al 1989: 25–26)

Moving into the 1990s, at a time following the 1993 NHS and Community Care Act, Peter Burke and Cathy Signo (1996) surveyed 67 parents of children with learning disabilities about their support networks. Once more, social work and social services departments came very low in the league of helping.

> 'Who do they think they are? I know what our needs are; I live them day by day.'

> 'They will come and take my child away if they see a bruise.'

> 'She [social worker] came to my house with a clipboard and asked me some questions. She seemed in a bit of a rush.'

> 'I rang for advice and they said they would ring back. Two months later there was still no reply. I rang again and they had no record of my call. I did not try again.' (Burke and Signo 1996: 98–99)

There was no sense of their being a preventative service in any of the responses received in this research.

There were some exceptions. MWO Neville Porter, who took up post in Lowestoft in 1954, focused on support for families: "This was vital in Suffolk ... the family was the key thing. If you supported the family you could keep a patient at home" (Rolph et al 2003: 347). To that end, Lowestoft set up a Home Help service administered by the MWOs, whose main role was to 'hold families in the community' (Rolph et al 2003: 347). But this is exceptional, and it may be, had we asked the beneficiaries, we'd have found a very different picture.

There is more in the vein of these rather depressing comments from families – see for example the stories collected by Rolph et al (2005) for their book *Witnesses to Change*, family accounts since the 1940s. Suffice to reiterate that the key messages are:

- Social workers do not (have time to) listen.
- Social workers are unresponsive and unreliable.
- Social workers change frequently, no time to build trusting relationships.
- Social workers only appear at times of crisis.
- Social workers do not tell families what support they can expect, or where to find it.
- Social workers leave families to struggle alone.
- Social workers are, by some, feared as they may only appear to remove their relatives (safeguarding).

Social work and parent advocacy

The advent of parent groups in the later twentieth century changed the picture and demanded a response from social work.

Parents have probably advocated for their relatives with learning disabilities since the beginning of time. But until the second half of the twentieth century such advocacy was muted and individual. Families were isolated with the shame of having a child with a learning disability. They were sometimes given the choice to put relatives into institutions, sometimes forced to do so (Thomson 1998; Walmsley 2000). There were very few special schools, or day centres, no voluntary organisations to represent their interests, no means of knowing about others in similar situations (Rolph 2002). Occasionally we hear a voice like this man requesting that his sister be allowed home from the institution for a holiday: 'I am the only one who goes to see her. I thought a change would do her good to being in there. She has never had a holiday' (Bedfordshire Mental Deficiency Committee correspondence 1937). His request was turned down. The home, reported the Visitor (predecessor of social worker), was dirty.

This is a further poignant example.

> My son has been away now from home since 1917, a lifetime really and there seems no hope of his ever coming home. It is nearly two years since we saw him as the train fare is so high and the train service so bad. I should love to see my only one. But I know it is awkward. I tries to send

him a packet of cigarettes every week. (Bedfordshire Mental
Deficiency Committee correspondence 1940)

Things changed after the Second World War. The second half of the
twentieth century saw a massive growth in parent advocacy. From
the later 1940s, families gradually came to be portrayed as burdened,
deserving of both sympathy and practical support (Castles 2004; Rolph
2002; Walmsley 2000). 'Little Stephen', Mencap's then logo, illustrates
this shift. The image is of a pathetic child, rather than the somewhat
threatening persona of the pre-war 'defective' (Walmsley 2000).

Collective parent advocacy in the second half of the twentieth
century was characterised by mutual support, the provision of services
in local communities, and campaigning (Rolph 2002). Across the
UK from 1946 onwards small local groups formed. Their early
efforts were focused on building holiday chalets, nurseries, residential
homes, occupation centres and training volunteer welfare visitors
(Rolph 2002). Contemporary large-scale provider organisations like
Hft and MacIntyre started as the initiatives of parent activists looking
for alternatives to hospital care in the 1960s. National campaigning
contributed to the 1970 Education Act (England and Wales) and the
Education (Mentally Handicapped Children) Act 1974 in Scotland,
which gave all children the right to an education for the first
time; and the 1971 White Paper Better Services for the Mentally
Handicapped (England and Wales) and Scotland's Services for the
Mentally Handicapped (1972), which both made commitments to
expand residential and day provision, in 'the community' (Welshman
and Walmsley 2006). Similar processes have been recorded in the USA
(Castles 2004), Australia (Johnson 2006) and Scandinavia (Grunewald
1978).

The need was great. Families could be incredibly isolated with their
disabled children (Harris 2005; Rolph 2002). "We never saw a soul.
We just had them at home. There was nothing. Nothing at all ... it
was a very dim period really for us in those days" (Rolph 2002: 52).
There was considerable stigma, which served to further isolate families.
Writing of the 1950s, when her son was born, Brenda Nickson (2005:
77) wrote: 'You felt you were pushing an empty pram because people
didn't know what to say to you.'

The difference made by coming together with others in similar
situations was considerable.

'Suddenly we realised we were not on our own ... It was
a great relief, we thought we must be the only parents

struggling like that … It did seem miraculous that we were going to these little functions where we were welcome, and our daughter Wendy was particularly welcome.' (Rolph 2002: 45)

There was a mixed response from social work to these newly energised parent groups.

Many local authorities were reluctant to embrace the parent advocacy movement. The newly formed Norwich and Norfolk branch of the National Association of Parents of Backward Children (NAPBC) was rebuffed for two years in seeking a place on the County Council's Mental Health subcommittee in 1954-1956 (Rolph 2005a: 32-33). When, in 1952, Bucks County Council took over the running of a day centre in Slough set up by local families, the families were denied a place on the committee supervising its rebuilding (Walmsley 2000: 110).

However, some MWOs saw the growing movement of parents as an asset rather than a threat. In Luton, parent Rene Harris was helped to set up the local branch of the NAPBC in 1955 by an MWO who, while he could not divulge names and addresses, instead sent a letter to families on his books inviting them to a party. The response was overwhelming, and the branch started from there (Harris 2005).

In Ipswich, MWO Harry Orme remembered working with the local NAPBC branch, listening to their problems, but, more importantly, securing money and premises for a two-week summer break scheme. They also adjusted the bus routes in response to family requests (Rolph et al 2003: 350).

In Bedfordshire in the 1960s the NAPBC set up a home visiting scheme to visit new parents with a child with learning disabilities. The Home Visitor's job was to liaise with the County Council Mental Health Department and to visit all new parents. Visitors interviewed in the early 2000s recalled the value of this service: "people would unburden themselves to you", "we were like a direction finder for them" (Rolph 2005b: 61).

The value of this cooperation was formally recognised: 'The support and practical help of the branch, both to the Authority and direct to patients is highly valued' (Beds M o H Report 1966 quoted in Rolph 2005b: 61).

Activists Michael and Ann Tombs, also in Bedford, recalled that David Clifton, first Director of Social Services, took an active interest in their work in the 1970s, gave them his private phone number and ensured that representatives of Mencap (the renamed NAPBC) were on a working party discussing the development of services (Tombs and Tombs 2005).

Can it be different?

I end this chapter with a reminder that at the time of writing there was an initiative to pilot a scheme to allocate named social workers to individuals with learning disabilities in England. It remains to be seen whether this initiative lived up to expectations – the pilots ended in March 2017 and the final evaluation is awaited. But there are examples which show that services can support families.

Linda Ward wrote extensively about the Wells Road Service in Bristol, set up in 1983 specifically to support all people with a learning disability in the area, and their families. Families reported overwhelming enthusiasm, both for the support it offered to their relatives – "now he's got more than a full social life" (Ward 1989: 193) – and for themselves – "It was the best thing that happened to me all year" (Ward 1989: 193).

In research conducted in the early 2000s, Sue Ledger considered why some people with complex needs living in an Inner London Borough did *not* get placed out of area when their domestic circumstances led to a crisis.

Her findings were that what prevented out of area placements were local services, including both Local Authority and Residential Social Workers, which made it their business to get to know families: "'I encouraged staff to build up relationships with carers so they knew to turn to us for help" (Manager short term break facility RBKC 1990s)' (Ledger 2012: Chapter 7).

Senior staff had been involved with the local parents' movement: "'Many of the … senior managers had served on the first Mencap Committee … This made it easier for families to approach them when there were difficulties at home" (Manager RBKC 1990s)' (Ledger 2012: Chapter 7).

Frontline staff had discretion to respond flexibly to families when necessary:

> 'I was allowed a tremendous amount of freedom … families did not need a .. referral. They would just ring us up …'
> (Senior Manager RBKC 1990s)

> 'I remember a carer ringing saying she had to go into hospital that day. I said leave it with me. In my head I was

thinking what am I going to do? We have no spaces' (Short breaks manager RBKC (1990s))

'If we were full and the situation was urgent we would simply put a mattress down' (RSW RBKC (1990s)). (Ledger 2012: Chapter 7)

The brother of Lenny, one of the people whose stories Ledger collected, recalled how it had worked when his mother, Lenny's main carer, became ill:

'When mum became ill Lenny went to stay at Piper House [hostel]. He would come back home at the weekends when Ewan, and Cahill [older brothers] were not at work. If mum was out of hospital and well enough Lenny would come home then too. During the week when we were out at work Piper House looked after him. This went on for over two years.' (Ledger 2012: 304)

As an example of a creative service response to a family crisis which might well have resulted in Lenny's being moved to an out of area placement this is hard to surpass.

Conclusion: a better future?

The lessons from this survey of the history of social work with the families of people with learning disabilities are sharp. The norm is:

- Learning disability is not a priority for social work unless a 'safeguarding' issue.
- There are never enough social workers, never have been, and probably never will be.
- Families bear the brunt, but struggle, get little help and fear for the future – when they are gone.
- Social work is reactive to crises, not proactive.
- Rapid staff turnover is detrimental to families.

If the situation is to improve then:

- There is potential in a partnership with the voluntary sector representing families, as in Bedfordshire in the 1960s.

- Support for families is vital, and can reduce costs in the long term, by supporting families when crises hit.
- Trusting relationships with families can make it possible to head off crises.
- Practitioners need discretion and a willingness to take risks.
- There needs to be some flexible capacity in local provision and discretion for frontline staff.

These lessons are not so very different from the recommendations of the 1982 Barclay Report on the roles and tasks of social workers in England and Wales which called for more emphasis on community engagement, and a new social work role of broker of resources (Barclay 1982). If Barclay's recommendations were ignored by government, it is unlikely that my conclusions will meet a different fate, but, although it is hard to imagine such changes in the context of present-day services, the lessons are clear. Things can be different.

Notes

[1] www.open.ac.uk/health-and-social-care/research/shld/
[2] Refers to the practice of identifying people who may be 'mentally defective' so that they could be dealt with.
[3] This information from Bundle 3937 in Northamptonshire's County Archives labelled Mental Deficiency: Files re Welfare of Defectives.

6

Social work by and for all

Peter Beresford

Introduction

Big claims have sometimes been made for social work. For example, leading up to the creation of large local authority social services departments in the UK in the early 1970s, it was suggested that it could have a major impact on poverty (Seebohm 1968). In the event, instead of the community-based, family social work that was hoped for, these hierarchical departments marked the beginning of the large-scale bureaucratisation of local state social work which has accelerated under the political New Right and neoliberal politics that have dominated in the intervening years. In England and Wales, we now have state social work that is tightly regulated and shaped by central government, where, as numerous reports have testified, the day to day social work task is dictated more by 'the bottom line' and the managerialist surveillance of social workers than by any independent social work values, ethics or discretion (Social Work Task Force 2009).

During this period social work has essentially been a marginalised and residual service, working primarily and often only with people seen as the most disadvantaged and marginalised. In their efforts to demonstrate the specific and unique role and tasks of social work, unintentionally or otherwise, policy makers and formal social work leaders have tended to emphasise its specific and control functions (Beresford 2007). While many of social work's formal leaders seem to have both advanced and supported this view of the profession, the aim of this discussion is to look more carefully at the assumptions that this is based upon and to critique how helpful they may be to social work, service users and the rest of us for the future.

In some ways my focus here is a simple, straightforward one, reflected in the title of this chapter: 'Social Work by and for All'. Starting with this premise, the importance of an inclusive, mainstream social work, I want to identify some of the principles which I believe underpin all that is best about social work and which offer us a helpful route map for the future, as well as looking at more problematic principles that have long troubled social work. But first, back to what I called my simple focus.

In truth, nothing is really simple or straightforward in social work. Nothing is made simple or easy for social work and social workers. Little can be treated at face value. Much of what is said about social work, many of the arguments used to attack and condemn it, or to justify doing it differently, bear little relation to what actually happens on the ground. In fact, very little is publicly known about what goes on routinely on the ground (Brindle 2017). Years ago the *Daily Mail* ran one of its frequent attacks on social work. My partner, longstanding face-to-face practitioner Suzy Croft (www.socialworkawards.com/previous_winners/lifetime-achievement-2/) contacted the paper and suggested they actually take a look at social work. They did. They came and interviewed her during a day's work as a specialist palliative care social worker. The journalist seemed interested and enthusiastic. She seemed personally to have gained a new understanding, beyond populist stereotypes. However, later she phoned to say they weren't going to use the article! Since then the *Daily Mail* has consistently maintained its hostile, damaging stance towards social work and social workers.

Not only can social workers expect to come under media attack. Additionally, they themselves now are frequently debarred from speaking to the media. Few are supported by their agencies and employers to take part in conferences and other key discussions. There tend to be very few practitioners at international events, like those organised by the International Federation of Social Workers, which tend instead to be dominated by researchers and educators. The latter are more likely to be funded to present papers, but few of them are able to remain in practice. To make matters worse, service users are still often not listened to, even if they may be increasingly heard. And then there is talk of social work needing a stronger voice!

It is only to be expected that there will be problems if the key actors and voices in any activity or profession are largely absent or excluded from its discussion and development This seems particularly to be the case with social work, where the viewpoints and experience of both current practitioners and service users have tended to be marginalised. Perhaps it is not surprising, with this gaping hole in the middle – the frequent exclusion of its key voices – that social work so often seems a matter of extremes. Let me give an example from research which I have been involved in carrying out. I want what I say in this chapter to be firmly based on research, so I will start with this example – as I mean to go on.

A case study of key issues for social work

Three of us carried out a UK-wide research project exploring what service users thought about palliative care/end of life social work (Beresford et al 2007). This was a large-scale qualitative project, supported by the Joseph Rowntree Foundation, involving more than 100 people as service users. By no means everyone who accesses palliative care gets social work support. It is the poor relation there, as in so many other policy contexts. So we only interviewed people either with life limiting conditions or facing bereavement who had received such social work support. What was interesting was how many told us that they had doubts about accepting the offer, because of their pre-existing views about social work. Some of these came from the media presentation of social work, some from family experience and some were first-hand. We couldn't know of course how many had turned down the offer of help for such reasons. But the project took us from one extreme to another. It quickly became apparent from the interviews that service users overwhelmingly had very positive things to say about the support they received from palliative care social workers. They were so positive and enthusiastic that we felt we had to introduce additional check questions to give them more opportunities to be critical and negative – but they weren't! This made us wonder even more about those who had decided not to access social work support because of their negative preconceptions about it and what problems this created for them. What might they have lost?

Social work and universalism

Another key issue associated with end of life social work, and it is the first of the issues of principle that I want to consider here, is that it has been universalist in principle, in the sense that it has been a service like the modern hospice movement, where the aim is to offer support to *all* who may need it, free and regardless of people's income, history or status. We all die and so the assumption has been that we all may need help to negotiate life's ending and the bereavement that goes with it. In this it reflects one of the fundamental principles of the post-war welfare state. The welfare state's key policies, from education and social security to housing and the NHS, rested on the belief that they were there to help anyone in need. This was a radical departure from the poor law, an essentially residual policy, based on deterrence and less eligibility; that is to say, on ensuring that the standards and opportunities it offered people were inferior to those they could secure without recourse to public support. The poor law was, of course, also associated with stigma, segregation and inferior life chances (Beresford 2016).

In reality, because palliative care, like all services, has been subjected to financial cuts and restrictions and medical advances have affected its role and meant that patients may live much longer, this goal of ensuring a truly universalist service is not routinely realised. The modern hospice movement largely began as an initiative to offer people with cancer support at the end of their lives, but it has extended its brief as the years have gone by. Some groups, though, continue to be less likely to access specialist palliative care support than others, notably people from black and minority ethnic (BME) communities and people with less valued life-limiting conditions, (compared with cancer), like heart failure and chronic obstructive pulmonary disease (COPD) (Gunaratnam 2007). But palliative care social workers can expect to work with rich and poor; refugees and asylum seekers. They may well work with people who are household names as well as prisoners released from incarceration to end their days in a humane and specialist setting. Our study included a diverse range of people in terms of health condition, class and culture, income, education and experience, gender and ethnicity, disability and age.

Thus, in principle, palliative care social work has developed as a needs based rather than means tested policy and service. You qualify for it if you need it, not because your income is at a defined low level or you are seen as problematic. The increasing aim has been for it to be available for all with need for end of life care and/or bereavement support. In this sense, it embodies the universalist principles of the post-war welfare state, which sought to replace those of the Victorian means-tested poor law, which determinedly restricted support to destitute or impoverished people and then imposed value judgements on whether they were 'deserving' or not. While it is important to acknowledge that cuts in health and social care spending under 'austerity' policies in the UK have increasingly restricted the role of palliative care social work, and in some cases caused loss of jobs and services, nonetheless its universality remains a common principle and goal. What this universalism highlights is how helpful social work can be – for anyone, rich or poor, marginalised or indeed advantaged. Many of the people we interviewed may never have imagined that they would be on the receiving end of social work, or that it could be helpful to them. Instead a common refrain was that the social worker offered them all that they would hope for from a *real friend*. But in the real world, it can often be difficult for a friend to take on the tasks the social worker would, or bring as much skill to bear. Equally, this sentiment did not mean that the social worker was unboundaried in their role, but rather frequently seen as having key valued human qualities, like warmth, empathy, reliability, having time, being non-judgemental and, perhaps above all, listening (Beresford et al 2008).

This characteristic, its universalistic nature, has set palliative care social work apart from much other modern statutory and voluntary social work. Social work's origins are largely rooted in regulatory and paternalist intentions. Yet in the UK at least, its flowering took place in the years following the creation of the universalist post-war welfare state. While we may challenge contemporary understandings of such 'universalism' (Beresford 2016), what is significant is that social work since then, by contrast, has largely been accepted as a residual and marginal service for those identified as marginal, deviant and disadvantaged. As New Right politics have increasingly predominated, the pressure to marginalise social work and extend its regulatory role, not surprisingly, have accelerated.

Driving in a different direction: from negative to progressive forces in social work

Historically, social work has largely been associated with being a response to marginalised, poor and disadvantaged people. We have not escaped that tradition. Often it seems to have been taken for granted. This was true of its origins in nineteenth century philanthropic, paternalistic and charitable utilitarian interventions like those of the Charity Organisation Society and Octavia Hill's housing management and rent collection schemes, and also of the schemes which grew out of socialist philosophy and working class self-organising. The great expansion of social work through the Seebohm reforms and the creation of social services departments in 1971 were focused on people conceived of as deprived. It was not so much 'family social work' as it was presented, as social work with poor people/families. As we have seen, a major criticism that has been made of the advocates of these reforms is that they over-claimed the capacity of social work to reduce poverty (Jones 1999).

Reactions to the managerialist, bureaucratic, hierarchical social work that resulted from those reforms ranged from the first emergence of radical social work in the 1970s with its commitment to equality and social justice, to the development in the 1980s of community and patch-based social work (Beresford and Croft 1986).

Social work, while largely led formally by traditional and consensual bureaucrats, has also been significantly influenced by radical practitioners and the service user movements that emerged during the last quarter of the twentieth century (Lavalette 2011). These have both created forces for resistance to the centralised and top-down pressures operating on social work, as well as highlighting and giving rise to alternative ideas, ways of learning, knowledge production, practice and organisation.

These progressive forces have been influential even if the dominant discourse has continued to be regressive. They point to a route to and a shape for a future social work, responding to the need for a truly universalist service, committed to sustainability, as part of a new user-led welfare state to challenge the present neoliberal running down and subversion of both the welfare state generally and social work specifically. I want next to highlight and explore these issues for the future, from the position of being committed to a social work by and for the people in their overlapping roles as service users, workers and other local people.

However, as I have already said, the dominant political response has been one of seeking to marginalise social work, cutting its funding and restricting its resources, imposing increasing control over social workers, weakening the independence of its organisations and 'othering', individualising and pathologising service users. Cuts have particularly affected social work with adults and fewer and fewer adults who might previously have accessed it as disabled people, mental health service users, people with learning difficulties, older people or people with long-term conditions are now less likely to do so. High-level political fears of a child protection tragedy and ensuing high-profile scandal on their watch have perhaps encouraged more caution among politicians in the context of social work with families and children. Nonetheless, fewer families are likely to access support and those that do can expect to get less, with increased adoption serving as policy makers' preferred ideological solution (Gallagher, 2017).

What this means is that statutory social work not only continues overall to be a residual service in the UK, but that it is increasingly residualised. It is increasingly restricted to people seen as poor and problematic. Now it is not only focused on what are seen as a minority population, but an ever-diminishing proportion of that minority are likely to access it. Also, because social work has few political friends, it has been the control rather than support role of social work which has commanded what political and policy support it has managed to retain. As has already been noted, when there is policy talk about the unique role and tasks of social work, what is special and signature about it, these are increasingly framed in terms of control. This is a further significant and worrying development.

There has perhaps rarely been a time when social work has been so contradictory. Progressive and reactionary seem to be operating cheek by jowl in increasingly stark contrast and contradiction. This is highlighted by my partner and colleague Suzy Croft, a practitioner with decades of experience of face-to-face work with highly diverse range of service users:

> 'One of the shocking things you have to struggle with is that you encounter other people, both directly and indirectly, who are employed as social workers who seem to have a very different notion of what that role is about to that set out in social work's own professional ethics and codes. I've worked with many people without citizenship status and there isn't a word less than shocking I'd use to describe social workers, badged as care managers, who collude, apparently without conscience, in the grim business of returning people to their country of origin, regardless of what discrimination and oppression they may have already experienced there and sought to flee from, or which they can expect to encounter on their return. Or social workers supposedly working with disabled people or mental health service users who do not act as advocates for them, but rather are merely part of the process of rationing rather than accessing them to support. How does this square with our role of speaking up for people, of supporting social justice, of challenging exclusion, discrimination and impoverishment?' (Personal communication with Suzy Croft, 18 July 2017)

Re-examining the social in social work

I want next to move on to the second underpinning principle of social work I am concerned with. I think it is particularly interesting to consider the development of social work – essentially as a residual service associated primarily with those seen as deprived – in relation to what has always also been the defining feature of social work: its *social* nature.

At the heart of social work's unique repertoire is its holistic approach, its social approach. This is a key underpinning principle. I am not saying, of course, that in practice social work hasn't deviated from this social approach. We know that it has. We know there has been a whole psychodynamic/psychoanalytic tradition which has focused narrowly on the individual. We know that policy makers have constantly tried to emphasise the individualised. But the core of the idea of social work, what distinguishes it from other occupational and professional approaches, is that it is as it says on the tin, in essence *social* work. It is concerned with the individual and their context; the psychological and the social; nature and nurture; the individual and their environment; structure and agency; and of course the interaction between, the intersection of, the two. Or as C Wright Mills (1959) put it when talking about his idea of sociological imagination, the conjunction of individual biography and history.

We should also take into account the lessons for social work to be learned from the social model of disability developed by the disabled people's movement. This has distinguished between the individual's perceived impairment and the negative or disabling societal response to it and over the years elaborated on the relationship between the two (Thomas 2007). Social work's concern with the personal, the social and the material, and their interactions with each other, has been the reason why social work at its best has always been concerned with both practical and emotional/psychological support, with the one often being the route into the other.

The range of social work support

So let me return for a moment to our study of what service users thought about specialist palliative care social work. What was also striking was the different kinds of support that service users talked about social workers offering them: practical support, emotional support, help with their family, with employment and benefit issues, in negotiating the health and service system, providing advocacy, information and advice. They offered direct support, support to people's family and friends – and group work. And also we know that there are elements of community work to be found here in social work more generally too. Different people valued different things, but the large menu that social workers could offer was one that was widely appreciated and drawn on (Beresford et al 2007: 68 and following).

This combination of practical and therapeutic work, following from social work's social understanding, distinguishes it from most if not all counselling. Of course there are many forms and schools of counselling. These may pay more or less attention to the structural issues affecting people's lives, as well as addressing their feelings, emotions and psychology. But putting to one side the particular enthusiasms or skills of individual counsellors or where counsellors have been influenced by social work, there is not the same engagement with the practical: the rolling up of sleeves, the wiping up of vomit, and all the rest that social workers know only too well.

Now I turn to the issue which I suspect has not been much discussed elsewhere: the relationship of social work's social orientation and its largely residual nature. We have tended to take this coupling for granted. I think we need to question it for the future.

Let me explain. It might initially seem a good thing to focus social work on poor and disadvantaged people. They can perhaps be seen as having most need of its support – which even in times of plenty will always be of finite quantity. It recognises and takes account of the damaging effects on their rights and needs through deprivation and inequality. This is something that social workers rightly stress and keep in their line of sight. But equally it can also be used in a different, negative way.

It becomes routine to associate poor and disadvantaged people with pathology and deviance and then, we know, it is a short step to say it is their fault. It can be a short journey from coupling personal problems with disadvantage to seeing it as in the nature of people's disadvantage to be problematic; that is to say, poor people have and are problems. And it is one thing to say their problems arise from poverty when we are talking about the effects of poor housing, of lack of food or clothes for their children. It is another when we associate what is judged as 'poor parenting' or child neglect and abuse crudely with material want, because quickly this can get translated into policy assumptions that poor parents are poor parents in the sense of being damaging to their children – with its extreme rendition of an abusive and destructive 'underclass' or notion of 'troubling families'. The Victorian reformers, for example, associated incest with poverty and bad housing and used this coupling ostensibly progressively as an argument for improving housing, while tacitly using it to condemn the working class and poorly housed as immoral.

Social work for all?

Let me begin with the broader issue that our damaging, oppressive, racist, homophobic, sexist, disablist, unequal, increasingly neoliberal society has destructive effects on many if not all of us. The influential text *The Spirit Level* made this point (Wilkinson and Pickett 2009). If we consider this argument then we might see how social work with its unifying focus on the personal and the political; the individual and their environment may have a valuable support role for many more of us.

Of course poverty is especially destructive for people made poor. But why should we think that an approach based on recognition of the important intersection of the personal and material should only work or be for those seen as deprived? It is as if human needs and rights are only denied those experiencing material deprivation and that all needs follow from that. Clearly this is not true from my research example of death, dying and bereavement. But we know that it is also true of problematic parenting, of child abuse, of child sexual abuse, of rape, of trauma, of relationship breakdown, of mental distress and madness, of disability and so on. They can befall any of us (even if poverty and disadvantage may expose people to them more and for different reasons) and we might all benefit from social work support.

Of course we know that more powerful people, people who are not materially disadvantaged who do the sorts of things that poor people can expect to be vilified for, may escape attention or be able to avoid the oversight of social work. Take the recent case of graphic designer Ben Butler, who murdered his daughter Ellie after a custody battle, where the *Daily Mail* campaigned against social workers for his right to keep his daughter – the daughter he went on to murder (O'Carroll and Taylor 2016).

So we should not make simplistic assumptions about the relation between disadvantage and the problems people may experience. I suspect that there may have been some of this within the founding welfare state post-Second World War. There seems to have been a sense that issues associated with poor law poverty, like the miserable conditions some older people lived in, or the impairments that some children experienced, would diminish and disappear as a fairer and materially more just society developed. But we know that medical innovation and other social changes have not necessarily diminished such challenges, but instead in some cases have increased their incidence, meaning that more people may need support, including social work support, as they encounter them.

I hope in this chapter that I have begun both to challenge those negative principles that social work has been vulnerable to, of residualism and individualisation, while also highlighting the need for more thought in relating the key principles of its social approach and modelling social work as a universalist service. I believe that only if we demarginalise social work, see it as something that may help any of us, that we will offer it true hope for a positive future.

Five key principles for future social work

So far I have taken considerable space focusing on two key principles for future social work: universalism and a social approach. But I believe that there are at least five key principles altogether that we must hold up as the basis for just and person-centred social work. I haven't left myself much space to explore these others, but then they are, I think, more often the subject of discussion and therefore are likely to be more familiar. So now let me briefly address them.

Treating diversity with equality

Social work's longstanding commitment to addressing diversity, framed in terms of anti-oppressive practice, signifies its fundamental recognition of the central importance of treating diversity with equality as a pillar of its philosophy and activity. It is not an easy principle to hold as central, in discriminatory times and discriminatory settings, even if it can make for easy rhetoric. Social work has not necessarily stood firm by this principle in its own operation. There are still glass ceilings and exclusions at work which need to be challenged. It is interesting to remember that the General Social Care Council tried to challenge mental health service users' capacity to be social work practitioners as a group, until legally challenged by the then Disability Rights Commission. It is also crucial to recognise all aspects of diversity: in relation to gender, sexuality, race, class, culture, belief, age, impairment and more. When Shaping Our Lives, the national user-led disabled people's organisation, carried out a four-year research and development project, in addition to exclusions that emerged in relation to equality issues, we identified major exclusions on four other bases. These were:

- Where people live: if they are homeless, in prison, in welfare institutions, refugees and so on.
- Communicating differently: if they do not speak the prevailing language, it is not their first language, they are deaf and use sign language and so on.
- The nature of their impairments, which are seen as too complex or severe to mean they could or would want to contribute.
- Where they are seen as unwanted voices: they did not necessarily say what authorities want to hear, are seen as a problem, and so on. (Beresford 2013)

All of these need to be recognised and addressed, and the complexities of ideas of intersectionality given more consideration and explored further.

Participation

Social work has been a pioneer in developing a participatory approach to its learning, its practice, its organisation and its research and knowledge development and exchange. It is still the only profession in the UK and beyond where there are both formal requirements through every aspect and every stage of its professional education for such involvement and where there is (in England and Wales at least) a central budget to support this. In an age where the effective discretion of social workers has increasingly been limited by political, funding and managerial constraints, they can expect to be offered some promise of professional power, but many are still not settling for less than partnership with service users. However, there are still many challenges. It is great that we now routinely have service users actively involved as educators in the classroom, but we know that much of what students are still learning from texts, notably in relation to disability and especially 'mental health' or madness and distress, still pathologises service users because of its reliance on medicalised individual models of understanding and 'treatment' (Beresford and Wilson 2000). Much has been learned from listening to and involving service users about what works and what they value from social workers and it is important to keep this in view. Repeatedly, in research and consultations, they highlight the value they attach to human qualities and skills of warmth, empathy, reliability, being non-judgemental, listening, honest, with a social understanding and commitment to equality (Beresford 2016).

Gap ending

Finally I want to turn to gap ending. This is a concept I find helpful which has grown out of another pioneered by the European network of educators and service users PowerUs – gap mending (http://powerus. eu). It connects with social work's commitment to user involvement. Originally funded by the European Union as a partnership between the UK, Sweden and Norway, PowerUs developed the idea of gap mending to challenge the taken-for-granted divisions that can exist in social work and indeed other helping professions. The first it focused on was between service users and social workers and social work students. Swedish academics at Lund University pioneered an empowerment programme as part of their qualifying social work courses which brought service users and students together, to work and learn together, both of them gaining better understanding and trust in each other as well as formal recognition. There are now 12 participating countries in the partnership and such courses in several UK and EU countries, and they parallel the more traditional UK approach to user involvement. In PowerUs we have begun to identify more and more gaps within social work, gaps which we believe it is important to mend and hopefully end (Askheim et al 2017). These include, as well as gaps between social work and service users, gaps between:

- practice and management
- education and practice
- research, practice and service users

Steps are being taken internationally to address these, but they are still powerful. It is difficult to stay in practice while working in social work education. Jobs in management tend to be out of practice. These gaps cannot be helpful to understanding, empathy and skill development. Pressures increasingly seem to be towards making gaps bigger and deeper. The Frontline training scheme with its aspiration to create an elite corps of managers is such an example.

We know that service users greatly value the relationship that they have with social workers and that being relationship-based is a great strength of social work, and historically is known to make for good social work. But now the policy emphasis is much more on short and time-limited contacts with service users; practitioners can expect to be criticised for maintaining relationships with service users and are often encouraged instead to bureaucratise and boundary them, when what service users highlight they value is the sense of being in equal relation with workers, who routinely 'go the extra mile', see them as human beings, with the relationship, while professional, being a two-way one – making practice a coproduction rather than an unequal imposition.

And perhaps the most exciting development we have seen in recent years has been the formal recognition that the experience people may have from being on the receiving end of social work, or being from one of those groups that social work has worked with – their lived experience and experiential knowledge - may bring particular gains to being a social worker, to add to the other skills that they may acquire. However, the pressure to restrict social work qualifying courses to 'fast track/elite' routes and masters courses, rather than undergraduate qualifications, putting more emphasis on formal qualification rather than such experiential knowledge, is another example of current strengthening and reinforcing of gaps rather than seeking to reduce them.

Conclusion

To recap briefly, this chapter has identified five negative principles or values that I believe have overshadowed social work and continue, in my view, to do so, to varying degrees. These are its:

- residualisation
- medicalised and pathologising individualism
- failure to address diversity
- limited participation
- gap maintenance

The five positive, enhancing principles I have discussed are its

- universalism
- social approaches
- the treatment of diversity with equality
- participation/user involvement
- gap mending and ending

Finally I want to put social work in the context of the post-war UK welfare state. There are some interesting connections and synergies to identify of international relevance. Three key failings of the post-war welfare state settlement were:

- its top-down non-participatory nature;
- its failure to address diversity;
- its frequent overreliance on medical models for example in relation to disability and distress. (Beresford 2016)

But at the same time:

- it pioneered and was committed to universalism;
- it sought to mend social and economic gaps, exclusions and inequalities;
- it was committed through its class analysis to a social approach in many of the things it did and sought to do, highlighting the social origins and social solutions needed for many problems.

96

If the current political and ideological attacks on the UK welfare state and indeed public services and support globally are to be resisted, then we will need to work for a welfare system based on all five of the virtuous principles I have highlighted. We will also need a social work for the future that is underpinned by and articulates these five positive principles. Such a social work will have a key role to play as part of a new welfare state, offering insights both into what that welfare state will look like and helping people negotiate it. It offers the promise of being a social work by and for all, advancing a welfare state and society by and for all, one which, as I have argued in my book *All Our Welfare*, is based not on traditional, often exploitative processes of production, but of progressive anti-sexist and anti-discriminatory *social reproduction* (Beresford 2016). In the book, I talk about a future social work, responding to the need for a truly universalist service, committed to sustainability, as part of a new user-led welfare state, to challenge the present neoliberal rundown and subversion of both the welfare state generally and social work specifically. I argue for us to commit ourselves to a social work by and for the people in their overlapping roles as service users, workers and other local people. Such a social work has the potential to be both a vehicle for and an expression of benign personal and social change.

7

Anti-oppressive social work, neoliberalism and neo-eugenics

Gurnam Singh

Introduction

When the corporate banks from Wall Street to Canary Wharf came tumbling down in 2008/9 many commentators were proclaiming that the neoliberal project had reached its endgame. It was none other than the Nobel Prizewinning economist Joseph Stiglitz who noted at the time that:

> Today, there is a mismatch between social and private returns. Unless they are closely aligned, the market system cannot work well. Neo-liberal market fundamentalism was always a political doctrine serving certain interests. It was never supported by economic theory. Nor, it should now be clear, is it supported by historical experience. Learning this lesson may be the silver lining in the cloud now hanging over the global economy. (Stiglitz 2008: 2)

However, far from heralding a new settlement, with the instigation of a dual-track policy of bailouts of the banks and austerity, as Belzer and Wayne (2017) note, since 2008 we have seen the 'greatest theft from the public in our entire history'. And far from witnessing its demise, we have seen an intensification of neoliberalism, with the consequences most acutely felt by those least able to resist its impacts, resulting, among other things, in a rapid rise in poverty and inequality. A report by Oxfam, for example, estimates that between 2010 and 2020, 25% of British children will be living in poverty and an additional '1.5 million working-age adults are expected to fall into poverty, bringing the total to 17.5 per cent of this group' (Oxfam 2013: 2). Other effects of austerity are a significant rise in suicide rates, particularly among older males and disabled people (Antonakakis and Collins 2015; MacKenzie 2015). A blog by the Social Workers and Service Users against

Austerity campaign outlines a growing evidence base of the direct impacts of austerity on children's social care practices. For children and families, this has led to increasing levels of mental and physical ill-health, powerlessness, loss of self-esteem and alienation, whereas practitioners with increasing caseloads and diminishing resources and frequent staff turnover are pushed towards narrow, time-limited and risk-averse models of intervention where relationship-based practice becomes a luxury (Gupta and ATD Fourth World 2017).

Such increasing levels of poverty, if not blaming the poor, are often rationalised in terms of a poorly performing economy. However, as Michael Lavalette argues in this book, it was not a shortage of money that has led to such devastating levels of inequality but, through the state bailout of the failing banks, a direct transfer of money from the most to the least needy. The policy of austerity that was instituted to pay for the bailout, as well as leading to levels of poverty comparable to the 1930s is accompanied by unprecedented cuts in social protection and new insidious attacks on those most reliant on public services and state protection (Stewart 2016). And so, while in some senses we are seeing history repeat itself, we are also witnessing a new world in which existing challenges faced by welfare professionals related to questions of human rights, social justice and ethical practice, are manifest in new and increasingly complex ways.

The basic premise of this chapter is that the unique location that social workers occupy, at the interface between state bureaucracies and the most vulnerable people in society, means they have the potential to do immense good, but also immense harm! Though social workers are theoretically bound by a set of independent professional ethics, one cannot deny the reality that social workers' autonomy is mediated by the objectives of the (neoliberal) state. However, as Comley (1989: 63) notes, 'social workers can make effective use of this position' only if they are able to think critically about 'welfare and the assumptions that mediate its forms' and only by doing so can they 'counteract their own involvement in the reproduction of oppressive social relations'. While perhaps there never was a perfect time to do social work, the question of whether social workers are agents of social change or social control comes sharply into focus when we consider the contemporary challenges facing the profession. Today, social workers are being confronted with a unique set of social, economic and political circumstances that are having profound effects on how we view and value human life. John Holloway, the Marxist lawyer and activist philosopher, captures the profundity of this sense of crisis when he notes that 'We have reached a stage where it is easier to think of the total annihilation of humanity than to imagine a change in the organisation of a manifestly unjust and destructive society' (Holloway 2010: 13).

This chapter argues that, in the light of the crisis of neoliberalism, the ruling elites are reconstructing a new common sense about the nature of both welfare and welfare recipients. This is built around a three-pronged strategy: first, there is an ongoing and sustained attack on progressive sociological critiques of power and oppression; second, in the attempt to develop holistic biopsychosocial approaches to understanding such things as human resilience and child abuse, there is a diminishing of focus on poverty and the damaging effects of structural inequalities (Garrett 2016; Hill and Hart 2017); and third, as an explanatory framework for the root cause of human problems and most worryingly a justification for social work intervention, we see an uncritical embrace of 'an increasingly political biology' in the guise of 'epigenetics', which seeks to link environmental factors to gene expression (White and Wastell 2016: 1). In contrast to the previous crude eugenics of the early twentieth century, that social destiny can be simply determined according to genetic makeup, this contemporary manifestation hides behind 'a vastly more complex biological cloak' (Dorling 2010: 113).

And so, as well as outlining the history and significance of the struggles for anti-oppressive social work, the chapter will uncover some of the worrying trends towards an altogether more sinister model of practice that is deeply implicated by what Katz (2013) terms 'neo-eugenics'. Having offered a critical analysis of the nature and scale of the challenge, the chapter concludes by offering some thoughts about how progressive anti-oppressive social workers can/should respond to these new and altogether more sophisticated manifestations of human oppression.

Capitalism, accumulation and dehumanisation

Throughout the past 200 years or so of capitalist development one of the challenges facing ruling elites was how to legitimise the impoverishment of populations and their own elite status. Whether this was at home in relation to the exploitation of the working classes, the Atlantic slave trade and the enslavement of black Africans or the process of colonisation and the expansion of empire, the elites had to devise some rationale for their wealth, power and status. Quite simply, they had to develop systems of thought that could not only justify inequality as a natural consequence of inherent differences but also that indeed such inequalities were beneficial (Dorling 2011: 103).

The only alternative explanation, and one that would completely delegitimise their claim to elite status, is one that rejects theories of biological determinism. Such a perspective would argue that there is nothing fixed about society and that the disparities in wealth and life chances are, as the Marxist scholar David Harvey suggests, a direct result of 'dispossession', which is accomplished through violence, war, enslavement and colonialism. Building on Marx's notion of 'primitive accumulation', this process begins by dispossessing and expelling people from the land, thus creating 'a landless proletariat, and then releasing the land into the privatised mainstream of capital accumulation' (Harvey 2005: 149).

It all sounds very simple, but without some form of rationalisation and arguably co-option of the oppressed in this process, the project of dispossession would simply not have succeeded. In other words, accumulation through dispossession needed to be defended, if not as a moral enterprise, then as one that was constituted in the natural order of things. This can be illustrated in the work of nineteenth century capitalist economist Adam Smith (1776) who, in his classic work *An Inquiry into the Nature and Causes of the Wealth of Nations*, invokes the concept of 'the invisible hand' to describe the unintended social benefits of individual self-interested actions. These same ideas were deployed by the neoliberal economist Friedrich Hayek (1944/2014) who, in his seminal text *The Road to Serfdom*, argues that markets should be unchained and left to the free-flowing 'natural order of the invisible hand'.

One of the most appealing and insidious theories to be developed to provide 'natural' justification for the dispositions of populations was that of Social Darwinism. This theory, based on Charles Darwin's theory of evolution, offered a simplistic yet seductive explanation for social inequalities, namely that they were essentially the result of biological natural selection resulting in the ascendency and survival of the fittest. This theory had the capacity to transcend many prevailing and developing ideas, from the philosophical underpinnings of scientific racism, through to ideas about human intelligence and inherited genetic traits in the nineteenth and twentieth centuries (Dickens 2000).

If scientific racism was later exposed to be based on dangerous myths and fallacies about innate human biological difference (Montagu 2001), this did and has not stopped those in power developing new and increasingly sophisticated ways to demonise the poor, minorities, women and indeed all groups that deviate from the prevailing mythical norms of society (Lorde 1984).

Beverly Skeggs argues that in the present moment we are witnessing a rearticulation of the 'theory of monstrosity' that was developed first in sixteenth century England to legitimate violence used against labour and the poor:

> No longer branded with burning metal, the unemployed and working-class mothers in the UK in the 2000s are now inscribed by the symbolic violence of government policy promoted and popularized by a media that subjects them to contemporary slow death (slow, because the welfare state offers some protection, as do charities). The working-class mothers and unemployed are blamed for the global structural problems made by capital, capitalists and the state. (Skeggs 2014)

Though we may have abandoned the crude scientific language of twentieth century Social Darwinism (imbecile, cretin, moron, retards, feeble minded, negro, mongoloid and so on), human oppression and social divisions continue to play a key role in determining life chances. Much of this progress was achieved through social movements that emerged in the post-war period (welfare activism, feminism, anti-racism, gay rights, disability activism, student activism and so on) confronting dehumanising ideologies and practices, by exposing 'common sense' ideologies about human difference and ability, they challenge systems of thought and classification of populations associated with biological determinism and in doing do made a powerful case for equality and social justice.

Neoliberalism and the welfare state

The three pillars of the 'post-war consensus' spanning a period between 1945 and 1980 emphasised the importance of collectivism, a mixed economy and a welfare state (Toye 2013). However, from the early 1980s we have seen a gradual erosion of all three aspects to a point where, particularly within the current climate of austerity, talk of a 'post-welfare' state can no longer dismissed as idle speculation. Whereas previously, social protection measures were seen to have a beneficial economic rationale, within a Keynesian framework, we now see the view that welfare cuts should not be viewed as an inconvenient necessity, but are rather a prerequisite for economic growth and development. Coining the notion of 'expansionary austerity', influential economists like Reinhard and Rogoff (2011) have argued that in consumer-based economies, austerity is a good thing because it can lead to lower interest rates and therefore a boost in investment. The articulation of ideas like this reveals how generalised the earlier work of Milton Friedman and the Chicago school of economics has become. Stuart Hall, originator of the term 'Thatcherism', argued in one of his final pieces of writing, that the period we are now living through represents nothing less than the creation of a new form of capitalist hegemony:

> in ambition, depth, degree of break with the past, variety of sites being colonised, impact on common sense, shift in the social architecture, neoliberalism does constitute a hegemonic project. Today, popular thinking and the systems of calculation in daily life offer very little friction to the passage of its ideas. Delivery may be more difficult: new and old contradictions still haunt the edifice, in the very process of its reconstruction. Still, in terms of laying foundations and staging the future on favourable ground, the neoliberal project is several stages further on. (Hall 2011)

The neoliberal project in the present moment is morphing into a new and intensified period of commodification that is analogous to past expansions of global capitalism where, as Marx and Engels described in *The Communist Manifesto*, the bourgeoisie had 'pitilessly torn asunder the motley feudal ties that bound man to his "natural superiors", leaving no other nexus between man and man than naked self-interest' (Marx and Engels 1848: 6). The new neoliberal hegemony of the present has the same logic of placing 'naked self-interest' at the centre of economic decision making, though in the present context it is the global corporate empires that have such enormous influence.

Among other things, this new phase is characterised by unprecedented attacks on the poor and vulnerable sections of society most reliant on systems of social protection. The feminist writer Bea Campbell has recently noted that this attack on welfare combined with declining household incomes has major implications for women:

> when neoliberal politics and the world's financial institutions marginalize state welfare, as well as depriving women of support in their role as carers, they reconstitute women care workers as the precariat – it is estimated that 300,000 care workers are on zero-hours contracts; and they also reinstate

patriarchal divisions of labour and redistribute incomes towards men. (Campbell 2014)

Inequality has returned at many levels on a scale that can be hard to imagine; according to a recent report by Oxfam, 'almost half of the world's wealth is now owned by just one percent of the population, and seven out of ten people live in countries where economic inequality has increased in the last 30 years' (Oxfam 2014).

This unravelling of the welfare state poses a fundamental problem for the state – what do we do with people who have welfare needs? In the present moment of austerity, as noted by the Archbishop of Canterbury Justin Welby, we are witnessing 'a quiet resurgence of the seductive language of "deserving" and "undeserving" poor'.

> Who are today's new undeserving poor? The familiar tabloid assumption is that you know them when you see them. The undeserving poor drink White Lightning in the daytime, have too many children, keep dangerous dogs and spend their lives lolling about on the sofa. Now as in the past, the undeserving poor make an easy and popular target, especially when public money is tight again. Which is why references to fecklessness and irresponsibility have become such effective drivers of the coalition's welfare reform legislation. (*The Guardian*, Editorial, 27 January 2012)

One strategy, as we have seen with the cuts in disability living allowance, is to force people back to work. However, as the government's own data, reported in *The Guardian* (Butler 2015) revealed, during the period December 2011 and February 2014, 2,380 people died after their claim for employment and support allowance (ESA) ended because a work capability assessment (WCA) found they were found fit for work. Similarly, in relation to asylum seekers, there is growing evidence that government policies, either by withdrawing entitlements to public funds or deliberately delaying asylum claims, are pushing many into destitution. A study by the British Red Cross noted between 2014 and 2015 a 15% increase in the number of asylum seekers using its services (Beswick and McNulty 2015). Though it may be argued that these examples represent a tiny proportion of the recipients of public services, the crucial point here is that the inhumane treatment that they experience acts as a moral barometer for the overall thrust of government policy. Marginalised groups, such as asylum seekers and those claiming ESA, are easy prey for tabloid demonisation and therefore become convenient test beds for pushing the boundaries of welfare cuts and worse.

Anti-oppressive social work and the neoliberal project

The intensification of the global neoliberal project has resulted in the withdrawal of the state from delivery of services and to severe cuts to social spending. These changes are legitimated through a duel strategy of demonisation of the poor and socially excluded on the one hand and spurious economic arguments for creating more dynamic wealth-creating economies through lowering of taxes and encouraging entrepreneurship. This is tantamount to what I term the 'commodification of human need', where essential human services are being subject to the logic of the market and those in need of services are being transformed into atomised 'citizen consumers' (Singh and Cowden 2015). The crucial point here is that these 'innovations' are presented as the new 'common sense' and those arguing for a difference collectivist approach as being out of touch or incompetent.

The wide-ranging attacks on the welfare state and those dependent on it clearly raises many ethical, moral and practical dilemmas for social workers. Running alongside this, though paradoxically today we have quite well-developed anti-discriminatory legislation, we have also seen sustained attacks on the underpinning ideas associated with anti-oppressive social work from the onset of neoliberalism in the late 1980s (Singh and Cowden 2009). Indeed, the clearest illustration of this can be seen in the way that subsequent renditions of professional social work competency and capability requirements, from the revised Central Council for Education and Training of Social Workers (CCETSW) Paper 30 in the mid-1900s through to the present Health and Care Professionals Council (HCPC) Capabilities framework, there is a marked shift away from an emphasis on power and oppression to one focusing on personal psychology and cultural sensitivity.

From the 1980s onwards the linked cocepts of diversity and anti-oppressive practice become pivotal to contemporary understandings of social work theory and practice. They occupied a central aspect of the discourse and political challenges mounted by a wide range of marginalised groups against what were deemed to be oppressive and discriminatory public services. This resulted in challenges to both the power that professionals exercise and the knowledge base from which they make judgements about diverse groups of service users (Singh 2002).

To counteract some of the stereotypical conceptions of human difference, progressive understandings of diversity sought to bridge the subjectivity/objectivity divide. Subjectively, alternative perspectives emerged out of struggles over personal identity linked to gender, ethnicity, race, religion, health status, class, sexuality and age. In the objective sense, diversity was understood as a social relation, reflecting experience that was a product of social and political discourses, and institutional practices (see Brah 2005). Similarly, the concept of 'oppression' was understood in two distinct ways. Historically, it resided within the field of political theory and has been deployed to characterise particular tyrannical regimes. In this context, the term is related to systematic acts of violent brutality, subjugation, dominance and conquest perpetrated by powerful rulers (Cudd 2006). In contrast to the classic construction, contemporary applications of the term oppression are influenced by new social movements in their quest for social justice. In this context, as Young (2013) suggests in her 'five faces of oppression' model, it should be understood along a continuum, ranging through 'exploitation', 'marginalisation', 'powerlessness', 'cultural dominance' and 'violence'.

Though discussions about anti-oppressive practice began to permeate social work literature and practice from the late 1980s, questions of social work and oppression have a longer history. Indeed, much of the radical social work literature of the 1970s was replete with references to racism, oppression, power and the state. However, among anti-racist, feminist (and later disability) activists there was a feeling that the anti-imperialist left-wing radicalism had an overreliance on questions of class at the expense of gender and race. Moreover, it was thought that, though important, there was too much emphasis on a monolithic conception of oppression and a lack of attention to relational elements and to questions of identity, behaviour and psychological manifestations of oppression that shaped the everyday lived experiences and encounters of women and black people.

In this regard we began to see the development of wider conceptions of anti-oppressive practice that sought to connect the various levels at which power functioned. As Dominelli (2002: 12–13) suggests:

> Oppressive relations are countered through anti-oppressive initiatives that are intended to eradicate the injustices that these produce in the routines of everyday life in both the private and public domains. Anti-oppressive measures aim to deconstruct and demystify oppressive relations – stepping stones on the road to creating non-oppressive ones.

Dalrymple and Burke (2006: 7), in their widely referenced book *Anti-Oppressive Practice: Social Care and the Law*, make an important observation that anti-oppressive practice belongs to a critical tradition that not only confronts 'social relations and structures' but 'social work itself'. In this regard, one can perhaps understand why advocates of anti-oppressive practice may be seen as 'the enemy within', working as it were in, for, against and beyond the profession. Hence, to avoid the instrumental 'tick box' approach, anti-oppressive practitioners will seek to 'construct and understand their place, position, purpose, role, practice and power within and in relation to organisation' (Fook 2004: 73).

Given that discussions about diversity and anti-oppression represent the 'real' and complex struggles of people for dignity and justice, the challenge for social work has been to avoid overly abstracting the concepts, on the one hand, and oversimplification on the other. Hence popular frameworks such as Neil Thompson's widely used Personal, Cultural and Structural (PCS) model (Thompson 2011), though very useful, were subject to criticisms that they were applied in a formulaic way devoid of the context of lived experiences and historical struggles of oppressed groups (see Heron 2004). In this regard, it is important to appreciate that anti-oppressive practice developed as a generic term that incorporated a wide range of other related struggles associated with, for instance, feminist social work, radical social work, anti-racist social work and black perspectives, disability activism and service user movements (Dalrymple and Burke 2006). In other words, anti-oppressive practice can and should never be abstracted into some general model of practice that is to be evidenced through a series of behavioural repertoires.

To illustrate this point, it is worth briefly recalling the history of anti-racist social work, without which it is all too easy to reduce the historical struggle against racism and European colonialism to the celebration of diversity. To have a true picture one would need to trace the roots of racism in the seventeenth century and the development of European mercantile capitalism, the Atlantic slave trade, empire and the development of industrial capitalism. Not only have these shaped the social and economic geography of the world as we know it, many ideas and theories about racial inferiority and superiority and of systems of classifications of the difference of so-called racial and ethnic groups were a product of this period.

Myths about 'black', 'brown', 'yellow' and 'red' men and women were generated to justify oppression. Indeed, the delusion was so insidious and powerful that European colonialism was presented as a moral duty. This idea is captured in the poem "The White Man's Burden" by Rudyard Kipling which was first published in the 10 February 1899 edition of the *New York Sun*. Replete with derogatory language about black people, the poem offers justification for imperialism as a noble enterprise of civilisation. Indeed, Kipling suggested that white men had a moral duty to rule black people, as a means to encouraging their economic, cultural and social progress through colonialism (Murphy 2010).

And so to understand contemporary anti-racist struggles one needs to have a sense of the dehumanising narratives of the oppressor and also to register ways in which the oppressed have sought to resist and fight back. In this regard, riots sparked off essentially by police brutality in inner cities throughout the UK in the summer of 1981 was a pivotal moment for social work in the UK. The subsequent independent judicial enquiry by Lord Scarman for the first time introduced into public discourse the notion of institutionalised racism. Social work, hitherto a mainly white middle class profession, became one of the most active and well-publicised sites for the struggle against institutionalised racism (Penketh 2000). However, as I have argued elsewhere:

> the employment of black social workers, rather than leading to the eradication of racism, resulted in the uncovering of previously unacknowledged and virulent forms, as well as creating new antagonisms centred on concerns about the mistreatment of black service users, care workers and professionals. (Singh 2014: 19)

Among other effects, the anti-racist challenge from within the profession generated its own resistance, though perhaps the most insidious attacks were made in the right wing media in the guise of 'political correctness gone mad'. And so rather than being celebrated as change agents, many anti-racist social workers, both black and white, were increasingly labelled as anti-racist zealots, fifth columnists or simply as being incompetent (Singh 1994; Walker 2002).

A consistent body of evidence points to the way neoliberal social policy has singled out moral panics about incompetence among social work professionals obsessed with political correctness and theory, and the inadequacy of professional training (Singh and Cowden 2009). Ongoing social work 'scandals' have been central to the creation of a commonsense discourse about social work professionals not able to be 'trusted' by the public. It is clear in retrospect that these periodic attacks on state social work, framed popularly as concern about child deaths, have represented a sustained neoliberal assault on a progressive non-punitive social work – see for example the 'independent review' of social work education by Martin Narey (2014), in which he attacks the emphasis on anti-oppressive practice, suggesting that it is stopping social workers doing their 'real jobs'.

What is it about social work that bothers these people? The answer is simple: one of the distinctive features of social work as a profession lies in the way it is defined through its engagement with the people and communities that have been most excluded and violated by the march of the neoliberal polity. The embodied suffering and distress of these individuals poses an implicit challenge to the mission of self-improvement within common-sense neoliberal discourse, just as the destitution of the Victorian poor did for the church-based charities of the past. How do we make sense of these people who simply fail to see what is best for themselves and their families? It is in this sense that the reconstruction of the social work project in the image of neoliberal ideas about human worth and dys/functionality has come to form such a central concern for politicians and policy makers. And it is this very desire to expunge social work of structural explanations that lies at the core of an altogether more sinister and dangerous articulation of a new or neo-eugenics oriented approach to social welfare.

Neoliberalism and neo-eugenics

Stuart Hall (2011) has drawn attention to the way neoliberalism becomes synonymous with notions of the 'free, possessive individual', and therefore, by negation, the (welfare) state and everything it represents, becomes cast as 'tyrannical and oppressive'. It goes without saying that a social work model that begins with an expressed concern with issues of vulnerability, dependence and care will jar with the neoliberal fetish of the resilient, autonomous and successful individual, a person imagined as existing in a masculinist world absent of relations of dependency or caring responsibilities on the one hand and possessing undiminishing optimism and self-esteem on the other.

Elizabeth McCreadie (2017) in her analysis of eugenics thinking, specifically in relation to people with learning disabilities, argues that, like a 'submarine', it has a tendency to operate by stealth to influence policy and practice. She notes that 'Whilst the terminology of "eugenics" is no longer an acceptable topic of conversation, the impact of the ideology continues to permeate the "collective unconsciousness" (doxa) of many including those who are involved in the decision making processes of individuals identified as learning disabled.' (p vii) Though most popular conceptions of eugenic science associate it with the murderous atrocities of the Nazi regime in the 1940s and their policy to create a 'super-race' by eradicating undesirables, ideas about 'racial hygiene' and the development of state policies to promote certain human characteristics deemed desirable through social policy interventions were being developed across Europe and North America.

Indeed, social work itself has been deeply implicated in such policies: for example, social workers were co-opted into the Nazi policy of the 'Volk community', which was defined as one of 'blood and soil'. Those of other 'races', those with disabilities, those who sought to question were not fit to be members, and there is much evidence that social workers (or social pedagogues, as they were called) were deployed to assist both in the training of Hitler's youth and also identification of 'unfit' mothers to be subject to sterilisation or worse (Sunker and Otto 1997).

If we look at the origins of the modern welfare state back in the early part of the twentieth century, we know that William Beveridge, and other 'progressives' at the time, were sympathetic to ideas associated with eugenics and scientific ways of improving the human race (*The Scientist* 1999).

> those men who through general defects are unable to fill such a whole place in industry are to be recognized as unemployable. They must become the acknowledged dependents of the State ... but with complete and permanent loss of all citizen rights – including not only the franchise but civil freedom and fatherhood. (Sewell 2009)

Likewise, it is also significant that the question of social work's discourse of 'professionalism' was initially an object of criticism for the Left and only later became incorporated in the neoliberal attack on welfare. And more recently, in my own work I have noted how the politicised discourses associated with progressive service users and survivors' movements have, through the 'personalisation agenda', gradually become emptied of their historical meaning and become passengers on the vehicle of neoliberal social policy (Cowden and Singh 2007 and 2014).

Based on the belief of the existence of superior and inferior biological inheritance, in the guise of 'racial typologies', as noted earlier, Social Darwinism had already been deployed by European colonialists as a scientific justification for racial oppression (see Husband 1982: 14-15).

However, this idea enters the sphere of welfare in two distinct ways; it offers an individual rationale for the existence of inequalities and, second, it provides a scientific basis for enacting a range of social policies to prevent the reproduction of 'degenerate' or 'abnormal' genes (Spektorowski and Mizrachi 2004). Social Darwinism emerged in the later part of the nineteenth century as an idea that could offer a scientific basis for understanding human societies and cultural development. Drawing on Charles Darwin's theory of evolution, and in particular 'natural selection' and the idea of the 'survival of the fittest', Social Darwinism sought to provide a positive basis for improving or evolving human populations. Politically, the theory provided a perfect scientific justification for the existence of social inequalities as the product of natural human differences correlated with such things as inherent moral attributes, intelligence and various physical traits (Diane 2003).

It was this promise of a theory to explain the scientific mechanism for human development that found resonance with the idea of eugenics – meaning literally 'good birth' – to produce better human beings. Though ideas associated with eugenics can be traced back to the ancient Greek philosophical thought of Plato and Aristotle, the idea was not adopted as a basis for social policy programmes until the latter part of the nineteenth century. It is the work of Francis Galton, a cousin of Charles Darwin, that is most credited with formulating quite detailed practical programmes for 'improving human stock' through selective breeding programmes, the ultimate goal being to create 'better human beings' (Kevles 1985).

In relation to policy programmes based on eugenics, broadly speaking one can see two distinct approaches, which are referred to in the literature as 'positive and negative eugenics'. Positive approaches, some of which are still practised within medical contexts, are associated with promoting good health and reproduction to produce 'good births' and to offer prenatal screening and encouragement to ultimately eliminate certain inherited conditions and diseases (Goering 2014). Negative eugenics has an altogether different and sinister image and is associated with forced sterilisations of men and women deemed unfit to reproduce – described variously as 'defectives', 'imbeciles', 'retarded', 'feeble-minded', 'idiots' and so on – through to mass genocide, as in the case of the Nazis' racial hygiene programme. It wasn't only biological 'defects' that eugenics was seeking to eradicate but cultural, behavioural and social traits such as poverty, vagrancy or prostitution, as it was felt that this could be passed from parent to child, inherited as traits rather than shared as common social situations (Goering 2014).

And so, though the kinds of 'negative eugenics' ideas described here have rightly been discredited, disowned and in many places made illegal, we feel that the ideas of 'social and cultural pathology', which was subject to powerful critiques by anti-oppressive social work movements in the 1980s and 1990s (Singh 2002), are being rehabilitated and reproduced in very subtle ways under neoliberalism. Pierre Bourdieu has insightfully pointed to the way today's poor are now characterised, arguing that this is based on:

> a *racism of intelligence*: today's poor are not poor, as they were thought to be in the nineteenth century, because they are improvident, spendthrift, intemperate … but because they are dumb, intellectually incapable, idiotic. (Bourdieu 2003: 34–35)

Rather than representing the dominance of privilege, the rule of the 'brightest and best' represents a rational form of natural selection, objectively justified through neoliberal economic theory. A 2013 speech by the London Mayor Boris Johnson exemplified exactly this point. Johnson stated that 'Whatever you may think of the value of IQ tests it is surely relevant to a conversation about equality that as many as 16% of our species have an IQ below 85'. The implication is clear here; those at the bottom of society are 'the stupid' and it is these people who are incapable of coping with the competitive globalised world we are now living in. He went on to argue that:

> No one can ignore the harshness of that competition, or the inequality that it inevitably accentuates, and I am afraid that violent economic centrifuge is operating on human beings who are already very far from equal in raw ability, if not spiritual worth. (quoted in Watt 2013b)

In this eugenicist world view it is a lack of intelligence that leads to people failing to become economically successful – not only are the poor 'stupid', but this stupidity makes them less worthy as people.

Neo-eugenics and social work

I now turn to a discussion of how key progressive social work concepts are being appropriated in ways that enable the reconstruction of social work as a punitive activity. The ideological role of language has been crucial in neoliberal social policy as a means of appropriating social work's historically progressive language of social transformation (Watkins 2010). One clear example is related the concept of 'resilience'. Most dictionary definitions of resilience tend to focus on an individual's capacity to resist, recover from or even flourish in adversity. Specifically in the context of social work, Fraser and colleagues (1999: 131) suggest that the term represents an individual's ability to adapt to 'negative life events, trauma, stress, and other forms of risk'. It follows that if it were possible to isolate those things that enable people to function despite the adversity, then this would be an important basis for developing appropriate practice interventions. If one aspect of resilience is concerned with 'surviving' then there is also the question of growth and of nurturing resilience or strengths. Indeed, much of the literature on resilience and social work is closely related to what is commonly termed a 'strengths perspective' (see Norman 2000).

A long-established current within the professional social work research is a curiosity about the kinds of personal qualities of those clients and families that appear to thrive against those that don't given a similar set of material circumstances. Why within family groups with similar high risk factors or low-support environments do some follow different trajectories? Why do some manage to survive and even thrive in the same kinds of stress-inducing situations whereas others do not? Though this research tends to be rooted in a psychological approach, more recently we have seen the emergence of psychosocial and ecological models that seek to develop perspectives on resilience that go beyond personal traits to environmental, cultural and in some instances economic factors (see for example Fraser 2004).

One might be excused for thinking: what can be wrong with this idea? But like the notion of empowerment, within vertical neoliberalism and particularly following the economic crisis of 2008 resulting in savage attacks on public health and welfare programmes and those most dependent on such services, the idea of resilience has been turned on its head. So, while it once was concerned with a framework for understanding and facilitating human flourishing and development, now the term is increasingly being used to categorise human beings according to their capability to survive in adversity. In what might be termed a survivalist doctrine of resilience, Gilligan (2008) notes that there is an increasing emphasis on the ability to 'bounce back' after adversity, or to thrive despite facing adverse or difficult circumstances.

This emphasis on self-improvement sits comfortably with the broader thrust of eugenics and its emphasis on biological and psychological functioning. It also acts to diminishing the impact that power, inequality and ideology, all ideas that form the basis for anti-oppressive practice, can play in both the social construction of who may or may not be seen as reliant or dysfunctional, and equally importantly in enabling people to meet the everyday challenges that life throws at them.

Neocleous (2013) notes how the idea of 'resilience is central not only to the self-help industry, but also to the wider 'happiness studies' now being peddled by politicians and academic disciplines such as psychology, economics and increasingly social work as well. Ian Ferguson (2008), in his book *Reclaiming Social Work: Challenging Neo-liberalism and Promoting Social Justice*, suggests that, in contrast to earlier philosophical discussions about happiness as a valued social good, the current preoccupation with 'happiness' reflects the commodification of human need as a major industry, through concepts of health, fitness and 'body beautiful' (Phipps 2014). And of more direct concern to social work are the real effects of neoliberalism associated with individualism and greed, in producing social isolation, depression and human misery in an objective and subjective manner.

Yet at the same time we are seeing a major trend in a wide range of fields, including education, health and welfare, where the assertion of psychological explanations for social needs, and in relation to the ongoing influence of the pharmaceutical companies, is entirely divorced from any social context. This was exemplified when the renowned sociologist Anthony Giddens made the astonishing claim that 'happiness and its opposite bear no particular relation to either wealth or the possession of power' (Giddens 1994: 181). In this sense, the quality of resilience is individualised and psychologised, coming to define a neo-Darwinian capacity for survival that denies the significance of wider social problems, such as psychosis, mental ill-health, child abuse and neglect, homelessness, family violence and so on. The danger is that without a social critique capable of resisting these constructions, what on the surface might appear to be reasonable explanations of people's problems and needs can mask dangerous new forms of oppression and justifications for exclusion.

Epigenetics and social work

The science of epigenetics is relatively recent and, as Waggoner and Uller (2015) note, there is no consensus on the precise definition. Nonetheless, as the word suggests, it has something to do with genes and their relation to the outside (epi) or the environment.

What distinguishes it from genetics more generally is the focus on how environmental factors, ranging from toxins in the atmosphere through to how 'stress, socio-economic status, bullying, racism and the lifestyles of our parents and grandparents, can all turn on or off certain genes in our DNA' (Meloni 2016). Moreover, by suggesting that our behaviour and ability are the product of an interaction between our genetic inheritance and the environment, epigenetics seemingly offers a resolution to the nurture versus nature conundrum (Katz 2013).

The seduction of this new biological modelling is that it apparently releases us from being simply determined our genes, which was the central assertion of old-style eugenics. That there can be 'non-genetic' influences on development and heredity, given the right environment, opens up the possibility of not only enabling one to become more functional but, because our genes become carriers, positive genetic development can also be transmitted through generations. However, most of the studies on epigenetic effects have focused on plants and animals and there are real uncertainties about the precise effects on humans. (Waggoner and Uller 2015). Yet, despite these uncertainties, the wider implications are often taken for granted and epigenetics is generally considered to be a basis for a better, more progressive, liberal and inclusive social policy (Meloni 2016).

One might be fooled into thinking that epigenetics is potentially an antidote to biological determinism. For example, if it can be proven that racism has a causal relationship with, for example, higher incidences of schizophrenia or lower educational attainment among black people, then doesn't this vindicate anti-racist arguments? However appealing this may be, there is a real danger of slipping back into biological determinism and eugenic reasoning – it really depends on how these ideas are implemented in practice. If one accepts that social inequalities can have a detrimental impact on our genes, unless there is a considerable effort to address structural inequalities that produce these effects, then epigenetics may provide a rationalisation for 'acquired pathology' in specific populations.

As Meloni (2016) notes:

> No doubt, by focusing on the environment as a cause for many unwanted conditions, epigenetics has the potential to advance social justice. But we need to remember that it is no guarantee of a more inclusive society. Social values often decide how we implement science, rather than the other way round.

Sue White and David Wastell argue that the implications of what they term a biology of social disadvantage for social work are far-reaching and that 'Epigenetics is part of a political biology with the potential to affect the moral direction of social work' (2016: 2256).

One of the appeals of epigenetics and related 'biosocial' models, such as some of the new developments in neuroplasticity, and the mapping of effects of maltreatment on brain development is that apparently one can develop quite precise measurements of effects and interventions. It is heralding a novel approach to evidence-based interventions where, for the first time, we are told that we can begin to offer concrete, quantitative, statistically significant data and perhaps even randomised control trials to determine 'what works'. The concern here isn't that some useful data might be generated, but what are the implications of focusing on what will inevitably be 'downstream solutions' at the expense of the mountains of data showing the powerful correlation between structural inequalities and health and social outcomes (Dorling 2010; Wilkinson and Pickett 2009).

Current research on the relationship between inequalities and child protection identifies some powerful evidence that increasingly poor families are being targeted by child protection services. Based on an analysis of over 35,000 children in the UK care system who were designated as 'looked-after' or on a 'child protection plan', a study by Bywaters and colleagues (2018) found that every '10% increase in deprivation rates saw a 30% rise in a child's chances of entering care' and lack of funding to provide appropriate services was the 'most likely' factor. Perhaps the most worrying finding in the study was, perhaps in the face of limited resources, the tendency by social workers to adopt a blinkered approach. As the study notes, 'Most social workers saw their core business as risk assessment, and regarded actions to address poverty (benefits advice, provision of food, rights advocacy) as services others should provide' (McNicoll 2017).

Conclusion: building an alternative project

To suggest that poverty and deprivation can lead to human dysfunctionality is not the same as saying that human dysfunctionality is the cause of poverty and deprivation. To do so would be to accept a slippery slope argument that can only lead to one conclusion, namely that some people and groups are naturally superior/inferior to others. However, historically, this reasoning error has not stopped policy makers framing a wide range of social problems, such as poverty, lower educational attainment, gender-based violence, mental ill-health and criminality, through the lens of 'nature' and biology. Running parallel to this framing of problems is a long history of oppression based on race, gender, class, disability, sexuality, religion and age being justified in terms of (pseudo)scientific truths. Until the 1970s and the period of decolonisation and emergence of anti-racist movements, most textbooks were replete with associations between biological attributes and 'racial' types. A classic example is a popular textbook in 1926 that stated: 'the Negro lacks in his germ plasm excellence of some qualities which the white race possesses, and which are essential for success in competition with the civilisations of the white races at the present day' (Popenoe 1926: 285).

Though eugenics was dislodged from the centre ground, primarily through progressive social movements in the post-war period, with current advances in molecular biology, neuroscience and epigenetics, as Katz (1996: 192) notes, 'a new wave of neo-eugenic scholarship flourishes'. It is not the science per se that should be the concern of social workers, but rather learning the lessons of history – the way in which scientific discoveries are deployed and presented as objective, dispassionate and apolitical.

At a time where social welfare is under severe attack, this chapter has sought to highlight three linked challenges confronting social workers. These are practical in relation to securing the resources to support vulnerable citizens, political in the ongoing assertion of neoliberal political ideology, and ideological in the ways in which dominant ideas about human difference and dysfunctionality are being reproduced through neo-eugenics. The wider political context is clear: we are seeing a deepening of global economic crisis and austerity programmes on the one hand, and the collapse of a progressive left alternative and the excision of even basic forms of sociological analysis from policy making on the other. This has created a dangerous situation, particularly for the most marginalised sections of modern developed societies.

By presenting a somewhat bleak analysis, my intention is not to imply that there are no alternatives. If one lesson of history is about the phenomenal power and influence that capitalism has had, another equally important lesson is, as John Holloway (2010: 250) reminds us, every system has its 'cracks' and the very brutality of neoliberalism creates new forms of refusal which represent the potential 'breakthrough of another world'. Specifically, for social work the challenge begins with a reclaiming of the title of the profession itself, namely that it is a 'social' profession. The idea of 'social' emerged in the twentieth century in parallel with the establishment of the welfare state and indeed social work itself. It was oriented towards moving away from punitive to progressive redistributive policy models and ideas like 'social security', 'social justice' or 'social inclusion' became the bedrock of approaches that rejected individualistic and biological explanations for human problems and need.

Similarly, anti-oppressive social movements were born out of the same desire to free human beings from the tyranny of state oppression, which was articulated through the brutal repression of targeted populations as well as subtler ideological strategies linked to the construction of 'common sense', human subjectivity, (dys) functionality and deviance. And so, as in previous times, those struggles against the mechanisms by which dominant discourses around normal/ abnormal are produced and reproduced, as well as the application of these in everyday societal and institutional settings, will continue. 'Anti-oppressive practice' emerged as a professional conceptual framework for making sense of the complex interplay between power, powerlessness, history, culture, identity and difference. However, given the constricted nature of professional social work roles, the scope of 'anti-oppressive practice' practitioners tended to focus on behavioural and attitudinal responses and reduce the history of various 'freedom struggles to struggles over individual privilege and state recognition of cultural difference' (Contaz 2012).

One of the most important contributions of service user movements that emerged in the 1970s was to challenge the legitimacy of 'expert knowledge'. Though today, albeit in a highly neoliberalised form, user perspectives are routinely sought out in policy formation, the reality is that, as I have noted elsewhere, these are increasingly used as a rubber-stamping exercise, often rendering the user as a kind of 'fetish' (Cowden and Singh 2007). Similar strategies have been deployed in the realm of race in the guise of 'race' experts and what are often handpicked 'community representatives'. It follows that the challenge for anti-oppressive social work today is to reconnect with 'social work from below', and some of this is already happening; we are seeing new alliances being formed between students, practitioners, service users and academics to not only confront the logic of neo-eugenics, but most importantly to articulate alternative models of social work that can be seen to be 'in, against and beyond' the neoliberal state. Ultimately, this may require a decoupling of the concept of social work from the straightjacket of local authority (or increasingly privatised) child protection social work. This is particularly so in the context of reforms to social work education and training that have significantly shifted power towards employers to dictate the kinds of knowledge, skills and dispositions they feel social work professionals need to have. While one shouldn't dismiss the value of robust partnerships between universities, employers and service users, it is important not to allow these structures to determine the priorities of the professional.

In this regard, anti-oppressive social work needs to be able to connect initiatives that are inspired by very localised groups campaigning, for example, to defend existing services, with struggles that are taking place across the globe. Indeed, arguably, it was through being inspired by social movements in other places that anti-oppressive social work in the UK was born. A prime example would be the ways in which Black Power movements inspired anti-racist and disability rights movements in the UK (see Oliver 1996) and Dalit liberation movements in India (Slate 2012). Similarly today, in developing anti-oppressive social work we need to take inspiration from the Black Lives Matter movement in the UK and the ongoing struggles of indigenous peoples, workers and migrants across the globe around questions of social and environmental justice, human rights and access to education and health care (see for example, Ferguson, Lavalette and Whitmore 2004).

One of the consequences of neoliberalism and managerialism has been to displace collective and critical forms of practice with individualised procedural models, what is disparagingly termed the 'tick-box' approach. Through the closing down of possibilities for creative and politically engaged practice, anti-oppressive social work has increasingly become reduced to individualistic acts of 'being good' or challenging certain behaviour deemed to be oppressive. However, such behavioural models, on their own, are likely to have a limited impact on the deeper structural aspects of oppression. Therefore, it is important that we seek to (re)build oppositional structures of anti-oppression, to reverse austerity policies and to resist the co-option of professionals in attacks on the most vulnerable. In terms of child care practice, this will require a radical departure from the current emphasis on 'downstream' risk assessment and child protection to upstream community-based preventative approaches.

Anti-oppressive practice is about doing but it is also about understanding the intricacies of power and how this can impact on all our actions and thoughts. This will require the nurturance of elevated levels of critical and reflective thinking. And only through maintaining a commitment to praxis can professionals avoid the slippery slope of cultural pathology and biological determinism. In a social media driven age, where mechanisms of social production and social control are more dispersed, anti-oppressive social workers will need to be constantly vigilant about the exercise of power and the way dominant discourses about clients and marginalised citizens are produced. And perhaps the greatest challenge for anti-oppressive social workers in times of increasing inequalities will be to find ways of building common cause and alliances with marginalised service users, workers and citizens and wider struggles for global social and environmental justice.

8

From Seebohm factories to neoliberal production lines? The social work labour process

John Harris

Introduction

When we think and talk about 'social work', we mostly focus on the first word. We read, discuss and write about the *social* problems and *social* issues addressed by social work or the *social* processes that are the focus of social work's intervention in people's lives and the vehicle through which that intervention takes place. In mainstream accounts of the development of social work after the Second World War, it was depicted as a demonstration of *social* responsibility: 'As the accepted areas of social obligation widened, as injustice became less tolerable, new services were separately organised around individual need' (Titmuss 1963: 21). In such accounts, social work, as part of the wider social services, was also extolled as the material expression of the *social* rights of citizenship:

> By the social element [of citizenship] I mean the whole range from the right to a modicum of economic welfare and security to the right to share to the full in the social heritage and to live the life of a civilised being according to the standards prevailing in the society. The institutions most closely connected with it are the educational system and the social services. (Marshall 1963: 74)

However, despite its embeddedness in many and various aspects of 'the social', social work is also a job. As a job it involves *work* and the focus of this chapter is on how the *work* of social work has been and can be understood from a critical perspective.

The conceptualisation of social work as work was developed in response to its organisational location in Social Services Departments

(SSDs) and this is, therefore, the starting point in what follows. The radical social work movement that emerged in the context of SSDs is then considered, followed by its articulation of an industrial labour process perspective in relation to social work, taken from the work of Braverman. Shortcomings in this perspective's ability to account for the nature of the social work labour process in this period, as revealed by empirical studies, are explored and Derber's analysis of professional labour processes is used to address the shortcomings. Having established an analytical framework, key developments in the social work labour process following the advent of neoliberalism are reviewed.

Social Services Departments

From the end of the Second World War the dominant professional interests saw their struggle to secure social work's legitimacy as linked to its incorporation in the welfare state (Jones 1999: 48). The range and responsibilities of social work grew slowly through its fragmented location in different departments of local government (in England and Wales), with administratively discrete, legislatively specific and professionally specialised services for children and families (Children's Departments), for people with mental health problems and learning disabilities (mental welfare services under the auspices of Medical Officers of Health), and for older people and people with physical disabilities (Welfare Departments). Social work broke out of its loci in these relatively marginal and dispersed roles and practices and was transformed into a central and systematically organised element of state welfare (in England and Wales) through the production of the Seebohm Report (Seebohm Committee 1968) and its implementation following the Local Authority and Allied Social Services Act (1970).

The Seebohm Committee's all-encompassing vision of social work's contribution to 'the social' is evident in the responsibility it saw the state as having for responding to the social problems of the citizenry and the building of solidarity:

> We recommend a new local authority department, providing a community-based and family-oriented service, which will be *available to all*. This new department will, we believe, *reach far beyond the discovery and rescue of social casualties*; it will enable the greatest possible number of individuals to act reciprocally, *giving and receiving service for*

the well-being of the community. (Seebohm Committee 1968: para 2, my emphasis)

However, the establishment of SSDs from 1971 onwards also had implications for the work of social workers, given that the structural reform of the personal social services and the professional unification of social workers occurred simultaneously, with social workers located unequivocally in the state's organisational and managerial structures. The analysis of these implications for social work came from the radical social work movement.

Radical social work

The wider context of the deliberations of the Seebohm Committee from 1965 onwards, and the production of its Report in 1968, was the wave of protest that was sweeping through the Western world. One of the by-products of this 'New Left' movement was entrants to social work who had backgrounds in student and other forms of activism. In the 1970s the loose-knit radical social work movement that emerged contained a variety of left-wing hues (Clark and Asquith 1975: 105–106) through which social work was scrutinised and recast. However, the central critique of existing social work was undertaken from the outset by Marxist-influenced variants of sociology (Langan 1992: 2; Langan and Lee 1989: 1). In these variants of sociology, social work was attacked as a form of social control and located within the ideological functions of welfare in a capitalist state (Clarke 1979: 125–126). As a consequence, the radical social work movement initially embraced class as the focal point of critical analysis (Day 1992: 12, 15; Hearn 1982: 22; Langan 1992: 2; Langan and Lee 1989: 9–10; Leonard 2004: 10).[1]

Although tensions existed between academics and practitioners in the radical social work movement concerning the relationship between radical theory and radical forms of practice (Clarke 1979; Cohen 1975; Hearn 1982), tensions were less evident between academics and practitioners in the class identification of social workers, first and foremost as *workers* (Langan and Lee 1989: 12). The underpinning of the radical paradigm by the theorists' analysis of social work as labour was endorsed by the activism of practitioners in the work setting. The latter were enjoined to adopt the mantra of Muhammad Ali in their employing organisations: 'float like a butterfly and sting like a bee' (Corrigan and Leonard 1978: 157). The proof of practitioners' radical credentials lay in the manifestation of an anti-management stance

(Clarke 1979: 131), with their agencies being regarded as 'just as big a problem as external factors' (Langan and Lee 1989: 5). The intellectual resource that was drawn upon to understand these developments in social work as work was Braverman's consideration of the labour process in *Labor and Monopoly Capital* (1974, republished 1998).

The labour process

Braverman's thesis has often been seen as representing the rediscovery of the labour process because Marx's (1974: Chapter 7) original formulation was the starting point for his work, which consisted of a review of Marx's theory of the labour process in the context of a detailed examination of changes in the organisation of production under capitalism. In a restatement and reaffirmation of Marx's theory, Braverman (1998: Chapters 1–3) emphasised the need to take the nature and purpose of production under capitalism into account when analysing the conditions of work. He saw the design of jobs, the division of labour and work organisation as all underpinned by the motive of accumulating capital through the extraction of surplus value. It was the logic of capital accumulation that dictated the organisation of work. The labour process could only be understood through an appreciation of its capitalist origins and its embodiment of the fundamental antagonism between capitalist and workers. This conflict, and in particular the employers' need to maximise profits, dictated the necessity for a management-initiated strategy to wrest control of the labour process from workers. As a part of this strategy, the scope for workers' control of and discretion in undertaking work had to be severely limited.

In specifying this management-initiated strategy, Braverman argued that in monopoly capitalism the necessity for capital to realise the potential of labour power contains an interlinked tendency towards the deskilling of workers through a different kind and scope of capitalist control by the division of labour. He describes the design of the labour process being fragmented into smaller, less skilled tasks that are more susceptible to coordination and control. As a result, only managers have an overall grasp of the labour process:

> Workers who are controlled only by general orders and discipline are not adequately controlled because they retain their grip on the actual processes of labour ... To change this situation control over the labour process must pass into the hands of management ... by the control and dictation

of each step of the process, including its performance. (Braverman 1998: 100)

Thus, the establishment and maintenance of managerial control was central to his analysis of 'scientific management': the separation of planning how to do a job (conception) from the doing of it (execution). As execution became increasingly separated from conception, the bulk of employees were involved in simple mundane tasks and discretion about how they undertook their work was removed. Accordingly, for Braverman, scientific management had become the pervasive, driving force of capitalist society. He sums up scientific management as follows:

> The first principle is the gathering together and development of knowledge of the labour process, and the second is the concentration of this knowledge as the exclusive preserve of management – together with its converse, the absence of such knowledge among workers – then the third step is the use of this monopoly of knowledge to control each step of the labour process and its mode of execution. (Braverman 1998: 119)

The social work labour process in the 'Seebohm factories'

Braverman's analysis of the labour process provided the analytical tools for radical social work's consideration of social work as work. As the position of social workers in SSDs and the forces that were exerted to manage and control them moved into prominence within radical analysis, the social work labour process was seen as being embedded in an industrial (Bravermanian) model (see, for example, Bolger et al 1981; Jones 1983; Joyce et al 1988; Simpkin 1983). In radical social work writers' formulation of the social work labour process, SSDs – frequently referred to on the Left as 'Seebohm factories' (see, for example, Simpkin 1983: 17) – were presented as having steadily eroded the discretion of frontline social workers through managers gaining control over their work. Following Braverman, writers pointed to two trends.

The first trend was an increasing separation between the processes of conception and execution. Bolger and colleagues considered that this Bravermanian concept had

> a direct, central and biting relevance to welfare work. The Seebohm Departments ... have increased their hierarchy

and their authoritarian nature ... This form has been directly lifted from the private enterprise arena where its main aim has been to increase control by a central management team ... The split is about knowledge of the whole process involved in the work. Some people have to carry out the work of the organisation and others plan it: the two groups are inevitably split and do not have a cross membership. Thus above team leaders there are very few people who ever meet clients; below team leaders there are very few people who structure, plan or co-ordinate ... We would underline the increasingly dominant trend in welfare work that separates control and practice further and further. (Bolger et al 1981: 66)

The split between those occupying roles of conception and those charged with execution was regarded as running through the social relations of the social work labour process in SSDs: 'The agency is not a whole; it contains an interiorised division between those working directly with clients and those responsible for management and rationing' (Simpkin 1983: 117).

The second trend radical writers identified was intensified detailed direction of the execution of day-to-day social work practice. This was considered to have resulted in management techniques that had reduced the day-to-day discretion of social workers because of a 'powerful de-skilling process' (Bolger et al 1981: 68). Jones (1983: 131) identified the control of social workers as one of the key factors limiting social workers' discretion:

One feature that stands out is the extent to which controls have been introduced for governing the activities and work of social workers. The range of measures has been wide and varied, and has included large-scale changes in the organisation of SSDs, with their expanded bureaucratic management hierarchies, more direct supervision over the social worker, and an expanded array of work processes which attempt to direct and regulate the social worker's contact with clients ... [There is] a gradual process of change which appears to be slowly ensuring greater employer control over the majority of social services workers ... In the main the major thrust of these changes appears to be in the direction of reducing further the already limited professional autonomy of social workers by introducing measures which will ensure more effective worker conformity to the policies of the employing agency. Such a process is by no means peculiar to social work, and writers such as Braverman have identified a similar process at work across the labour market, particularly in areas of skilled labour. The name given to the developments is that of 'proletarianisation'. For many social workers proletarianisation has become an increasing feature of their experience of work within a local authority SSD. (Jones 1983: 94, 122)

Simpkin (1983: 93–94) similarly contended that social workers were 'more and more members of a new proletariat ... as ever tighter control is exerted over their work process'. He considered that this managerial control meant that 'such occupational skills as social workers believed they possessed became diffused and lost' (Simpkin 1983: 94). He made a direct analogy with the industrial sphere:

> The cumulative effect of the [Seebohm] reorganisation upon social workers was little dissimilar from the introduction of the assembly line by Henry Ford ... From being a craft motor engineering had become the repetition of a detailed operation ... workers ... found that the same mode of production had encroached on every sphere of production. (Simpkin 1983: 19)

The radical literature lacked research that tested the applicability of Braverman's thesis to social work. Writers assumed that pervasive managerial control was a universal process across occupations and so they were concerned with outlining general features of developments in the social work labour process, which they saw as the playing out in a specific context of the broader tendencies Braverman had identified in the world of work. However, research was undertaken in this period that did shed light on the social work labour process.

Empirical studies

The twin trends of the separation of conception from execution and management control over day-to-day practice were presented in the radical social work literature as pervasive. However, there was little elaboration about the way in which these trends were being accomplished. It seems crucial, then, to turn to empirical studies of the nature of day-to-day social work in this period.

These studies suggested, contrary to the radical social work literature, that autonomy was the order of the day for teams of social workers. For example, in a study of a London borough's SSD, Satyamurti found that team leaders did not view the wider department as an object to which they owed loyalty or with which they identified. There was little scrutiny of their work with social workers and they could disregard specific departmental rules without negative consequences (Satyamurti 1981: 35). Similarly, Pithouse's study of a Welsh SSD found that in supervision meetings between team leaders and social workers the 'good practice' aspects of social work were looked at as much as, or more frequently than, looking at work from a managerial point of view (Pithouse 1987: 73–74). This permissive form of supervision in social work was well entrenched and Pithouse found that team leaders demonstrated to their teams their 'independence from higher management and their disinclination to intrude overly in the worker's day to day practice' (Pithouse 1987: 65). He stressed the existence of negotiable working arrangements in social work offices, rather than formal rules or objectives; social workers and team leaders saw themselves as definers of good practice as a result of the insulation of the area office from the rest of the department (Pithouse 1987: 47-49). Harris, in a study of an English SSD in 1980, found that frontline managers did not approach supervision on the basis of a superior-subordinate relationship in which they prescribed and judged social workers' practice, but as a meeting of two colleagues: 'I see social workers as autonomous. They should accept the responsibilities they have and supervision should be sharing those situations that they feel they need to talk over ... You have to allow social workers their autonomy' (Team manager, in Harris 1997: 98). Howe's study of 285 social workers and social work assistants in three English SSDs, undertaken in 1979, had similar findings (Howe 1986: 79).

Parsloe, drawing on the findings of research into the practice of 33 area teams, concluded:

> Sometimes we felt that a kind of Berlin Wall existed between each team and every other part of the department within which it was situated. It was particularly high and well-guarded between teams and what team members always called 'the hierarchy', which meant everyone above team leaders ... It was apparent that, in general, management had laid down few policy guidelines for the way teams undertook their work. Decisions about the way duty, intake and allocation were managed seemed to be made

> by the teams themselves ... Teams often appeared to make decisions in a vacuum which was seldom filled by guidance from headquarters. (Parsloe 1981: 92–93)

Parsloe identified some of the features of the permissive culture that existed behind the 'Berlin Wall',[2] in particular the absence of detailed forms or guidelines in relation to undertaking assessments, no shared criteria for deciding who in the team should do what work and no shared ideas about the kind or amount of work members should undertake (Parsloe 1981: 60). The research found 'little evidence of any systematic planning by supervisors to acquaint themselves with information about all the cases being supervised by individual social workers' (Parsloe and Stevenson 1978: 53) and the common pattern was for social workers to decide what they wanted to talk about in their supervision sessions. It was unusual for team leaders to even use lists of cases as a basis for keeping a check on work being done on each case (Parsloe 1981: 131).

As these studies illustrate, frontline managers were guardians of a permissive supervision tradition that carved out the discretionary space for social workers' sphere of discretion. There appear to have been few limitations on this discretion, either from senior managers attempting to control social workers through frontline managers' supervision of them or as an outcome of any initiative by frontline managers themselves to exercise control. Rather, social workers could define problems and the priority allocated to them, choose their preferred methods of work, control how they rationed their time and paced their work, decide the strategy to be adopted with people with whom they were working and even, in some cases, whether they would provide a service at all.

These findings from empirical studies are difficult to square with the radical social work literature's depiction of strictly controlled practice in the 'Seebohm factories'. Instead, they indicate the existence of a 'parochial professionalism' in this era (Harris 1998). This parochial professionalism had nothing to do with the grandiose aspirations to elite status and professional self-determination associated with the established professions. Rather it was a way of team leaders and social workers attempting to construct a shared view of social work as a key aspect of their working relations. In supervision, team leaders who had been promoted on the basis of judgements made about their competence in practice stressed their seniority as practitioners, rather than their managerial position. Parochial professionalism in the supervision of social workers was geared to developing the personalised and discretionary nature of social workers' contact with service users, rather than the imposition of control.

Professional labour processes

The discrepancy between the radical social work literature's account of the social work labour process in SSDs and the picture of their day-to-day operation provided by empirical studies suggests that an alternative formulation is needed to make sense of professional labour processes. Derber (1982, 1983) has provided an analysis that sets out the distinctiveness of professional work, an analysis that has the capacity to address the discrepancy that has been identified in the original consideration of social work as work.

In contrast to the universal industrial model of the labour process advanced by Braverman (and, as we have seen, by radical social work writers), Derber argued for the distinctiveness of the labour processes of professional workers, which, he maintained, had not followed the industrial model. In order to demonstrate the distinctiveness of professional labour processes, Derber posed a central question: what does lack of control over work mean? Braverman followed Marx in suggesting that lack of control has two components: lack of control over the process of labour and lack of control over the product. The first component highlights the tendency for the purchasers of labour power to impose their own conception of how to organise and execute the job (the separation of conception and execution). The second component points to the purchasers' control over what is produced and the purpose for which it is used (Derber 1983: 312). In other words, Derber argued, the first component is about the means and the second component is about the ends of the labour process (Derber 1983: 313). The labour process perspective developed around issues which addressed the first component, the means (execution) of the labour process and managerial control over it. Derber argued that the emphasis in the labour process perspective on this first component – lack of control over the process of work, which he terms 'technical proletarianisation' – had come to be synonymous with proletarianisation itself (Derber 1983: 315). As a result, the second component – lack of control over the ends of work – had been ignored. Derber refers to this second component as 'ideological proletarianisation', the management control exerted over the goals and purposes of work. As Derber emphasised, most industrial workers experience both the technical and ideological components of control simultaneously and this allowed the labour process perspective to concentrate its attentions on the former (Derber 1983: 313).

However, having disaggregated technical and ideological proletarianisation, Derber suggested that in the case of professional work:

> Ideological proletarianisation creates a type of worker whose integrity is threatened less by the expropriation of his [sic] skill than his values or sense of purpose. It reduces the domain of freedom and creativity to problems of technique ... It is the lack of control over the ends to which work is put that, in the current period, defines most centrally their [professionals'] proletarianisation. (Derber 1983: 316)

Thus, Derber argued, professional workers maintained a considerable degree of technical discretion. He further suggested that professional workers could adapt to ideological proletarianisation through ideological co-optation, a process of redefining the goals of their work so that the disparities between professional and organisational interests were minimised and their employing organisations were perceived as committed to professional workers' underlying values and purposes: 'Ideological co-optation reflects the new hybrid identity in which professionals take their moral values and objectives from their new institutional employers, but sustain an identity separate from other employees by their investment in technical expertise' (Derber 1983: 330-331). As far as social work was concerned Derber (1983: 333) argued that 'The therapeutic [casework] approach formed the basis for a highly sophisticated ideological co-optation, where social workers' moral concerns for the well-being of their clients could be accommodated in a form of practice that served institutional ends'.

Derber's distinction between ideological and technical proletarianisation suggested that professionals like social workers had retained considerable degrees of technical autonomy in determining service users' needs and responses to them. His analysis suggested that the labour process of such workers should not have been seen as automatically subject to the loss of control over work that the Bravermanian approach adopted by the radical social work writers saw as the central development. With the benefit of hindsight we can go further and suggest that social workers not only had some technical autonomy but also had some ideological autonomy in relation to the goals and outcomes of their work. Indeed, it is difficult to make sense of the phenomenon of radical social work, were this not the case.[3]

The neoliberal social work labour process

The context of the literature we have been considering was the tail-end of post-war social democracy, since which successive Conservative (1979–1997), New Labour (1997–2010), Conservative-Liberal Democrat coalition (2010–2014) and Conservative (2014–) governments have pursued a broadly neoliberal approach including towards the operation of the state. Although the initial impact of Thatcherism on social work (and other areas of the state) from 1979 onwards was seen as a ferocious and intrusive attack, neoliberalism gradually achieved hegemonic status, positioning itself as having no alternative and as being the taken-for-granted way of understanding the world and acting in it (Harris 2014). This has had significant consequences for the social work labour process, not least because a crucial element in achieving neoliberalism's hegemonic status has been the heightened managerialisation of state labour processes.

In the neoliberal political mainstream, managerialism has been regarded as a dynamic transformative process, needed to demolish the lingering structures of post-war social democracy:

> [*State organisations*] were seen as like a dinosaur, too big, too slow-moving, too insensitive, insufficiently adaptable, and seriously underpowered as far as brains are concerned ... Better management is seen as providing an effective solvent for a wide range of economic and social ills. (Pollitt 2003: 32)

Accordingly, as an aspect of these wide-ranging changes in state labour processes, managerialism has been the means through which the structure and culture of social work have been recast (Clarke et al 1994: 4). Management has been seen as constituted by generic knowledge and skills that can be applied to any activity in any circumstances (Harris 2003; Harris and White 2009). These generic models of management regard private sector practices as applicable to the public sector, claim to provide skills relevant in all circumstances and present a management solution to any problem (Du Gay 2000: Chapter 4; Rees 1995: 15–17). Such models have been represented as capable of rescuing the public sector from the dead weight of the social democratic welfare state's faith in professionals (Pollitt 2003: 27). Thus, being like management in the private sector has involved being 'free to manage', including being free to manage professionals (Pollitt 2003: Chapter 1). As part of this management freedom, greater control has been exerted over the social work labour process – the 'professional space' represented by the relationship between the social worker and the service user. This control has been achieved by a number of interlocking developments.

Developments in the social work labour process

An early shift in the labour process was the creation of neoliberalised managers. Managers were seen by the Thatcher governments as deeply implicated in the failings of the social democratic welfare state but were also seen as central to its dismantling and reconstruction. Senior managers became responsible for securing commitment to Conservative policies and were expected to take the lead in challenging power structures and vested interests left over from the social democratic regime (Audit Commission 1992: 27). They were required to meet targets and achieve strategic objectives, now well-established and taken-for-granted aspects of management. In order to achieve objectives, it was seen as important to remove intermediaries between those responsible for strategy and planning and those responsible for providing services (O'Higgins 1992: 48), so that senior management could take the lead in establishing strategy, planning change, defining and measuring needs and establishing priorities and targets. This aped the centralisation of management command that characterised capitalist enterprises (Hoggett 1991). Frontline management was also transformed. Although these managers could still be seen as senior manager/social worker go-betweens, they were now collecting information on team performance for senior management and were made responsible for improving overall achievements. Previously carriers of the parochial professional culture of social work, they were made responsible for transforming the labour process and giving it a managerial orientation. There was a fundamental shift away from the dominance of the professional culture: 'The team leader is now less a professional supervisor and more a manager with financial responsibility' (Lewis and Glennerster 1996: 143).

Neoliberal managers can be regarded as having introduced what we might term 'quasi-capitalist rationality' into the social work labour process (Harris 2003: Chapter 3). However, the Thatcher governments and their successors did not simply rely on persuading managers ideologically about delivering this rationality, although this was an important aspect of the discourse that changed the balance between managerialism and professionalism. Powerful material constraints were also introduced that reinforced the ideological direction. Cash limits were set on the budgets available to local authorities responsible for providing social services. These ceilings on central government income streams to local government contained assumptions about efficiency gains in percentage terms. This measure exerted general downward pressure on costs in services such as social work. With the advent of austerity, this long-term financial pressure has been intensified. 'Austerity' is used as shorthand for the principle that underpins policies and programmes that have been put in place following the crisis in the financial system in 2007/08. While the initial focus was on how to rescue the banks from disaster and restore financial stability, the economics and politics of austerity quickly shifted to a concern with government debt, which included the phenomenal amounts involved in saving the banks. In the process, the cause of and blame for the crisis shifted from the private sector (the high-risk strategies employed by the banks) to the public sector (the wasteful and expensive state). As a consequence, austerity amplified existing neoliberal themes in which public spending, public debt and public benefits and services are viewed as problematic and as obstructing growth and enterprise. The UK has cut public benefits and services more deeply than most European countries, justified by the argument that this is both economically necessary and morally desirable, as the actions of citizens are called upon to replace the activities of the state. This has resulted in workers in the public sector and recipients of its benefits and services bearing the brunt of austerity. While at first sight austerity may seem to belong to the realm of economics and to have little to do with social work, its impact has been far-reaching in shaping the social work labour process following the financial crash.

The straitened circumstances of the social work labour process intensified the existing neoliberal managerial trend towards commodification. This involves identifying discrete problem categories and corresponding service options (Ponnert and Svensson 2016) in order to quantify and cost service outputs. This tends to reduce social work to a series of one-off transactions, depriving it of meaningful working relationships with and commitments to service users, despite rhetoric to the contrary. The labour process is fragmented into a series of tasks, such as assessment, planning, intervention(s) and review, often with different social workers undertaking these tasks as separate functions, curtailing social work's aspirations to deal with 'the whole person' (Broadhurst and Mason 2014; Trevithick 2014). This development stems from a firmly held neoliberal belief that the life situations of service users can be classified into discrete problem categories that are susceptible to the strictures of management in terms of setting criteria for initial decisions about access to assessment for services, the service options made available following assessment and the quantifying and costing of service outputs. This shift in the labour process is reductionist: it disregards the potential complexity of service users' lives and circumstances that contribute to the causes of the problems they present, thus obscuring broad individual and social issues arising from social work. This has required a shift in orientation from social workers. They have been turned into (micro-)managers responsible for scrupulous gate-keeping and strict rationing of scarce resources, working within complex procedures for regulating their dispersal of services, based primarily on budgetary considerations (Jones and Novak 1993: 202). An extreme example of commodification is provided by 'Skylakes', which provides hit-squads of social workers to come into local authorities and blitz backlogs of particular kinds of work: 'Skylakes undertakes an agreed volume of work to a set timescale and at an agreed price upon delivery ... Our services are entirely bespoke to your needs, from piece work [*sic*] and project work to long-term support' (www.skylakes.co.uk).

The developments discussed thus far have been rooted in and routed through the IT systems that now dominate the social work labour process. IT has been crucial in monitoring social workers' rationing of resources and prioritising budgetary considerations in the allocation of services. In the process, social workers' recording has been constrained by standardised procedures for information processing, as Sapey anticipated it would:

> The use of computers therefore reduces the scope for interpretation of data and, in so doing, is transforming organisations from professionalised bureaucracies to centrally controlled administrative activities. While the rules and regulations of agencies will increase, adding controlling bureaucratic features, their flexibility and responsiveness to individuals in need will decrease. The primary task of the organisation may also be changed ... from one of welfare provision to the collection of data to regulate and determine eligibility for such provision ... Social workers will find themselves ... part of a machine that has achieved an objective reality ... Such systems will inevitably result in greater control over the interpretation of data and consequently over the activities of practitioners. (Sapey 1997: 809)

Earlier debates about social work methods and theoretical perspectives have been largely replaced by approaches embedded in computer systems controlled by managers, with social workers following through the actions required by IT systems in the space they previously largely controlled. Fabricant and Burghardt anticipated the nature of such developments from their research into parallel trends in the American context:

> The structure of work is redefined, breaking it down into ever more discrete and measurable elements. Then, this structure limits the worker's capacity to exercise independent judgement or discretion by mandating what can or cannot be done at each stage of the process. (Fabricant and Burghardt 1992: 86)

Converting social work tasks into IT-based processes means that the social work labour process has a modular design that requires social workers to execute tasks flexibly, unemotionally and in a time-efficient fashion (Hirst and Humphreys 2015), with the logics of managerialism built into the systems (Gillingham and Graham 2016). This changes the nature of the tasks and the way that social workers undertake and think about their work (Gillingham 2016).

By such means, IT has led to the reification of control in the labour process. Over time there has been a proliferation of protocols, procedures and tasks that have to be followed, according to the dictates of voluminous online manuals. Much of the work of social workers that previously had to be managed interpersonally is now managed by these systems, without the need for any overt human managerial intervention, except for electronic authorisation of end-stage outputs. As a consequence, when social workers experience control of their practice, they are likely to see it as simply a computer requirement, as part of the assembly-line character of IT systems, with certain tasks just having to be done at specific points. Rather than experiencing this in straightforward managerial terms – as a superior coercing a subordinate to undertake work in a particular way – the IT system appears to be requiring workers to perform 'neutral' 'technical' tasks. Thus, the codification of social work in IT systems is a managerial process that has provided a crucial opportunity for rationalising, routinising and controlling social workers. Increasingly this control is capable of being exercised at a distance; the introduction of 'remote' or 'agile' working means that IT requirements can be fulfilled anytime, anywhere. This is often promoted as freeing up the social worker, which in some respects it may do, but it also impacts on social workers' experiences of practice, interactions with colleagues and practice knowledge (Jeyasingham 2016). In addition, working remotely heightens the sense of existing simply as an individual worker in the labour process with an employment relationship mediated by IT.

As well as shaping the actions and personae of social workers, IT systems track what social workers do, opening them up to closer scrutiny through more continuous, more intense surveillance through tools such as 'dashboards'[4] that provide data about individual workers and aggregate data about groups of social workers. Social workers do not know when surveillance will take place, but have to comply with the computerised requirements on the basis that surveillance could take place at any time. IT systems generate data about social workers, such as the number of assessments undertaken over a given period, the number of activities carried out on a particular case and the number still outstanding, the time taken to follow up cases picked up on duty and so on. Of course, this data sheds no light on the qualitative nature of social workers' interactions with service users or the actual outcomes, rather than the outputs, of the work undertaken. In addition, it constrains frontline managers to act more like progress chasers than the peer consultants associated with the parochial professional supervisory relationships described earlier.

IT systems have been a crucial component in neoliberal managerialism's institutionalisation of performance management, through which organisational objectives are identified, performance indicators (PIs) are developed to reflect the objectives, targets are set in terms of the PIs and progress is reviewed. In the social work labour process, performance management creates what counts as social work by determining which specific forms of practice social workers are accountable for and are therefore authorised to undertake. In this way the social work labour process is reconstituted. Whereas early incarnations of managerialism were concerned with establishing the legitimacy of the right to manage, contemporary performance management seeks to secure the right to manage anything and everything, to bear down on workers and work processes in pursuit of the required performance indicators. In this sense, the emphasis on performance 'sustains managerialism, emphasising the value, authority and autonomy of managers' (Clarke 2004: 31). The managerial language reflects this, with managers referring to 'driving down', 'drilling down', 'tying down'; the phrases always seem to express forceful intentions and those intentions are always travelling down organisations in pursuit of the satisfaction of performance indicators.

Performance management presents measures of performance, and identification of the extent to which they have been met, as readily identifiable through the use of what is portrayed as a technical, objective, neutral approach to which all can subscribe and in which all can be actively involved. In contrast, we might point to 'the ineliminable place of conflict' (Mouffe 2000) in the constitution of anything so politically, ethically and morally charged as social work.

IT systems have also underpinned the introduction of call centres into the social work labour process. They are probably the most fundamental change to accessing social work that has ever taken place (Coleman and Harris 2008). They introduce a process for dealing with services users taken from the business sector that ignores the potential complexity of their 'transactions' and jettisons social work's emphasis on seeking to establish trust with, and appreciating the unique circumstances of, the service user. Call centres are much vaunted by their proponents because they overcome barriers of place and time. However, a sense of place and locality has other connotations in terms of service users' identities and where and how they want services to be provided. These kinds of concerns were traditionally seen as integral to the nature of social work. In many progressive aspirations for social work, the notion of responsiveness to the local community has had pride of place. With the advent of call centres, the ability of social workers to be aware of and utilise local networks and resources is rendered unimportant.

Concluding comments

The overall impact of the neoliberal developments in the social work labour process that have been considered is twofold: increased separation of conception and execution and increased control of, and decreased discretion for, social workers. It seems that the radical social work writers' analysis was not wrong; it was simply premature.

As we have seen, before the advent of neoliberalism social work can be regarded, in Derber's terms, as not having been subjected to technical control. It was subjected to ideological control in working to the broad ends and purposes defined for it by the state and expressed in legislative mandates, but social workers were left to determine the means by which those ends and purposes were achieved. However, even in relation to ideological control there was apparently some room for manoeuvre, otherwise it is difficult to account for the emergence of, for example, radical social work, feminist social work and anti-racist social work as perspectives explicitly concerned with alternatives goals and purposes for social work. This suggests that social work's location in the legislative and organisational base of the social democratic welfare state was compatible with considerable professional discretion, particularly after the implementation of the Seebohm Report had delivered resources that consolidated social work's control over its area of work. In contrast, neoliberalism has resulted not only in the tightening of ideological control but also the imposition of technical control over the social work labour process, displacing the parochial professional culture with a workplace culture of control.

The response to the developments reviewed can, understandably, be pessimistic (Leonard 2004), if they are viewed as unequivocal accomplishments that have produced a compliant workforce (Jones 2001): robotic social workers employed on neoliberal production lines. An alternative is to see social workers as interpellated[5] by neoliberalism, being called to get on board with its propositions and the processes that flow from them and to adopt specific identities within them. However, social workers may be called by the neoliberal agenda but may respond to it in ways that are not anticipated. This is because although neoliberal managerialism has curtailed social work discretion, it is impossible to eliminate it altogether (for a detailed discussion see Evans and Harris 2004). The potential gap between neoliberalism's intentions and accomplishments needs to be exploited not only by social workers struggling to work in the interests of service users in their day-to-day practice (Carey and Foster 2011; Ferguson 2013; Fine and Teram 2013; Rogowski 2012; White 2009) but also through collective struggles (see, for example, Social Work Action Network, www.socialworkfuture.org). Despite neoliberalism's attempts to establish itself in a position of settled and unquestioned hegemony in the social work labour process, tensions and contradictions in its attempts to do so inevitably remain. Analysis of these tensions and contradictions is a basis from which to be (to quote an earlier formulation of the position of state workers) in and against the neoliberal social work labour process (London Edinburgh Weekend Return Group 1980).

Notes

1   Subsequently there was growing recognition that a class analysis could only proceed with accompanying analyses of the impact of other social divisions (age, disability, ethnicity, gender, 'race', sexuality) on people's lives with regard to experiences of domination, subordination, exclusion and resistance.

2   This 'Berlin Wall' can be seen as a direct consequence of the Seebohm Report seeing decentralisation as the key to successful reorganisation of the personal social services. The Report gave strong support to the case for decentralised

141

offices staffed by professional social workers: 'We attach great importance to the comprehensive area team approach in the search for an effective family social service and, as a concomitant, the delegation of the maximum authority for decisions to the area office' (Seebohm 1968: para 392). Geographical decentralisation, and the accompanying delegation of functions and power from the centre to the periphery, was presented as the first and foremost element in attaining service user-oriented objectives: 'All the personal social services should be located under one roof wherever possible and they should be decentralised to bring them nearer to the public and make them more accessible' (Seebohm 1968: para 108), 'with the maximum amount of responsibility delegated to them from the headquarters of the social service department' (Seebohm 1968: para 19).

[3] In my own case, as a local authority social worker I was involved in benefit takeup campaigns, the setting up of a Claimants' Union, various campaigning groups of service users and forms of direct action. While this was not characteristic of the practice of every social worker at the time, it did not feel out of the ordinary in terms of what many of my fellow social workers were doing.

[4] Software that presents data in displays that simulate gauges and dials, and that looks like a car dashboard.

[5] Interpellation is a concept that was introduced by Althusser (2001: 115-118) to explain the way in which ideology enters individual consciousness and affects people's lives so that ideologies are experienced as their own ideas, as part of their makeup. He saw ideologies as addressing or calling to people and offering them a particular identity, which they are encouraged to accept. Accepting or not accepting dominant ideologies and the identities they offer places someone in a particular relationship with power.

9

Social work and the refugee crisis: reflections from Samos in Greece

Chris Jones

Introduction

Our work with refugees on Samos has been rooted in our common humanity and informed by mutual respect, solidarity and empathy. In Samos we have come to recognise that these human qualities are shaped by where you stand with the refugees. If you stand shoulder to shoulder as brothers and sisters it nearly always followed that relationships form where people connect, despite massive differences in background and experience. Even in 2015 when the average stay of the refugees on Samos was two to three days it was astonishing to see so many friendships made between the refugees and the local activists who met them on the beaches and helped provide clothes and food. Even two years later many of these connections have endured.

On the other hand we also saw many 'helpers' who did not stand with and alongside the refugees. These people could talk the talk of their concern for the refugees but they saw themselves as both different and superior. Such an attitude prevented meaningful contact with the refugees and often led to 'help' being given in ways which were humiliating and disrespectful. This was evident in many ways. Refugees for example were and are viewed as supplicants with almost no rights to even choose the clothes they were given. If a young male refugee refused a needed pair of jeans, for example, he was immediately seen as ungrateful. The very idea that refugees should care about how they looked or comment on the labels/brands on offer was seen as outrageous. Yet in so many ways the young adult refugees are just like their European counterparts in that they do obsess about labels and brands and do care greatly about their appearance – one of the very few parts of their lives they now have any sort of control over. Virtually every other aspect, from what they eat to where they sleep and when they can move are under the complete control of others.

Since the EU/Turkey pact in March 2016 refugees have been detained for months on Samos and it is possible to see more clearly how refugees fight to hold on to some control. At the cricket matches organised by the Pakistani refugees the hairstyles of many of the players are stunningly fashionable. These are all done within the camp and those with the skills and equipment are in high demand. Their clothes and shoes are not up to much – they never get to choose the clothes that are handed out in the camp – but their hairstyles are top drawer. And this is true for the majority of young male refugees on Samos. Control over their hairstyle is about all they have!

Here they come!

The summer of 2015 marked the beginning of a new period in Samos' long history of being a gateway into Europe for undocumented migrants. The massive increase in arrivals with over 90,000 coming to Samos – three times the population of the island – precipitated by the devastating war in Syria simply overwhelmed the already feeble capacity of the authorities. It was an experience which was repeated again and again as the tidal waves of refugees swept northwards out of Greece during that summer.

On Samos, the previous practice of detaining refugees in a camp that looked like Guantanamo Bay surrounded by a double fence topped with coiled razor wire had to be abandoned. The camp built in 2007 (replacing an equally horrendous ex-police station) had a capacity for 240 detainees and despite the warnings of the impending increase of refugees about to cross the Aegean from nearby Turkey, no additional provision (such as opening closed military camps and empty hotels) had been made.

The decision was taken that the only way to manage was to move the refugees off the island as quickly as possible. Of course, there were other options, but on Samos at least those with power and authority were firmly of the view that anything which made Samos look positive to the refugees would result in even more arrivals. This they wanted to avoid at all costs. So from early summer 2015 all the daily arrivals were no longer taken to the camp but were immediately directed either to the port in Karlovassi or in Samos Town where they could get a ferry to Piraeus/Athens. At the outset the authorities privileged the refugees fleeing from Syria, who were considered to be the most vulnerable. While Syrians constituted around 80% of the arrivals, there were also significant numbers of refugees from Afghanistan, Iraq, Somalia, north Africa and Iran. The plan was that Syrians would be 'fast tracked' at the port and on to Athens within 72 hours of arrival. All other nationalities were to be detained in the camp, where a more intense processing would take place.

But it was not to be so simple and it was only ever partially implemented. For a start the refugees are not stupid. Most of them knew that the Samos authorities had implemented the Syria-first approach. So apart from those whose skin colour (black) indicated that they were unlikely to be Syrian, all other refugees quickly realised that it was best to declare themselves as Syrian if they wanted to avoid being delayed. (Just as in 2006 most of the refugees coming then declared that they were Palestinian because they knew that to be Palestinian meant they wouldn't be deported.)

Most of the police at the ports clearly knew what was going on and often encouraged refugees from elsewhere (Iraq and Afghanistan) to declare themselves as Syrian because it meant that they avoided the hassle of detaining them in the camp and they could rapidly move them on. For some, however, this was taken as further illustration of the widely held assumption by the authorities that refugees lie; they are never to be believed. It is an assumption which can have fatal consequences, as our friend Wasim discovered: in 2013 the police refused to believe him when he told them that his wife and two young children were trapped in the forest in a remote part of Samos. Not only did the police take no action, they handcuffed Wasim to a chair for over 24 hours as he protested in vain. His wife and children died in the forest.

Refugees rarely travel 'alone'. Most of the refugees are with others, either friends or family, and these are vital forms of support. But through their smartphones they are also in contact with a much wider network of others, including those who have gone before them. These networks were and remain extremely important and valuable to the refugees. They provide information about routes, about smugglers and other contacts necessary to their onward journeys. It alerts them to what they can expect from the authorities they will be forced to deal with en route. It did not take long for some of the mainstream media to suggest that owning a smartphone indicated that the refugees were not having such a hard time, if they could afford such a gadget. They wilfully ignored how vital they were to the refugees' survival. We met many refugees who told us how their family had all chipped in to buy the phone before they left home and many we discovered were paid for by their mothers. The phones were lifelines. This is why one of the most pressing needs expressed by the refugees shortly after arriving here was phone charging and access to free Wi-Fi. The phones and networks created by the refugees became crucial 'intelligence' resources in their hands.

In the summer of 2015 the two ports on Samos and not the camp became the focus of the islanders' efforts to help the refugees. It was here that the refugees were corralled, waiting to be photographed and have their basic details (name, birth, country and so on) recorded before being given a 'white paper' which allowed them to move on to Athens. Once there they were expected to continue with their applications for asylum. Very few wanted to stay in Greece so there was no question of lingering in Athens for further processing. They were not interested in seeking asylum in Greece. They could see that the Greek economy was in ruins and that there was little or no chance of decent work. They wanted to move on and join the wave of refugees pushing northwards. In any event the Greek asylum service had collapsed, and through a newly introduced application system operated through Skype it was virtually impossible to obtain even an initial interview to kick-start the procedure.

The boat groups

The scenes at the two Samian ports for much of summer 2015 were extraordinary, with hundreds of refugees milling around waiting to be dealt with by the police. Every available fence was used for drying the clothes that had been soaked during their crossing and every place that offered some shade was occupied. The great majority of refugees stayed together with those they had travelled with, especially during the sea crossing from Turkey. Some of the groups were mixed and included a variety of nationalities but mostly they were from the same countries – Syrians with Syrians, for example. Within each group, of usually around 40 to 60 people, there would be subgroups of friends and families. But the solidarities that formed as a result of the sea crossing, which threw people together who were often meeting for the first time, were exceptionally strong and significant.

At this time the 'boat groups' became the most important survival resource for the refugees. With the authorities offering nothing in terms of food, shelter, clothing and comfort of any kind, the well-being of the refugees depended largely on themselves. There were no NGOs on the island, and not only did the authorities do nothing, nor did other significant local actors such as the army and the ubiquitous Greek Orthodox Church, which turned their backs on the refugees. It was in the boat groups that money was shared so food could be bought, or hotel rooms could be booked for those who were most in need of a proper bed and toilets – young children, those with disabilities, and those with the greatest trauma. It was from within the boat groups that money was raised to pay for the ferry tickets for those who had lost everything. And it was in these groups that compassion and support was offered. Oftentimes boat groups refused to leave on the ferries until all their group had been issued with the necessary authorisation to leave Samos. Nobody was to be left behind.

Representatives/spokespeople always emerged from the boat groups, usually selected on their ability to speak English. In Karlovassi port we had the enormous advantage of having an Arabic speaker who had come to Samos as a refugee in 2006. Creating effective communication systems with the boat groups was crucial. They were able to identify those within their groups who needed special attention, usually medical but also financial. Our involvement needed to be fully engaged with the boat groups and directed to supporting and deepening their solidarities. For example, it was evident from the beginning that in order to avoid chaos and mobbing over food and clothing distributions the refugees themselves had to be involved and given responsibilities. The boat groups became vital in this effort and they created effective systems for ensuring that food was shared and distributed with dignity and respect. They also organised the lunches, setting up lines of sandwich makers. And they were especially important in terms of maintaining some semblance of hygiene in a very difficult situation.

The negligence of the authorities seemed to have no limits and this extended to a complete disregard for the hygiene and cleanliness of the ports. In Karlovassi, for example, apart from the quayside bars, some of which allowed the refugees to use their toilets, there was a single broken toilet in an abandoned port police building at the harbour. Yet there were often 200 to 300 refugees staying there. Within days this single toilet and the empty rooms in the building were a public health disaster area. Under pressure from the locals, the local authority announced that it would install portaloos in the harbour. They promised immediate action. But as ever, nothing materialised. No portaloos ever came. To do nothing quickly became impossible. The health risks from this stinking excrement filled building in the very centre of where the refugees stayed at the port were extreme. With nothing forthcoming from the system, the activists at the port took over the abandoned police building, cleaned it out, painted the rooms and got the single toilet working again. In the meantime another local group had managed to raise enough money to install additional toilets and outside washing sinks. No permission was sought. Direct action was taken.

Although driven by the immediate health needs of the refugees, both they and the activists were well aware of the broader context where refugees are routinely demonised as being dirty and diseased. The disgusting state of the port police building was taken as yet further proof of this stereotype. In Karlovassi, the importance of keeping the area free of garbage and keeping the restored building and toilets clean became a daily refrain. It was not only about keeping themselves as healthy as possible but it was also a conscious fightback against one aspect of their demonisation.

This was the broad context in which islanders responded to the needs of the refugees. It took various forms and was spontaneous. There was no overall coordination, although a web of relationships formed between the various groups which helped with effectiveness. Nor was there any time when any individual or group attempted to take control. This in part might be explained by the absence of the organised left-wing parties such as the Communist Party (KKE) and Syriza in these initiatives. As anyone with any familiarity of the Greek Left knows, their thirst to manage and control is (in)famous. Their absence was justified largely on the grounds that these popular interventions allowed the authorities both in Greece and the EU to evade their responsibilities for the refugees. And with some justification they argued that the explosion of popular action across Europe in response to the refugees deflected attention from the machinations of imperialism and neoliberalism which were at the root of the refugee crisis. But for the islanders who were at the ports, the all too evident suffering of the refugees demanded immediate action. And for many it was never a question of either helping the refugees or criticising the neglect of the authorities or the evils of imperialism and global capital; both were seen as necessary. There was also some hope that their example would shame the authorities into doing something humane for the refugees. This never materialised.

Criminalising help

Help for the refugees came from a range of quarters on Samos. For example, before the NGOs arrived at the end of the summer, a collection of tourists and regular summer visitors to Samos (between 15 and 40 at any one time) made a crucial contribution in meeting the refugees when they landed on the beaches. A phone rota was created so that when refugee boats were spotted coming into land, usually between 4am and 7am, they could be called on to drive down to the beaches and help both with the landing and above all to take them to the nearest port. Despite the high summer temperatures the authorities made no provision for either the landings (need for water and dry clothes) or transport to the ports. Without the drivers and their vehicles, the already exhausted refugees faced a walk of up to 20 kilometres to get to the nearest port. Furthermore, public transport was not an option as the bus company refused to carry refugees. The same applied to the taxis, although that changed later in the summer as it became evident that they were missing out on a highly lucrative source of income. But worse still was a longstanding law in Greece which criminalised giving any lifts to refugees by car, boat or even donkey. Even though this restriction was lifted in the early summer of 2015 (although you were still expected to inform the police every time you took a refugee) the police took a great deal longer to accept that the law had changed. So drivers were often stopped and told that they were breaking the law; they had to report to police stations with their documents and were generally harassed.

The tourists and holiday visitors were not so fearful of this law or of the Greek police and saw it as an outrageous attempt to curb their humanity. Not only did they continue to drive in the face of police harassment but they often came down to the ports with food once the refugees had settled in. Moreover, once they returned home many of those people continued to offer valuable financial support by fundraising for refugees on Samos, and some have linked up with refugees whom they first met on Samos and who successfully made it to northern Europe.

As always it was the refugees who suffered most from these laws. Countless cars and pickups with room for passengers never stopped to pick up refugees tramping to the ports. Many islanders reported of being afraid of the consequences if they stopped to help. As recounted in detail on the blog Samos Chronicles, for some refugees the consequences have been fatal – as in the case of Wasim, who was not helped by the local fishermen as he swam along the coast looking for help for his wife and two young children trapped in the forest by the shore. Boats would approach him but turn away once they saw he was a refugee. They feared that if they helped they would be arrested as smugglers and lose their boat. It was not an idle threat as confiscations had happened and had been widely reported. But for Wasim it was a contributory factor in the death of his family. Similarly, when a motor launch capsized in 2014 and led to the deaths of over 22 refugees locked in the cabin, none of the small fishing boats in the nearby fishing village were prepared to go out and take part in the search and rescue of survivors. When pressed, they all expressed fear that they would be arrested and risk the loss of their boats. For over two hours, from the vantage point of our home, we watched in mounting horror as this drama unfolded and we could see no attempt at rescue.

Laws criminalising refugee help, seeing it as an aspect of smuggling, are widespread in Europe and not confined to Greece. But there can be no doubt that here on Samos it has been a contributory factor in making locals fearful of helping refugees. The islanders live under an unrelenting drizzle of propaganda which demonises refugees. They are dirty, they are diseased and a threat to our health, they are violent, they are selfish, they are sexual predators, they are terrorists and not least they are mainly Muslim. The list is endless and changes depending on the latest 'outrage' and moral panic. It has many consequences, and generating fear among the people is one. It was evident in the small numbers of islanders who offer lifts to the refugees, which was not just the consequence of the law. It was evident in some of the ways in which much-needed clothes, food and water were distributed at the ports. Cars would arrive and simply leave a pile of clothes or fruit with no attempt to make direct contact with the refugees and help ensure its fair distribution. Similarly, very few refugees were ever invited to stay or visit the homes of islanders. The lack of a common language did not help but the fear element also played a role.

The nervousness of many local people wanting to help the refugees was in fact easily overcome. Those who crossed the line and sat and talked with the refugees soon found themselves in conversations like those they would have among themselves. Again and again islanders exclaimed that the refugees 'are just like us' after spending time with them at the ports. For so many this was a life-changing revelation, especially given the intensity with which refugees are portrayed as being not like us - as different and often dangerous. It was a revelation which energised activists, who flourished as friendships with the refugees deepened. It was just as well, for with hundreds arriving every day and with the rapid turnover as the refugees moved on to Athens, systems had to be recreated almost on a daily basis.

Help from 'below'

Scores of islanders came to help the refugees in whatever ways they could. It was all the more impressive given that Samos, as throughout Greece, was in its sixth year of devastating austerity which had seen wages and pensions slashed and jobs evaporate. Poverty on Samos is acute and widespread and if it were not for the gardens that so many islanders cultivate and the high level of homeownership the situation here would be utterly desperate. With many having given up their cars and pickups, and with a bus service that (poorly) connects the main towns, leaving the smaller villages isolated, going to the ports to offer direct support to the refugees was not an option for many. But even so many organised clothing collections in their villages, others collected fruit and tomatoes from their gardens and some became involved in cooking groups and clothes washing and drying. In other words, they 'dug where they stood' and contributed with great generosity and with love. It was exemplified by one older woman in one of the villages who after going through her few possessions came up with a pair of women's shoes. They were leather, in good condition but there were some scuff marks on the heels. So she had her friend re-dye the shoes before giving them. As far as she was concerned, giving scuffed shoes would be an insult. This concern with the dignity of the refugees was common and reflected in the quality of the clothing donated. It was very rare to find rubbish.

Those who came down to the ports represented only a fraction of the local people who helped the refugees. Those who were there distributing food, especially cooked meals, commonly had behind them a network of women who in their homes and villages were preparing meals and who had organised rotas which allowed their efforts to be sustained over the summer months. Others spent hours washing, drying and recycling clothes. Family relationships and friendships with those in local businesses were also activated with great effect. Some pharmacies either donated or massively discounted essential medicines and first aid materials. The same was true for some of the locally owned (not the big, national/multinational chains) supermarkets and fruit sellers and one businessman gave rent-free a large modern warehouse to be used as a refugee clothing and equipment store.

So much was learnt during those days. We learnt about the importance of working together with the refugees; of the myriad ways in which to communicate when there is no common language; of the power of humour; of the bonds which unite us despite our differences and of the importance of working in ways which strengthened refugee solidarity. During that summer it became clear that personal contacts with the refugees were as important as providing meals and shoes. Landing on the beaches of Samos in the early hours of the morning is a tumultuous experience for the refugees. There is the relief at surviving an often terrifying journey through the night. Low in the water, packed in small underpowered rubber dinghies, being steered by another refugee who might have had five minutes practice with the engine before leaving the Turkish coast, most of the refugees pray their way through the 4–8 hours it takes. Not surprisingly, they are overwhelmed when they arrive, with some just sitting sobbing while others who have got a signal on their phones are shouting with joy to friends and family as they tell them that they are alive and now in Europe. Not knowing what reception to expect, it meant so much when they were met by those who gave them a hug, which is such a powerful act of fellowship and solidarity and was just as important as the dry clothes and snacks provided. The arrivals often had no idea who we were. Many had endured months of being scared of strangers as they made their way to the Turkish coast. Some had been attacked and robbed. In this context an embrace, a hug and a smile can almost instantaneously vaporise their anxieties. They were at least for the moment with people who cared for them and who didn't see them as garbage.

Abusive authority

The contrast with the state authorities could not be greater. Newly arriving refugees were and still are met by police and other officers wearing masks and rubber gloves and in lieu of a common language revert to shouting at the refugees. 'Malaka' is one of the first Greek words many refugees learn. It is a vulgar term of abuse and is widely used by the police when talking to refugees. It resonates disrespect, of refugees 'counting for nothing'. Surgical gloves and masks are also powerful symbols. The police on Samos never tire of telling us and our friends that we should not take refugees in our cars because of the health risks. In this context, then, an embrace and simply being with and among the refugees is a powerful and necessary act of solidarity as well as a repudiation of the state's propaganda.

Abusive behaviour towards refugees is not unique to the police, who in any event should never have been given such a key role in the management of refugees coming to Samos in the first place. The Greek police has its own particular history, which includes a significant longstanding connection with fascism, reflected in such facts as that over 50% of the police in Athens voted for the openly fascistic Golden Dawn party in the last general election. Given a long and well-documented history of endemic racism within much of the Greek police, which includes deaths, severe injuries, torture and routine neglect of refugees and migrants, it is astonishing that the police were given such a crucial role in the management of refugees. But with no papers, refugees are still considered to be illegal arrivals to be managed by police and so placed within a penal rather than welfare framework.

That they are refugees, traumatised and frightened, leaving everything behind as they fled to safety, is not the starting point.

The arrival of the NGOs

The humanitarian NGOs began to arrive in numbers from late 2015, including Médecins Sans Frontières (MSF), Red Cross, Save the Children, in addition to a number of Greek-based NGOs. During the same period, the UN Refugee Agency greatly expanded its involvement, especially in the provision of tents and temporary structures which made up the so-called 'Hotspot' which was initially constructed in the port area of Samos Town. The arrival of the NGOs took the major burden of care off the shoulders of the locals, as they took over trying to meet the basic needs of the refugees. While the NGOs have benefited the refugees, their impact has also been problematic in a number of ways for both the refugees and the local activists.

For many of the big international NGOs such as MSF this was the first time they had ever operated in western Europe as it was widely believed that this part of the world was more than capable of dealing with such humanitarian challenges. That it was in fact incapable was not just a matter of politics but also a reflection of the extent to which neoliberalism had hollowed out the social capacity of many European governments. They no longer had the agencies or the personnel to respond and were already overcommitted to providing what shredded social services survived to their own vulnerable populations. This is spectacularly true for Greece, where austerity has almost done away with state public services. Into this vacuum stepped the NGOs acting in much the same way as privatised contracted out companies which have taken over and richly profited from the vanishing social state. They may not be motivated by generating profits, but it was evident on Samos that not only are the international NGOs big business but they have come to form one part of the 'system's' response to the 'refugee crisis' which was reflected in their ambiguous stance towards the refugees and the local activists and also in their relationships with the Greek authorities.

Obsessed by their concern to stay in control, the authorities in both Samos and Athens have placed all kinds of limits on the NGOs. Basically, every NGO action needs official permission, which in Samos means endless delays, countless meetings and unimaginable amounts of paperwork. Obey us or leave was basically the Greek state's message to the big NGOs. Despite their size and influence, the extent to which the NGOs submitted to the control of the Greek authorities was surprising. It was exemplified in the contracts issued to their staff, which required them to comply without comment with the demands of the authorities and on no account to speak or disclose anything of their work. In short, gagging contracts. We witnessed many examples where the NGOs failed to speak out so as not to upset the Greek authorities. Even though some did make an eventual stand over the EU/Turkey pact in March 2016 and declared that they could not countenance working in locked camps, this should not be allowed to blind us to their temerity and concern not 'to rock the boat'. To many on Samos, the NGOs showed a remarkable lack of political 'nous' and courage.

But it was their failure to stand full-square, shoulder to shoulder with refugees that represented one of the most serious flaws in the NGO interventions. Refugees are routinely excluded from any involvement in setting the priorities and then the planning and implementation of NGO operations. While the NGOs never hesitate to claim that they speak for the refugees, they seem incapable of engaging with or even listening to them. Since the EU/Turkey pact of March 2016, refugees on Samos no longer move on to Athens after 48–72 hours as was common throughout 2015. Instead they are stuck here for months. Many have been here for nine months, which is more than enough time for the NGOs to build relationships directly with refugees and to get them actively involved. This has not happened.

The arrival of the NGOs significantly changed the nature of the refugee experience, both for the refugees and the islanders. Help has been professionalised, with all that entails. Despite the presence of some truly inspirational workers, it was surprising how many NGO staff kept their distance from refugees. It is unusual on Samos to see an NGO worker sitting with refugees offering them a coffee or juice in a café or in the squares. Groups of 10–20 NGO workers can be seen every day in the summer months meeting up for a drink and a meal (on expenses in many cases). Never a refugee in sight. There was one notable occasion when the refugees forced open the gates to the camp in Samos town. It was a carnival atmosphere as the refugees flooded out of the open gates. Families with young children filled the streets as they made their way down to the sea front where they sat and enjoyed their freedom. In reality only a small victory but much enjoyed. However, what stood out was that while the refugees and their friends sat on the sea wall all the NGO workers who came down were standing apart on the pavement and looking over to where we sat. None of them came over. That so few of the NGOs get close to the refugees, staying deskbound in their offices, has led them to being nicknamed 'Never Go Out' by the refugees.

In addition, top-down social work has long been infected by infantilising those it seeks to help. Clients, in all shapes and forms, are frequently viewed as children (often insulting children in the process): immature, lacking in judgement and prone to unreasonable and irresponsible behaviour and so on. There is more than a hint of these perspectives thriving in Samos, where refugees are not valued and their voices are rarely heard. This in turn contributes to an almost total disdain, which sees refugees as having nothing to offer. For months the clothing store managed by 'volunteers' (mainly short-stay visitors from the USA and Europe who come to 'help' the refugees) refused to allow refugees to either help in or even visit the store. What made this worse was that refugees are beside themselves with frustration and want to do something. The store could have offered one such opportunity for meaningful activity. The reasons given for this refusal was that the refugees could not be trusted not to thieve and/or to take more than they needed – reasons that had added irony given that everything in the store was donated for the refugees. It was their stuff! And this was not an isolated example. Workers in one of the more respected NGOs even ran a 'book' betting on how long another, smaller clothing store would stay open because it was managed by one of their workers who believed in working with the refugees. It was a joint initiative in which she gave refugees control over its organisation, access and distribution. In fact the store flourished and was more effective precisely because the refugees were involved.

Disdain for the refugees also characterised the NGOs' relationships with the activists on the island whose core work they now took over. Of course this was an enormous relief but it also led to a significant withdrawal of islanders from working with refugees. In the main the NGOs referred to the local activists as volunteers and through their behaviour indicated that the time had come for the 'experts' to run the show. It was a process which not only discarded a valuable resource for the refugees but had profound consequences in widening the distance between the islanders and the refugees, which is currently being exploited by the authorities on Samos. Diminishing numbers of islanders are now involved with the refugees and, like them, they are not routinely included in determining the activities of the NGOs. That wide web of relationships that had emerged in 2015 which connected so many local people to the realities of the refugees has largely disappeared. This disconnection between the locals and the refugees is now being relentlessly exploited by the island authorities.

In the past six months, for example, the authorities have found it easier to claim that the island has to be rid of all refugees because they have made life almost intolerable for the locals. Although tourism on Samos was declining long before the numbers of refugee arrivals exploded in 2015, it is now the common belief here that refugees are exclusively to blame for its current dire state. But as a consequence of the arrival of the NGOs and their style of expertise they have marginalised an important countervailing voice. All kinds of resentments are now being actively promoted as islanders read about resources supposedly being devoted to refugees while they get nothing. At the same time nothing is heard of the refugees' resentment that these very same resources rarely get to them and simply support an ever growing number of people who do nothing for them.

A different way of working

Again and again the interventions most valued by the refugees were those in which they had involvement and shared responsibility. And none of these came from the official system, whether an NGO or state agency. There were two outstanding examples and both involved anarchist groups, one from Germany and the other from Switzerland, who set up kitchens on the island and provided the best food that Samos refugees have had in their history here. The key to their success was linked with what they did and how they did it. It is never a matter of just what you do but how you do it.

The two open kitchens were brilliant for the refugees and it was a sad time in early 2016 when the army took control of food provision for the camp. Understandably, the kitchens decided to leave and go to where they were most needed. These kitchens were much more than just about providing freshly cooked nutritious meals. From the outset they involved the refugees in shopping, storage, cooking, food preparation and menus. The volunteer workers stood side by side with the refugees in all these activities, working and talking, laughing and joking. Unlike so many of the NGO workers as well as many of the newly arriving 'volunteers' the core staff did not stand apart from the refugees.

The kitchens were happy places. A characteristic that can be rarely applied to the NGOs and state agencies here on Samos, or even within many if any contemporary organised social work settings. It was in the refugee camps of the West Bank in Palestine that I first understood the importance of jokes and laughter as one of the means of surviving the intolerable oppression of the Israeli occupation. Alongside deep hurts the Palestinians had great jokes. I still don't fully understand how this all hangs together but I do know that laughter draws people together in a myriad of ways and is a source of great strength.

Both kitchens created seating areas around an ever-ready supply of tea. Noticeboards were created for sharing information and the kitchens rapidly became the most important centres for the refugees to meet, relax and to do something. The importance of activity cannot be underestimated and it is no exaggeration to say that the enforced idleness of being detained on Samos for months, with no idea when they will have their asylum claims assessed, drives them crazy with frustration. And guess what? The refugees had talent. Refugees came forward who had worked in kitchens and restaurants, who knew how and what to cook to satisfy their compatriots; others had skills in IT and were experts at trawling the net for information, especially concerning the routes to follow once released from the island; others organised backgammon competitions, all of which made the kitchens places where you wanted to spend time.

The 'politics' of the open kitchens were critical to their success and saturated everything they did. They knew that the 'system' was inhumane and had no care for the well-being of the refugees. They were explicit in seeing borders and papers as cruel and unnecessary. They knew much about the ways in which our world creates refugees through wars and exploitation. They were angry at the hurts and injustices and the pain of the refugees. They felt this pain. They did not pity but were full of empathy and rage at the inhumanities before their eyes. They stood shoulder to shoulder with refugees as human beings.

And then came the volunteers

The media spotlight on the Greek frontier islands such as Samos in 2015 drew individuals who wanted 'to help' the refugees. They have come to be termed the volunteers. At any one time there can be up to 50 volunteers here. They are overwhelmingly middle class and tend to be either young people from Europe or the USA and Australia, with many having just completed a university course, or newly retired. They stay for anything from two or three days to a month, and a few even longer. They are a mixed group with different motivations for their interventions.

The volunteers do not come here as part of an organised intervention. They travel often on their own or as a couple. Few if any questions are asked of their competence. The very fact that they have volunteered seems to be enough to allow them to intervene. Some are excellent and stand full-square with the refugees. Others are not. Some, for example, seem to be trophy hunters, such as the young German couple who spent just under one hour with refugee children getting them to paint pictures of their experiences which were then gathered together to be taken back to Germany to show to their friends. Fortunately these volunteers were prevented by activists who asked whether they had sought the permission of the kids to keep their paintings. Of course they hadn't. For most, however, it was their endless photographs/selfies, posing with refugees as they handed out bottles of water or snacks, which are then posted on their Facebook pages that were most prized. Not only did these photographs elicit effusive responses as to their heroic actions but they also helped the volunteers raise funds for their stay.

Driven by their desire to do something, anything, when they arrive also led to the volunteers falling into the embrace of the authorities on the island. For the system, the volunteers were rapidly seized upon as being useful as a form of bottom-tier labour that could undertake some of the dirty work such as cleaning rubbish in and around the camp. As the numbers increased, the authorities made available a warehouse and entrusted the distribution of clothes, shoes, tents, sleeping bags and the like to the volunteers. (It was the local authority which insisted that the refugees should not be allowed in the store either as casual visitors or to help in its work. This injunction was not challenged by the volunteers.)

As with the NGOs, the arrival of the volunteers has been a mixed blessing. As they themselves are now realising, their contributions allow the funded agencies to evade some of their core responsibilities. This, coupled with the experience of only being allowed to undertake work sanctioned by the authorities, has pushed the volunteers into a fundamental review of their purpose which at the time of writing is yet to be resolved.

But as with the NGOs the volunteers have inadvertently contributed to the distancing of the islanders from the refugees. For a variety of reasons there are virtually no locals working with the volunteers and similarly little interaction between the islanders and the volunteers, who tend to stick together even when socialising. Furthermore, the island authorities have now created a system whereby all those who wish to work with refugees and are not employed by an appropriate agency are expected to register and be approved. Few local activists are prepared to seek permission to engage with refugees from the very authorities which are so patently part of the problem.

Some final reflections

There can be no conclusion as the inhumane treatment and management of refugees on Samos is still ongoing and the situation here continues to unfold according to the shifting policies of the EU and the other power brokers involved. As for the refugees, it remains a tortuous time in which their humanity is routinely denied. Nobody any longer denies that the conditions for the refugees on the Greek frontier islands are deplorable. Refugees are dying every week from these conditions. Detained for months, never knowing when they will be either deported to Turkey or allowed asylum is torture for them. Their lives in a sense have stopped.

There is still no evidence of any compassion in the ever-shifting policies towards refugees. As ever, so-called security concerns always trump refugee welfare. So this winter we have seen hundreds of refugees living in tents during freezing weather but at the same time no hesitation in deploying additional police. Samos is awash with police. The authorities on all the Greek frontier islands insist that their populations can take no more of the refugees and are trying to drive new wedges between the refugees and the islanders. On places such as neighbouring Chios we are seeing clear collusion with the fascist Golden Dawn, who have been organising attacks on the refugees and their camps. These crimes are taken as a sign of the islanders' frustration and anger at the presence of the refugees, who have apparently destroyed their crucial tourist economy. It is scapegoating of a classic form, channelling the desperation and misery of seven years of austerity on to the shoulders of refugees.

We are also witnessing a renewed focus on the so-called 'economic migrants' from Pakistan and north Africa who, without papers and authorisation, are a significant part of the refugee population on Samos. That poverty and absence of any possibility for a reasonable life in their home countries drives them to the dangerous and expensive clandestine routes to Samos counts for nothing. Who would risk such a journey if they could flourish at home? Instead, they are dismissed as selfish vermin with no right at all to seek sanctuary in Europe. At this time, international law still allows all refugees to make a claim for asylum. One wonders how much longer this right will remain. Even so, the EU and its constituent governments have made it clear that those who are not basically fleeing war will have their asylum claims dismissed and be subject to deportation.

At the same time over 200,000 young people have left Greece in the past five years in search of work and a better life. It is a cause of sadness but never a cause for their demonisation as selfish free-loaders. But it also illustrates in part the huge commonalities which are shared by the islanders and the refugees in terms of the causes and the consequences of their ongoing misery.

Today the ' European Refugee Crisis' has moved down the mainstream media's agenda as the number of new arrivals has dropped, especially via the 'Eastern Route' across the Aegean to places like Samos. There is still considerable movement, mostly clandestine, but there has also emerged, especially in the borderlands of Greece and the Balkans, places where refugees are detained, fenced and stopped. These peripheral places, unlike the squares and railway stations of Germany, Austria, Sweden and the rest of the more prosperous north, are easier to ignore and easier to manage. They are dark places and they need to be illuminated.

We have come to expect nothing of value and benefit to the refugees coming from the top whether it be an NGO or governmental welfare agency. They are part of the problem and certainly not the solution. On the other hand, we have seen the power and effectiveness of interventions which work with and alongside the refugees as people 'just like ourselves'. But if it is to be more compelling, we should recognise that we must also shed light on these darkest of places. It is a huge challenge. But it is necessary if the barbarism of the system is to be halted.

Conclusion: the road to an alternative future?

Michael Lavalette

In Reisch and Andrews' (2002) classic book on the history of social work in the US the authors look at the 'road not taken'. Their argument is that there has been a rich and varied past within social work, and that, at key turning points, the profession followed certain 'roads' or 'paths' which has led us to where we are today. By following these roads, however, alternative approaches and visions regarding what social work could or should be were closed down. Reisch and Andrews make clear that the development of the social work profession is not a simple linear process. Knowing our (contested) histories, recognising how things have been different in the past, enables us to consider the possibility of a different present and an alternative future. And there are always alternatives: different ways of conceptualising social problems, different priorities for social engagement, different values to shape our practice, different goals to social intervention. It is possible to do social work in diverse ways; it doesn't have to be like this.

Collectively, the authors in this book share a concern that we are fast approaching a key fork in the road, with the social work profession facing a question over which road to take: what kind of social work do we want to see, and what kind of a profession do we want to be part of? Is it one shaped by targets and markets, with workers processing people at the behest of an increasingly brutal and brutalising 'welfare' state? Or is it one that, in the face of the present crisis (of cuts, austerity and managerialism) asserts its independence, its values and its belief that 'another social work is possible'?

Collectively we are of the view that the years of austerity need to be brought to an end – urgently. Collectively we believe that the growth of inequality, poverty and, in contrast, the obscene 'conspicuous consumption' of the fabulously wealthy is damaging to the fabric of our society. Collectively we believe that years of cuts, marketisation, welfare transformation and restructuring are damaging people's lives. Collectively we believe that urgent action needs to be taken to stop the erosion of 'the welfare state' (though that doesn't mean we simply want to move back to some 'golden age' that, in reality, never existed). Collectively we want 'more and better' welfare, a welfare system that listens and responds to the needs of service users and workers and puts people before profit.

And within this context we want to argue that there is a place for social work. All the chapters have emphasised that, at its best, social work is a valuable profession. It requires workers who are committed to understanding people's complex lives in an unequal and divided society, and workers who are determined to support service users at times of difficulty, offering solidarity and empathy to people when they decide to bring about change to their lives. Yet the chapters have also emphasised that the social work task, in the present, is being narrowed down, increasingly being reduced to a narrow set of skills and work tasks.

Jones' chapter draws this debate out by offering a perspective on his work alongside refugees on the Greek island of Samos. Here Jones posits the great potential for a social work that is humane, that works in solidarity alongside refugees and that is developed organically out of communities and social movements committed to open borders and free movement. But Jones contrasts this with the role of the state and state agencies, with 'volunteers' and NGOs who too often work for their own interests, or work to control and criminalise vulnerable refugees fleeing oppression and poverty to try and build a better life.

Harris draws on his work over several years to look at the ways in which social work is being 'degraded', from the 'professional craft' of the street-level bureaucrat to an increasingly technicist work task. He plots the ways in which the social work labour process is impacting upon frontline workers, reducing the space for professional discretion over the work task and allocation of resources, to a task that is increasingly regulated and controlled by social work managers and by managerial authority embedded in policy and IT systems. The implication is that, if we want to defend social work as a value-driven profession, we need to work, alongside frontline workers and their unions, to defend working practices and the skills, knowledge and craft of the profession.

Beresford and Walmsley in their chapters look at the various ways that the social work profession has learned (and could learn more) from working alongside service users, carers, families and communities, in the promotion of social work and social policies that promote service users' voices, rights and independence. But such principles cannot be delivered via marketisation which reduces rights and choices to 'consumer-led' interventions into a care market. Instead we need a properly funded and resourced welfare system, attuned to meeting people's needs, and led and shaped by the demands of service using communities.

Singh's chapter is incredibly timely. In the late 1980s social work was accused of 'political correctness' because the Diploma in Social Work (the qualifying programme at the time) described Britain as an institutionally racist society and demanded that social workers implement 'anti-racist social work'. The assault on social work forced too many into silence. But now is not the time to be quiet. Levels of racism, Islamophobia and anti-Semitism are rising across Europe, America and much of the world. In Brazil, the US, Hungary, Austria and Poland populist and far-right politicians sit in government. The UK is not immune. The Brexit vote of 2016 was motivated by very many things, not just, or simply, racism, but there is no doubt that the levels of racism in Britain have risen in the aftermath. Yet it is not just the growth of the far right or increasing levels of racist attacks that we need to confront: increasingly social workers are being asked to implement policies that are, in themselves, inherently racist. Policies around Prevent or age assessments of asylum seekers are institutionally racist and, as a profession, social work needs to make clear that ours is an explicitly anti-racist profession.

Featherstone, Lymbery and Ferguson in their chapters similarly argue for models that focus on the 'social': addressing the public causes of so much individual pain and trauma. Further, all three emphasise that social work must, by necessity, be political. In a sense we occupy a position of privilege — service users let us into their lives; we see, at first-hand, the impact of inequality, poverty and discrimination on people's lives. This brings with it a responsibility, to identify social harm and to speak out, to 'speak truth to power' and to promote the interests of the many — and not simply the few who have so enriched themselves over the 'neoliberal' decades.

References

ADCS (2017) *A Country that Works for All Children*, www.adcs.org.uk,

Alejo Vázquez Pimentel, D., Macías Aymar, I. and Lawson, M. (2018) 'Reward Work Not Wealth': Oxfam Briefing Paper. Oxford: Oxfam International.

Allcock Tyler, D. (2016) 'In four years there will be no grants for charities – it will destroy communities', *The Guardian*, 11 February, www.theguardian.com/voluntary-sector-network/2016/feb/11/grants-local-charities-campaign-appeal-government-cuts

Althusser, L. (2001) *Lenin and Philosophy and Other Essays*, New York: Monthly Review Press.

Alzheimer's Society (2014) *Dementia UK: Second Edition*, London: Alzheimer's Society.

Antonakakis, N., and Collins, A. (2015) 'The impact of fiscal austerity on suicide mortality: evidence across the "Eurozone periphery"'. *Social Science & Medicine*, 145: 63–78.

Ash, A. (2013) 'A cognitive mask? Camouflaging dilemmas in street-level policy implementation to safeguard older people from abuse'. *British Journal of Social Work*, 43(1): 99–115.

Askheim, O.P., Beresford, P. and Heule, C. (2017) 'Mend the gap: strategies for user involvement in social work education'. *Social Work Education*, 36(2): 128–140.

Association of Directors of Adult Social Services/Department of Health/Skills for Care/British Association of Social Workers/Social Care Association (ADASS/DH/SFC/BASW/SCA) (2010) *The Future of Social Work in Adult Social Services*, London: ADASS/DH/SFC/BASW/SCA.

Asthana, A. (2017) 'Council funding freeze "means cuts to many essential services"', *The Guardian*, 21 February, www.guardian.co.uk/society/2017/feb/21/lack-council-funding-essential-services-slashed

Atkinson, D. (1993) *Past Times*, Aldershot: Ashgate.

Atkinson, E. (2005) 'You do as well as you can for them', in S. Rolph, D. Atkinson, M. Nind and J. Welshman (eds), *Witnesses to Change: Families, Learning Difficulties and History*, Kidderminster: BILD, pp 133–142.

Audit Commission (1992) *The Community Revolution: Personal Social Services and Community Care*, London: HMSO.

Bamford, T. (2015) *A Contemporary History of Social Work: Learning from the Past*, Bristol: Policy Press.

Barclay, P. (1982) *Social Workers: Their Role and Tasks*, London: Bedford Square Press.

Bayley, M. (1973) *Mental Handicap and Community Care: A Study of Mentally Handicapped People in Sheffield*, London: Routledge and Kegan Paul.

BBC (2006) 'UK settles WWII debts to allies', 29 December, news. bbc.co.uk/1/hi/uk/6215847.stm

BBC (2016) 'Income tax powers officially devolved to Holyrood', 30 November, www.bbc.co.uk/news/uk-scotland-scotland-politics-38150285

BBC (2018) 'Reality check: what's happening to defence spending?', 22 January, www.bbc.co.uk/news/uk-42774738

Bedfordshire Mental Deficiency Committee: report of Voluntary Visitor (1936) Mental Deficiency Papers, MDP 23, Bedfordshire and Luton Archive and Record Office.

Bedfordshire Mental Deficiency Committee correspondence (1937) Mental Deficiency Papers, MDP 23, Bedfordshire and Luton Archive and Record Office.

Bedfordshire Mental Deficiency Committee correspondence (1940) Mental Deficiency Letters MDL 41, Bedfordshire and Luton Archive and Record Office.

Bell, D. (2018) 'Free personal care: what the Scottish approach to social care would cost in England', *The Health Foundation*, 18 May, www. health.org.uk/newsletter/free-personal-care-what-scottish-approach-social-care-would-cost-england

Belzer, R. and Watyne, D. (2017) *Corporate Conspiracies: How Wall Street Took Over Washington*, New York: Skyhorse Publishing.

Bentall, R. (2004) 'Does "schizophrenia" exist? Reliability and validity', in J. Read, L. Mosher and R.P. Bentall (eds). *Models of Madness*, London: Routledge, pp 43–56.

Beresford, P. (2007) *The Changing Roles and Tasks of Social Work from Service-Users' Perspectives: A Literature-Informed Discussion Paper*, London: Shaping Our Lives.

Beresford, P. (2011) 'Radical social work and service users: a crucial connection', in M. Lavalette (ed), *Radical Social Work Today: Social Work at the Crossroads*, Bristol: Policy Press.

Beresford, P. (2013) *Beyond the Usual Suspects: Towards Inclusive User Involvement*, Research Report, London: Shaping Our Lives.

Beresford, P. (ed) (2014) *Personalisation*, Bristol: Policy Press.

Beresford, P. (2016) *All Our Welfare: Towards Participatory Social Policy*, Bristol: Policy Press.

Beresford, P. and Croft, S. (1986) *Whose Welfare? Private Care or Public Services*, Brighton: Lewis Cohen Urban Studies Centre at University of Brighton.

Beresford, P. and Wilson, A. (2000) '"Anti-oppressive practice": emancipation or appropriation?', *British Journal of Social Work*, 30: 553–573.

Beresford, P., Adshead, L. and Croft, S. (2007) *Palliative Care, Social Work and Service Users: Making Life Possible*, London: Jessica Kingsley.

Beresford, P., Croft, S. and Adshead, L. (2008) '"We don't see her as a social worker': a service user case study of the importance of the social worker's relationship and humanity"', *British Journal of Social Work*, 38(7): 1388–1407.

Beswick, J. and McNulty, A. (2015) 'Poor health, no wealth, no home: a case study of destitution', South Yorkshire: British Red Cross.

Bilson, A., and Martin, K. (2016) 'Referrals and child protection in England: one in five children referred to children's services and one in nineteen investigated before the age of five', *British Journal of Social Work*, 47, 3(1): 793–811.

Bilson, A., Featherstone, B. and Martin, K. (2017) 'How child protection's "investigative turn" impacts on poor and deprived communities', *Family Law*, 47: 316–319.

Bisman, C. (2004) 'Social work values: the moral core of the profession', *British Journal of Social Work*, 34(1): 105–123.

Blyth, M. (2013) *Austerity: The History of a Dangerous Idea*, Oxford: Oxford University Press.

Bolger, S., Corrigan, P., Docking, J. and Frost, N. (1981) *Towards Socialist Welfare Work: Working in the State*, London: Macmillan.

Borland, B. (2018) 'Investors are raking in MILLIONS in dividends from taxpayer-funded PFI projects', *Daily Express*, 21 January, www.express.co.uk/news/uk/907613/scotland-snp-labour-party-pfi-projects-taxpayer-Private-Finance-Initiative-contracts

Bourdieu, P. (2003) *Firing Back: Against the Tyranny of the Market 2* (Vol 2), London: Verso.

Brah, A. (2005) *Cartographies of Diaspora: Contesting Identities*, London: Routledge.

Braverman, H. (1998) *Labor and Monopoly Capital: The Degradation of Work in the Twentieth Century* (25th anniversary edn), New York: Monthly Review Press.

Brindle, D. (2017) 'Good social workers are invaluable, so let's give them proper support', *The Guardian*, 21 March, www.theguardian.com/society/2017/mar/21/social-workers-proper-support-morale-pride

Broadhurst, K. and Mason, C. (2014) 'Social work beyond the VDU: foregrounding co-presence in situated practice – why face-to-face practice matters', *British Journal of Social Work*, 44(3): 578–595.

Brown, G. and Harris, T. (1978/2011) *The Social Origins of Depression*, London: Routledge.

Buchan, L. (2017) 'Tax avoidance cost UK economy £13bn in five years, say Labour', *The Independent*, 5 September, www.independent. co.uk/news/uk/politics/tax-avoidance-cost-uk-economy-13-billion-labour-peter-dowd-a7929666.html

Burchardt, T. (2004) 'Capabilities and disability: the capabilities framework and the social model of disability', *Disability & Society* 19(7): 735–751.

Burchardt, T., Obolenskaya, P. and Vizard, P. (2016) 'The coalition's record on adult social care: policy, spending and outcomes 2010–2015', in R. Lupton, T. Burchardt, J. Hills, K. Stewart and P. Vizard (eds), *Social Policy in a Cold Climate: Policies and Their Consequences since the Crisis*, Bristol: Policy Press.

Burke, P. and Signo, K. (1996) *Support for Families*, Aldershot: Avebury.

Burns, T. (2014) *Our Necessary Shadow: The Nature and Meaning of Psychiatry*, London: Penguin.

Butler, P. (2015) 'Thousands have died after being found fit for work, DWP figures show', *The Guardian*, 27 August, www.theguardian. com/society/2015/aug/27/thousands-died-after-fit-for-work-assessment-dwp-figures

Butler, P. (2018) 'Welfare spending for UK's poorest shrinks by £37bn', *The Guardian*, 23 September, www.theguardian.com/politics/2018/ sep/23/welfare-spending-uk-poorest-austerity-frank-field

Butler, P. and Foster, D. (2017) 'Two Shelter board members quit after Grenfell Tower fire', *The Guardian*, 23 June 2017, www.theguardian. com/uk-news/2017/jun/23/two-shelter-board-members-derek-myers-tony-rice-quit-after-grenfell-tower-fire

Bywaters, P. (2017) 'What the new looked-after children statistics don't tell us', *Community Care*, 3 October.

Bywaters, P., Bunting, L., Davidson, G., Hanratty, J., Mason, W., McCartan, C. and Steils, N. (2016) *The Relationship between Poverty, Child Abuse and Neglect: An Evidence Review*, www.jrf.org.uk/report/ relationship-between-poverty-child-abuse-and-neglect-evidence-review

Bywaters, P., Brady, G., Bunting, L., Daniel, B., Featherstone, B., Jones, J., Morris, K., Scourfield, J., Sparks, T. and Webb, C. (2018) 'Inequalities in English child protection practice under austerity: a universal challenge', *Child and Family Social Work*, 23(1): 53–61.

Campaign against Climate Change (CCC) (2014) *One Million Climate Jobs: Tackling the Environmental and Economic Crises*, 3rd edn, London: CCC, www.campaigncc.org/sites/data/files/Docs/one_million_climate_jobs_2014.pdf

Campbell, B. (2014) 'After neoliberalism: the need for a gender revolution', in *Soundings 56*, www.eurozine.com/after-neoliberalism-the-need-for-a-gender-revolution/

Carey, M. (2016) 'Biomedical nemesis? Critical deliberations with regard to health and social care integration for social work with older people', *International Social Work*, 61(5): 651–664.

Carey, M. and Foster, V. (2011) 'Introducing "deviant" social work: contextualising the limits of radical social work whilst understanding (fragmented) resistance within the social work labour process', *British Journal of Social Work*, 41(3): 576–593.

Carrell, S. (2017) 'Call for inquiry into privately financed public projects in Scotland', *The Guardian*, 18 October, www.theguardian.com/business/2017/oct/18/expert-report-calls-for-inq

Carrell, S. (2018) 'Glasgow strike: union told it faces legal action over "illegal pickets"', *The Guardian*, 24 October, www.theguardian.com/uk-news/2018/oct/24/schools-remain-closed-glasgow-equal-pay-strike-continues

Castles, K. (2004) 'Nice average Americans: postwar parents' groups and the defense of the normal family', in S. Noll and J. Trent (eds) *Mental Retardation in America*, New York: New York University Press.

Child Poverty Action Group (CPAG) in Scotland (2018) 'Child poverty in Scotland', www.cpag.org.uk/scotland/child-poverty-facts-and-figures

Clark, C.L. and Asquith, S. (1975) *Social Work and Social Philosophy*, London: RKP.

Clarke, J. (1979) 'Critical sociology and radical social work: problems of theory and practice', in N. Parry, M. Rustin and C. Satyamurti (eds), *Social Work Welfare and the State*, London: Edward Arnold.

Clarke, J. (2004) *Changing Welfare, Changing States: New Directions in Social Policy*, London: Sage.

Clarke, J., Cochrane, A. and McLaughlin, E. (eds) (1994) *Managing Social Policy*, London: Sage.

Cohen, S. (1975) 'It's all right for you to talk', in R. Bailey and M. Brake (eds) *Radical Social Work*, London: Edward Arnold.

Coleman, N. and Harris, J. (2008) 'Calling social work', *British Journal of Social Work*, 38(3): 580–599.

Comley, T. (1989) 'State social work: a socialist-feminist contribution', in C. Hallett (ed), *Women and Social Services Departments*, Hemel Hempstead: Harvester Wheatsheaf.

Contaz, J. (2012) 'The limits of contemporary anti-oppression theory and practice', *Libcom.org*, 9 May, https://libcom.org/library/limits-contemporary-anti-oppression-theory-practice

Cooper, C. (2015) 'Iain Duncan Smith's tougher fit-to-work tests "coincide with 590 additional suicides"', *The Independent*, 16 November.

Cooper, V. and Whyte, D. (eds) (2017) *The Violence of Austerity*, London: Pluto.

Corby, B. (2005) *Child Abuse: Towards a Knowledge Base* (3rd edn), Milton Keynes: Open University Press.

Corrigan, P. and Leonard, P. (1978) *Social Work Practice under Capitalism: A Marxist Approach*, London: Macmillan.

Cowburn, A. (2015) 'IFS report dispels Osborne myth that we're "all in it together"', *New Statesman*, 23 January, www.newstatesman.com/politics/2015/01/ifs-report-dispels-osborne-s-myth-we-re-all-it-together

Cowden, S. and Singh, G. (2007) 'The "user": friend, foe or fetish? A critical exploration of user involvement in health and social care', *Critical Social Policy*, 27(1): 5–23.

Cowden, S. and Singh, G. (2014) 'A critical analysis of service user struggles', in C. Cocker and T. Letchfield (eds), *Rethinking Anti-Discriminatory and Anti-Oppressive Theories for Social Work Practice*, Basingstoke: Palgrave.

Cree, V. (2018) 'A history of social work in Scotland', in M. Smith and V. Cree (eds), *Social Work in a Changing Scotland*, London: Routledge.

Cribb, J. and Johnson, P. (2018) '10 years on – have we recovered from the financial crisis?', 12 September, www.ifs.org.uk/publications/13302

Croft, S. (2019) Personal communication to the author, 3 May 2019.

Cudd, A.E. (2006) *Analyzing Oppression*, Oxford: Oxford University Press.

Cunningham, I. (2008) 'A race to the bottom? Exploring variations in employment conditions in the voluntary sector', *Public Administration*, 86(4): 1033–1053.

D'Arcy, C. (2018) *Low Pay Britain 2018*, London: Resolution Foundation, www.resolutionfoundation.org/app/uploads/2018/05/Low-Pay-Britain-2018.pdf

Dalrymple, J. and Burke, B. (2006) *Anti-Oppressive Practice: Social Care and the Law*, Maidenhead: McGraw-Hill Education.

Daly, M. (2016) 'Liverpool City Council tender adults with a learning disability to the cheapest bidder' (blog), 30 November, http://michelledaly.blogspot.co.uk/

Dartington, T. (2012) 'The therapeutic fantasy, self-love and quick wins', in S. Thompson, and P. Hoggett (eds), *Politics and the Emotions, the Affective Turn in Contemporary Political Studies*, London: Continuum.

Davidson, S. and Rossall, P. (2104) *Evidence Review: Loneliness in Later Life*, London: Age UK.

Day, L. (1992) 'Women and oppression: race, class and gender', in M. Langan and L. Day (eds), *Women, Oppression and Social Work*, London: Routledge.

Department for Education (DfE) (2016) *Putting Children First: Delivering our Vision for Excellent Children's Social Care*, www.gov.uk/government/publications/putting-children-first-our-vision-for-childrens-social-care

Department of Health (2011) *No Health Without Mental Health*, www.gov.uk/government/publications/the-mental-health-strategy-for-england

Derber, C. (1982) 'Managing professionals: ideological proletarianization and mental labor', in C. Derber (ed), *Professionals as Workers: Mental Labor in Advanced Capitalism*, Boston: G.K. Hall.

Derber, C. (1983) 'Managing professionals: ideological proletarianization and post-industrial labor', *Theory and Society*, 12(3): 309–341.

Diane, P.B. (2003) 'Darwin, Social Darwinism and Eugenics', in *The Cambridge Companion to Darwin*, Cambridge: Cambridge University Press.

Dickens, P. (2000) *Social Darwinism: Linking Evolutionary Thought to Social Theory*, Milton Keynes: Open University Press.

Dingwall, R., Eekelaar, J. and Murray, T. (1983) *The Protection of Children: State Intervention and Family Life*, Oxford: Blackwell.

Dominelli, L. (2002) *Anti-Oppressive Social Work Theory and Practice*, Basingstoke: Palgrave Macmillan.

Dorling, D. (2010) *Injustice: Why Social Inequality Persists*, Bristol: Policy Press.

Dorling, D. (2018) *Peak Inequality: Britain's Ticking Time Bomb*, Bristol: Policy Press.

Dorling, D., Gordon., Hillyard, P., Pantazis, C., Pemberton, S. and Tombs, S. (2008) *Criminal Obsessions: Why Harm Matters More Than Crime*, London: Centre for Crime and Justice Studies.

Du Gay, P. (2000) 'Entrepreneurial management and public management: the anti-bureaucrats', in J. Clarke, S. Gewirtz and E. McLaughlin (eds), *New Managerialism, New Welfare?*, London: Sage.

Duffy, S. (2013) *A Fair Society? How the Cuts Target Disabled People*, Sheffield: Centre for Welfare Reform.

Ellis, M. (2017) 'Public sector workers doing £11 billion in unpaid overtime every year', *Daily Mirror*, 24 July.

Equality Trust (2018) 'UK rich increase their wealth by £274 billion over five years', 13 May, www.equalitytrust.org.uk/wealth-tracker-18

Evans, T. and Harris, J. (2004) 'Street-level bureaucracy, social work and the (exaggerated) death of discretion', *British Journal of Social Work*, 34(6): 871–895.

Fabricant, M. and Burghardt, S. (1992) *The Welfare State Crisis and the Transformation of Social Service Work*, New York: M.E. Sharpe.

Fahmy, E., Williamson, C. and Pantazis, C. (2015) *Evidence and Policy Review: Domestic Violence and Poverty. A Research Report for the Joseph Rowntree Foundation*, www.jrf.org.uk

Featherstone, B., White, S. and Morris, K. (2014) *Re-imagining Child Protection: Towards Humane Social Work with Families*, Bristol: Policy Press.

Featherstone, B., Gupta, A., Morris, K. and Warner, J, (2016) '"Let's stop feeding the risk monster": towards a social model of child protection', *Families, Relationships and Societies*, 7(1): 7–22.

Featherstone, B., Gupta, A, Morris, K. and White, S. (2018) *Protecting Children: A Social Model*, Bristol: Policy Press.

Ferguson, I. (1999) *The Potential and Limits of Mental Health Service User Involvement*, unpublished PhD thesis, University of Glasgow.

Ferguson, I. (2008) *Reclaiming Social Work: Challenging Neo-Liberalism and Promoting Social Justice*, London: Sage.

Ferguson, I. (2013) 'Social workers as agents of change', in M. Gray and S.A. Webb (eds), *The New Politics of Social Work*, Basingstoke: Palgrave Macmillan.

Ferguson, I. and Lavalette, M. (2013) 'Crisis, austerity and the future(s) of social work in the UK', *Critical and Radical Social Work*, 1(1): 95–110.

Ferguson, I., Lavalette, M. and Whitmore, E. (2005a) *Globalisation, Global Justice and Social Work*, London: Routledge.

Ferguson, I., Petrie, M. and Stalker, K. (2005b) *Developing Accessible Services for Homeless People with Severe Mental Distress and Behavioural Difficulties*, Stirling: University of Stirling.

Fine, M. and Teram, E. (2013) 'Overt and covert ways of responding to moral injustices in social work practice: heroes and mild-mannered social work bipeds', *British Journal of Social Work*, 43(7): 1312–1329.

Finkelstein, V. (2001) 'A personal journey into disability politics', *The Disability Studies Archive UK*, Leeds: Centre for Disability Studies, University of Leeds, www.independentliving.org/docs3/finkelstein01a.pdf

Fitzpatrick, S., Bramley, G., Sosenko, F., Blenkinsopp, J., Wood, J., Johnsen, S., Littlewood, M. and Watts, B. (2018) *Destitution in the UK 2018*, York: Joseph Rowntree Foundation.

FitzRoy (2015) *Who Will Care After I'm Gone? An Insight into Pressures Facing Parents of People with Learning Disabilities*, www.fitzroy.org/wp-content/uploads/Who-will-care-after-im-gone.pdf

Fook, J. (2004) 'Critical reflection and organisational learning and change: a case study', in N. Gould and M. Baldwin, (eds) *Social Work, Critical Reflection and the Learning Organisation*, Aldershot: Ashgate.

Foundation for People with Learning Disabilities (2012) *Learning Disability Statistics: Support*, www.learningdisabilities.org.uk/help-information/Learning-Disability-Statistics-/187696/

Fraser, M.W. (2004) *Risk and Resilience in Childhood: An Ecological Perspective*, 2nd edn, Washington, DC: NASW Press.

Fraser, M.W., Richman, J.M. and Galinsky, M.J. (1999) 'Risk, protection, and resilience: Toward a conceptual framework for social work practice', *Social Work Research*, 23(3): 131–143.

French, C. (1971) *A History of the Mental Health Services in Bedfordshire*, Bedford: Bedfordshire County Council.

Fromm, E. (1955/2001) *The Sane Society*, London: Routledge.

Gallagher, B. (2017) 'Fewer staff, dwindling services: how austerity has hit child protection', *The Guardian*, 17 July, www.theguardian.com/social-care-network/2017/jul/17/impact-austerity-child-protection

Garthwaite, K. (2016) *Hunger Pains: Life Inside Foodbank Britain*, Bristol: Policy Press.

Garrett, P.M. (2016) 'Questioning tales of "ordinary magic": "resilience" and neo-liberal reasoning', *British Journal of Social Work*, 46(7): 1909–1925.

Giddens, A. (1994) *Beyond Left and Right: The Future of Radical Politics*, Redwood City: Stanford University Press.

Gilburt, H. (2015) *Mental Health Under Pressure*, London: King's Fund.

Gillies, V., Edwards, R. and Horsley, N. (2017) *Challenging the Politics of Early Intervention: Who's Saving Children and Why?*, Bristol: Policy Press.

Gilligan, R. (2008) 'Promoting resilience in young people in long-term care: the relevance of roles and relationships in the domains of recreation and work', *Journal of Social Work Practice*, 22: 37–50.

Gillingham, P. (2016) 'Technology configuring the user: implications for the redesign of electronic information systems in social work', *British Journal of Social Work*, 46(2): 323–338.

Gillingham, P. and Graham, T. (2016) 'Designing electronic information systems for the future: social workers and the challenge of New Public Management', *Critical Social Policy*, 36(2): 187–204.

Glasby, J. (2017) 'The holy grail of health and social care integration', *British Medical Journal*, 356. DOI: https://doi.org/10.1136/bmj.j801

Goering, S. (2014) 'Eugenics', *Stanford Encyclopedia of Philosophy*, http://plato.stanford.edu/entries/eugenics/

Gosling, P. (2011) 'The rise of the public services industry', updated edition, London: Unison, https://www.cheshireeastunison.org.uk/files/resources/19.pdf.

Gove, M. (2013) 'Getting it right for children in need', speech to the NSPCC, www.gov.uk/government/speeches/getting-it-right-for-children-in-need-speech-to-the-nspcc

Grunewald, K. (ed) (1978) *The Mentally Handicapped: Towards Normal Living*, London: Hutchinson and Co.

Guardian, The (2012) Editorial, 'Rich and poor: deserving and undeserving', 27 January, www.theguardian.com/commentisfree/2012/jan/27/rich-poor-deserving-undeserving

Gupta, A. and ATD Fourth World (2017) 'Giving poverty a voice', blog published 1 February, http://givingpovertyavoice.weebly.com/blog/the-impact-of-austerity-on-childrens-social-care-and-practice

Gupta, A., Featherstone, B. and White, S. (2014) 'Reclaiming humanity: from capacities to capabilities in understanding parenting in adversity', *British Journal of Social Work*, 46(3): 339–354

Gunaratnam, Y. (2007) *Improving the Quality of Palliative Care: A Race Equality Foundation Briefing Paper*, London: Race Equality Foundation.

Hall, S. (2011) 'March of the neoliberals', *The Guardian*, 12 September, www.theguardian.com/politics/2011/sep/12/march-of-the-neoliberals

Hardy, D. (2005) 'Our life with Margaret', in S. Rolph, D. Atkinson, M. Nind and J. Welshman (eds), *Witnesses to Change: Families, Learning Difficulties and History*, Kidderminster: BILD, pp 41–46.

Harman, C. (2009) *Zombie Capitalism: Global Crisis and the Relevance of Marx*, London: Bookmarks.

Harris, J. (1997) *Managing State Social Work*, Aldershot: Ashgate.

Harris, J. (1998) 'Scientific management, bureau-professionalism, new managerialism: the labour process of state social work', *British Journal of Social Work*, 28(6): 839–862.

Harris, J. (2003) *The Social Work Business*, London: Routledge.

Harris, J. (2014) '(Against) neoliberal social work', *Critical and Radical Social Work*, 2(1): 7–22.

Harris, J. and White, V. (eds) (2009) *Modernising Social Work: Critical Considerations*, Bristol: Policy Press.

Harris, R. (2005) 'I don't think I'll give up till I die', in S. Rolph, D. Atkinson, M. Nind and J. Welshman (eds), *Witnesses to Change: Families, Learning Difficulties and History*, Kidderminster: BILD, pp 47–54.

Harrop, A. and Reed, H. (2015) *Inequality 2030: Fabian Policy Report*, London: Fabian Society.

Harvey, D. (2005) *The New Imperialism*, Oxford: Oxford University Press.

Hastings, A., Bailey, N., Bramley, G., Gannon, M. and Watkins, D. (2015) *The Cost of the Cuts: The Impact on Local Government and Poorer Communities*, York: Joseph Rowntree Foundation.

Hayek, F.A. (1944/2014) *The Road to Serfdom: Text and Documents. The Definitive Edition* (Vol 2), London: Routledge.

HealthWatch Oxfordshire (2014) *A Local Experience of National Concern*, Oxford: HealthWatch Oxfordshire.

Hearn, J. (1982) 'Radical social work: contradictions, limitations and political possibilities', *Critical Social Policy*, 2(1): 19–38.

Heron, G. (2004) 'Evidencing anti-racism in student assignments: where has all the racism gone?', *Qualitative Social Work*, 3(3): 277–295.

Heslop, P., Blair, P., Fleming, P., Houghton, M., Marriot, A. and Russ, L. (2013) *Confidential Inquiry into Premature Deaths of People with Learning Disabilities (CIPOLD)*, Bristol: Norah Fry Research Centre.

Hill, L. and Hart, A. (2017) 'Gaining knowledge about resilient therapy: how can it support kinship carers?', *British Journal of Social Work*, 47(5): 1–20.

Hirst, A. and Humphreys, M. (2015) 'Configurable bureaucracy and the making of modular man', *Organization Studies*, 36(11): 1531–1553.

Hofmann, S. (2014) 'Tracing contradictions of neoliberal governmentality in Tijuana's sex industry', *Anthropology Matters*, 15(1): 62–89.

Hoggett, P. (1991) 'A new management in the public sector?', *Policy & Politics*, 19(4): 243–256.

Holloway, J. (2010) *Crack Capitalism*, London: Pluto Press.

Hood, R., Goldacre, A., Grant, R. and Jones, R. (2016) 'Exploring demand and provision in English child protection services', *British Journal of Social Work*, 46, 4(1): 923–994.

Howe, D. (1986) *Social Workers and Their Practices in Welfare Bureaucracies*, Aldershot: Gower.

Howe, D. (1996) 'Surface and depth in social work practice', in N. Parton (ed), *Social Theory, Social Change and Social Work*, London: Routledge.

Hudson, B. (2012) 'What can England learn from Scotland on integrating health and social care?', *The Guardian*, 17 September, www.theguardian.com/healthcare-network/2012/sep/17/england-scotland-policy-nhs-integration-markets

Hudson, B. (2018) 'Adult social care: is privatisation irreversible?', *British Politics and Policy*, http://blogs.lse.ac.uk/politicsandpolicy/adult-social-care-is-privatisation-irreversible/

Hughes, J. (2017) 'Why the "Dementia Tax" debate can't be over', *The Huffington Post*, 16 June, www.huffingtonpost.co.uk/jeremy-hughes/dementia-tax_b_17124134.html

Hughes, M. and Heycox, K. (2006) 'Knowledge and interest in ageing: a study of final-year social work students', *Australasian Journal on Ageing*, 25(2): 94–96.

Husband, C. (1982) *'Race' in Britain: Continuity and Change*, London: Hutchinson.

Ife, J. (1997) *Rethinking Social Work*, Melbourne: Addison Wesley Longman.

Innes, D. and Tetlow, G. (2015) 'Delivering fiscal squeeze by cutting local government spending', *Fiscal Studies*, 36(3): 303–325.

Institute for Fiscal Studies (IFS) (2015) 'Recent cuts to public spending', www.ifs.org.uk/tools_and_resources/fiscal_facts/public_spending_survey/cuts_to_public_spending

Jay, P. (1979) *Report of the Committee of Enquiry into Mental Handicap Nursing* (Cmnd 7468), London: HMSO.

Jeyasingham, D. (2016) 'Open spaces supple bodies? Considering the impact of agile working on social work office practices', *Child and Family Social Work*, 21(2): 209–217.

Johnson, K. (2006) 'The mirror cracked: care in the community in Victoria, Australia', in J. Welshman and J. Walmsley (eds) *Community Care in Perspective: Care, Control and Citizenship*, London: Palgrave Macmillan, pp 146–158.

Johnson, T. (1972) *Professions and Power*, Basingstoke: Macmillan Education.

Jones, C. (1983) *State Social Work and the Working Class*, London: Macmillan.

Jones, C. (1999) 'Social work: regulation and managerialism', in M. Hexworthy and S. Halford (eds), *Professionals and the New Managerialism in the Public Sector*, Milton Keynes: Open University Press.

Jones, C. (2001) 'Voices from the front-line: state social workers and New Labour', *British Journal of Social Work*, 31(4): 547–562.

Jones, C. and Novak, T. (1993) 'Social work today', *British Journal of Social Work*, 23(3): 195–212.

Jones, K. (1975) *Opening the Door: A Study of New Policies for the Mentally Handicapped*, London: RKP.

Jones, O. (2018a) 'Fat Cat Friday should shatter the myth that Britain's bosses deserve their pay', *The Guardian*, 4 January, www.theguardian.com/commentisfree/2019/jan/04/fat-cat-friday-britain-bosses-pay-executives-worker

Jones, R. (2015) 'Plans to privatise child protection are moving at pace', *The Guardian*, 12 January, www.theguardian.com/social-care-network/2015/jan/12/child-protection-privatisation-ray-jones

Jones, R. (2018b) *In Whose Interest? The Privatisation of Child Protection and Social Work*, Bristol: Policy Press.

Joseph Rowntree Foundation (JRF) (2017) *UK Poverty 2017: A Comprehensive Analysis of Poverty Trends and Figures*, York: Joseph Rowntree Foundation.

Joyce, P., Hayes, M. and Corrigan, P. (1988) *Striking Out: Trade Unionism in Social Work*, London: Macmillan.

Jutte, S., Bentley, H., Tallis, D., Mayes, J., Jetha, N., O'Hagan, O., Brookes, H. and McConnell, N. (2015) *How Safe are Our Children? The Most Comprehensive Overview of Child Protection in the UK*, London: NSPCC.

Katz, M.B. (1996) *In the Shadow of the Poorhouse: A Social History of Welfare in America*, New York: Basic Books.

Katz, M.B. (2013) 'The undeserving poor: America's enduring confrontation with poverty', *Social Work & Society*, 11(1), www.socwork.net/sws/article/view/359/709

Kevles, D. (1985) *In the Name of Eugenics: Genetics and the Uses of Human Heredity*, Berkeley: University of California Press.

Kimber, C. (2011) 'The welfare stakes', *Socialist Review*, 357: n.p.

Kimbrough-Melton, R.J. and Melton, G.B. (2015) '"Someone will notice, and someone will care": how to build strong communities for children', *Child Abuse and Neglect*, 41: 67–78.

Klein, N. (2008) *The Shock Doctrine: The Rise of Disaster Capitalism*, Harmondsworth: Penguin.

Kollewe, J. (2018) 'IFS: UK wages have not recovered to pre-crisis levels', *The Guardian*, 13 September, www.theguardian.com/business/2018/sep/12/uk-wages-have-not-yet-recovered-to-pre-crisis-levels-says-ifs

Konzelmann, S.J. (2014) 'The political economics of austerity', *Cambridge Journal of Economics*, 38(4): 701–741.

Langan, M. (1992) 'Introduction: women and social work in the 1990s', in M. Langan and L. Day (eds), *Women, Oppression and Social Work*, London: Routledge.

Langan, M. and Lee, P. (eds) (1989) *Radical Social Work Today*, London: Unwin Hyman.

Larson, M.S. (1977) *The Rise of Professionalism: A Sociological Analysis*, Berkeley: University of California Press.

Lavalette, M. (ed) (2011), *Radical Social Work Today: Social Work at the Crossroads*, Bristol: Policy Press.

Ledger, S. (2012) *Staying Local: Support for People with Learning Difficulties in Inner London, 1971–2007*, unpublished PhD thesis, Milton Keynes: Open University.

Leonard, P. (2004) 'The uses of theory and the problems of pessimism', in L. Davies and P. Leonard (eds), *Social Work in a Corporate Era: Practices of Power and Resistance*, Aldershot: Ashgate.

Lewis, J. (2001) 'Older people and the health-social care boundary in the UK: half a century of hidden policy conflict', *Social Policy and Administration*, 35(4): 343–459.

Lewis, J. and Glennerster, H. (1996) *Implementing the New Community Care*, Milton Keynes: Open University Press.

Local Government Association (LGA) (2014) *LGA Adult Social Care Efficiency Programme: The Final Report*, London: Local Government Association.

London Edinburgh Weekend Return Group (1980) *In and Against the State* (2nd edn), London: Pluto Press.

Lorde, A. (1984) *Sister Outsider: Essays and Speeches*, Trumansburg, NY: Crossing Press.

Lymbery, M. (2004) 'Managerialism and care management practice with older people', in M. Lymbery and S. Butler (eds), *Social Work Ideals and Practice Realities*, Basingstoke: Palgrave.

Lymbery, M. (2005) *Social Work with Older People: Context, Policy and Practice*, London: Sage.

Lymbery, M. (2006) 'United we stand? Partnership working in health and social care and the role of social work in services for older people', *British Journal of Social Work*, 36(7): 1119–1134.

Lymbery, M. (2008) *Social Work with Older People: Context, Policy and Professional Status*, Submitted towards the Award of PhD by Published Work, University of Nottingham.

Lymbery, M. (2010) 'A new vision for adult social care? Continuities and change in the care of older people', *Critical Social Policy*, 30(1): 5–26.

Lymbery, M. (2013) 'Reconciling radicalism, relationship and role: priorities for social work with adults in England', *Critical and Radical Social Work*, 1(2): 201–215.

Lymbery, M. (2014a) 'Austerity, personalisation and older people: the prospects for creative social work practice in England', *European Journal of Social Work*, 17(3): 367–382.

Lymbery, M. (2014b) 'Social work and personalisation: fracturing the bureau-professional compact?' *British Journal of Social Work*, 44(4): 795–811.

Lymbery, M. (2014c) 'Understanding personalisation: implications for social work', *Journal of Social Work*, 14(3): 295–312.

Lymbery, M. and Butler, S. (eds) (2004) *Social Work Ideals and Practice Realities*, Basingstoke: Palgrave.

Lymbery, M. and Postle, K. (2015) *The Social Work Role in Transforming Adult Social Care: Perpetuating a Distorted Vision?*, Bristol: Policy Press.

MacAskill, E. (2016) 'Trident renewal: would £205bn be a price worth paying?', *The Guardian*, 17 July, www.theguardian.com/uk-news/2016/jul/17/trident-renewal-205bn-arguments-for-against

Macias, J.J. (2014) 'Why private companies are taking on social workers', *The Guardian*, 6 October, www.theguardian.com/social-care-network/2014/oct/06/private-companies-social-workers

MacKenzie, D. (2017) 'Analysis links 590 suicides to push to get disabled working', *New Scientist*, 17 November, www.newscientist.com/article/dn28499-analysis-links-590-suicides-to-push-to-get-disabled-working/

MacLachlan, M., Dennis, P., Lang, H., Charnock, S. and Osman, J. (1989) 'Do the professionals understand? Mothers' views of families' service needs', in A. Brechin and J. Walmsley (eds), *Making Connections*, London: Hodder and Stoughton, pp 24–28.

Marmot, M., Allen, J., Goldblatt, P., Boyce, T., McNeish, D., Grady, M. and Gedded, I. (2010) *Fairer Lives, Healthy Society: Strategic Review of Health Inequalities in England Post-2010*, London: Marmot Review.

Marshall, T.H. (1963) 'Citizenship and social class', in *Sociology at the Crossroads*, London: Heinemann.

Marx, K. (1974) *Capital: Volume One*, London: Dent Dutton.

Marx, K. and Engels, F. (1848) *The Communist Manifesto*, www.marxists.org/archive/marx/works/1848/communist-manifesto/index.htm

Matthews, F.B. (c. 1948) *Mental Health Services*, London: Shaw and Sons.

McCall, A. (2018) '30 years on: how the Rich List has undergone a social revolution', *Sunday Times*, 13 May, www.thetimes.co.uk/article/sunday-times-rich-list-2018-30-years-undergone-social-revolution-b0dl7gl06

McCreadie, E.A. (2017) *Doxa Disability and Discrimination*, Doctoral dissertation, Brighton: University of Sussex, http://sro.sussex.ac.uk/id/eprint/66873/1/McCreadie%2C%20Elizabeth%20Ann.pdf

McCusker, P. and Jackson, J. (2016) 'Social work and mental distress: articulating the connection', *British Journal of Social Work*, 46(6): 1654–1670.

McDonald, C., Harris, J. and Wintersteen, R. (2003) 'Contingent on context? Social work and the state in Australia, Britain, and the USA', *British Journal of Social Work*, 33(2): 191–208.

McNicoll, A. (2015) 'Mental health trust funding down 8% from 2010 despite coalition's drive for parity of esteem', *Community Care*, 20 March, www.communitycare.co.uk/2015/03/20/mental-health-trust-funding-8-since-2010-despite-coalitions-drive-parity-esteem/

McNicoll, A. (2016) 'Landmark deal for private firm to run social work service approved', *Community Care*, 11 November, www.communitycare.co.uk/2016/11/11/landmark-deal-private-firm-run-social-work-service-approved/

McNicoll, A. (2017) 'Children in poorest areas more likely to enter care', *Community Care*, 28 February, www.communitycare.co.uk/2017/02/28/children-poorest-areas-likely-enter-care-finds-study/

McPhail, M. (2008) *Service User and Carer Involvement: Beyond Good Intentions*. Policy and Practice in Health and Social Care, Edinburgh: Dunedin Academic Press.

Means, R. (2007) 'The re-medicalisation of later life', in M. Bernard and T. Scharf (eds), *Critical Perspectives on Ageing Societies*, Bristol: Policy Press.

Meloni, M. (2016) 'If we're not careful, epigenetics may bring back eugenic thinking', *The Conversation*, 15 March, http://theconversation.com/if-were-not-careful-epigenetics-may-bring-back-eugenic-thinking-56169

Mills, C.W. (1959), *The Sociological Imagination*, Oxford: Oxford University Press.

Milne, A., Sullivan, M.P., Tanner, D., Richards, S., Ray, M., Lloyd, L., Beech, C. and Phillips, J. with the College of Social Work (2014) *Social Work with Older People: A Vision for the Future*, London: The College of Social Work.

Mitchell, B.R. (2011) *British Historical Statistics* (revised edn), Cambridge: Cambridge University Press.

Mitchell, D. and Welshman, J. (2006) 'In the shadow of the Poor Law: workforce issues', in J. Welshman and J. Walmsley (eds), *Care, Control and Citizenship: Community Care in Perspective*, London: Palgrave, pp 187–200.

Monbiot, G. (2016) 'Neoliberalism is creating loneliness. That's what's wrenching society apart', *The Guardian*, 12 October, www.theguardian.com/commentisfree/2016/oct/12/neoliberalism-creating-loneliness-wrenching-society-apart

Montagu, A. (2001) *Man's Most Dangerous Myth: The Fallacy of Race*, Walnut Creek, CA: AltaMira Press.

Mouffe, V. (2000) 'For an agonistic model of democracy', in N. O'Sullivan (ed), *Political Theory in Transition*, London: Routledge.

Murphy, G. (2010) *Shadowing the White Man's Burden: US Imperialism and the Problem of the Color Line*, New York: NYU Press.

National Audit Office (NAO) (2018) 'Taxpayer support for UK banks', www.nao.org.uk/highlights/taxpayer-support-for-uk-banks-faqs/#

Narey, M. (2014) *Making the Education of Social Workers Consistently Effective: Report of Sir Martin Narey's Independent Review of the Education of Children's Social Workers*, London, Department for Education, https://assets.publishing.service.gov.uk/government/uploads/system/uploads/attachment_data/file/287756/Making_the_education_of_social_workers_consistently_effective.pdf

Neocleous, M. (2013) 'Resisting resilience', *Radical Philosophy*, 178, www.radicalphilosophy.com/commentary/resisting-resilience

New Economics Foundation (2015) *Fairness Commissions*, www.nef.org.uk

NHS Digital (2016) *Adult Psychiatric Morbidity Survey: Mental Health and Wellbeing, England, 2014*, 29 September, www.gov.uk/government/statistics/adult-psychiatric-morbidity-survey-mental-health-and-wellbeing-england-2014

Nickson, B. (2005) 'Never take no for an answer', in S. Rolph, D. Atkinson, M. Nind and J. Welshman (eds), *Witnesses to Change: Families, Learning Difficulties and History*, Kidderminster: BILD, pp 77–86.

Nixon, J. and Humphreys, C. (2010) 'Marshalling the evidence: using intersectionality in the domestic violence frame', *Social Politics: International Studies in Gender, State and Society*, 17(2): 137–158.

Norman, E. (ed) (2000) *Resiliency Enhancement: Putting the Strengths Perspective into Social Work Practice*, New York: Columbia University Press.

North, O. (2009) 'Seize the crisis', *Washington Times*, 29 March.

Nottinghamshire County Council (2014) *Adult Social Care Strategy*, Nottinghamshire.

O'Carroll, L. and Taylor, D. (2016) 'Ben Butler, the violent criminal who posed as a doting father', *The Guardian*, 21 June, www.theguardian.com/uk-news/2016/jun/21/ben-butler-violent-posed-doting-family-man

O'Higgins, M. (1992) 'Effective management: the challenges', in T. Harding (ed), *Who Owns Welfare? Questions on the Social Services Agenda*, Social Services Policy Forum Paper No 2, London: National Institute for Social Work.

Office for Budget Responsibility (OBR) (2013) 'Post-World War II debt reduction', July, https://obr.uk/box/post-world-war-ii-debt-reduction/

Office for Budget Responsibility (OBR) (2018) 'An OBR guide to welfare spending', March, https://obr.uk/docs/dlm_uploads/An-OBR-guide-to-welfare-spending-March-2018.pdf

Office of National Statistics (ONS) (2016a) 'Population estimates for UK, England and Wales, Scotland and Northern Ireland: mid-2015', www.ons.gov.uk/peoplepopulationandcommunity/populationandmigration/populationestimates/bulletins/annualmidyearpopulationestimates/mid2015#uk-population-continues-to-age

Office of National Statistics (ONS) (2016b) 'Local area life expectancy at birth', https://www.ons.gov.uk/peoplepopulationandcommunity/birthsdeathsandmarriages/lifeexpectancies/bulletins/lifeexpectancyatbirthandatage65bylocalareasinenglandandwales/2015-11-04#local-area-life-expectancy-at-birth

Office of National Statistics (ONS) (2018a) 'Time series: PS: Net Debt (excluding public sector banks) as a % of GDP: NSA', www.ons.gov.uk/economy/governmentpublicsectorandtaxes/publicsectorfinance/timeseries/hf6x/pusf

Office of National Statistics (ONS) (2018b) 'UK government debt and deficit: March 2018', www.ons.gov.uk/economy/governmentpublicsectorandtaxes/publicspending/bulletins/ukgovernmentdebtanddeficitforeurostatmaast/march2018

Ofsted (2016) *Social Care: The Report of Her Majesty's Chief Inspector of Education, Children's Services and Skills*, London: Ofsted.

Ofsted (2017) *The Multi-Agency Response to Children Living with Domestic Abuse*, London: Ofsted, Reference no 170036.

Oliver, M. (1983) *Social Work with Disabled People*, Basingstoke: Palgrave Macmillan.

Oliver, M. (1996) *Understanding Disability: From Theory to Practice*, New York: St Martin's Press.

Osborne, H. (2017) 'UK workers' wages fell 1% a year between 2008 and 2015, TUC says', *The Guardian*, 27 February, www.theguardian.com/money/2017/feb/27/uk-workers-wages-fall-one-per-cent-year-since-financial-crisis-tuc-analysis

Oxfam (2013) 'The true cost of austerity and inequality: UK case study', www.oxfam.org/sites/www.oxfam.org/files/cs-true-cost-austerity-inequality-uk-120913-en.pdf

Oxfam (2014) 'Working for the few', www.oxfam.org/en/research/working-few

Oxfam (2017) *Building a More Equal Scotland: Designing Scotland's Poverty and Inequality Commission* (Oxfam Scotland Research Report, April 2017), https://oxfamilibrary.openrepository.com/bitstream/handle/10546/620264/rr-building-more-equal-scotland-270417-en.pdf;jsessionid=56A6F527F31698F71BE7B9EA85070F41?sequence=1

Parsloe, P. (1981) *Social Services Area Teams*, London: George Allen and Unwin.

Parsloe, P. and Stevenson, O. (1978) *Social Services Teams: The Practitioners' View*, London: HMSO.

Parton, N. (1985) *The Politics of Child Abuse*, Basingstoke: Macmillan.

Parton, N. (2014) *The Politics of Child Protection*, Basingstoke: Palgrave/Macmillan.

Payne, M. (2006) *What Is Professional Social Work?* (2nd edn), Bristol: Policy Press.

Peacock, M., Bissell, P. and Owen, J. (2014) 'Shaming encounters: reflections on contemporary understandings of health', *Sociology*, 48(2): 387–402.

Pemberton, S. (2016) *Harmful Societies: Understanding Social Harm*, Bristol: Policy Press.

Penketh, L. (2000) *Tackling Institutional Racism: Anti-Racist Policies and Social Work Education and Training*, Bristol: Policy Press.

Philpott, T. (2000) *Political Correctness and Social Work*, London: IEA.

Phipps, A. (2014) *The Politics of the Body: Gender in a Neoliberal and Neoconservative Age*, London: Polity.

Pithouse, A. (1987) *Social Work: The Social Organisation of an Invisible Trade*, Aldershot: Gower.

Pollitt, C. (2003) *The Essential Public Manager*, Milton Keynes: Open University Press.

Ponnert, L. and Svensson, K. (2016) 'Standardisation – the end of professional discretion?', *European Journal of Social Work*, 19(3–4): 586–599.

Popenoe, P. (1926) *The Conservation of the Family*, Baltimore: The Williams Wery and K. Postle (eds), *Social Work: A Companion for Learning*, London: Sage.

Quinn, A. (2000) 'Reluctant learners: social work students and work with older people', *Research in Post-Compulsory Education*, 5(2): 223–237.

Ray, M., Milne, A., Beech, C., Phillips, J. Richards, S., Sullivan, M.P., Tanner, D. and Lloyd, L. (2015) 'Gerontological social work: reflections on its role, purpose and value', *British Journal of Social Work*, 45(4): 1296–1312.

Read, J. and Sanders, P. (2010) *The Causes of Mental Health Problems*, Ross-on-Wye: PCCS Books.

Rees, S. (1995) 'The fraud and the fiction', in S. Rees and G. Rodley (eds), *The Human Costs of Managerialism: Advocating the Recovery of Humanity*, Leichhardt: Pluto Press.

Reinhart, C. and Rogoff, K. (2011) 'Growth in a time of debt', *American Economic Review: Papers and Proceedings*, 100: 573–578.

Reisch, M. and Andrews, J. (2002) *The Road Not Taken: A History of Radical Social Work in the United States*, London: Routledge.

Richards, S., Sullivan, M.P., Tanner, D., Beech, C., Milne, A., Ray, M., Phillips, J. and Lloyd, L. (2014) 'On the edge of a new frontier: is gerontological social work in the UK ready to meet twenty-first-century challenges?', *British Journal of Social Work*, 44(8): 2307–2324.

Roberts, M. (2016) *The Long Recession*, Chicago: Haymarket.

Rogowski, S. (2012) 'Social work with children and families: challenges and possibilities in the neo-liberal world', *British Journal of Social Work*, 42(5): 921–940.

Rolph, S. (2002) *Reclaiming the Past: The Role of Local Mencap Societies in the Development of Community Care in East Anglia 1946–1980*, Milton Keynes: Open University Press.

Rolph, S. (2005a) *Captured on Film: The History of Norwich and District Mencap Society 1954–1990*, Milton Keynes: Open University Press.

Rolph, S. (2005b) *Building Bridges into the Community: The History of Bedford and District Society for People with Learning Disabilities 1955–1990*, Milton Keynes: Open University Press.

Rolph, S., Atkinson, D. and Walmsley, J. (2003) '"A pair of stout shoes and an umbrella": the role of mental welfare officers in delivering community care in East Anglia 1946–1970', *British Journal of Social Work* 33(3): 339–360.

Rolph, S., Atkinson, D., Mind, M., Welshman, J. (eds) (2005) *Witnesses to Change: Families, Learning Difficulties and History*, Kidderminster: BILD Publications.

Rose, S. (2004) 'Introduction: the new brain sciences', in D. Rees and S. Rose (eds) *The New Brain Sciences: Perils and Prospects*, Cambridge: Cambridge University Press.

Rose, S. and Rose, H. (2016) *Can Neuroscience Change Our Minds?* London: Polity.

Ryan, F. (2017) 'Whether its teachers' pay or disability payments – the freeze is chilling', *The Guardian*, 13 July, www.guardian.co.uk/commentisfree/2017/jul/13/public-sector-teachers-pay-benefits-freeze-carers-disabled-hardworking-britain

Ryan, S. (2013) 'Whose best interest?', mydaftlife (blog), 14 April, https://mydaftlife.com/2013/04/14/whose-best-interest/

Sanctuary, G. (1984) *After I'm Gone What Will Happen to My Handicapped Child?*, London: Souvenir Press.

Sapey, B. (1997) 'Social work tomorrow: towards a critical understanding of technology in social work', *British Journal of Social Work*, 27(6): 803–814.

Satyamurti, C. (1981) *Occupational Survival*, Oxford: Basil Blackwell.

Schraer, R. (2015) 'Councils still in funding crisis despite welcome recognition for adults' social care', *Community Care*, 1 December, www.communitycare.co.uk/2015/12/01/councils-still-funding-crisis-despite-welcome-recognition-adults-social-care/

Scientist, The (1999) 'Five years of Darwin seminars: a paradigm shift?', *Times Higher Education*, 12 March.

Scottish Government (2017) *Mental Health Strategy 2017–2027*, www.gov.scot/Resource/0051/00516047.pdf

Seebohm Committee (1968) *Report of the Committee on Local Authority and Allied Personal Social Services*, Cmnd 3703, London: HMSO.

Sen, A. (1983) 'Poor, relatively speaking', *Oxford Economic Papers*, 35: 153–169.

Sen, A. (1999) *Development as Freedom*, Oxford: Oxford University Press.

Sewell, D. (2009) 'How eugenics poisoned the welfare state', *The Spectator*, 25 November, www.spectator.co.uk/2009/11/how-eugenics-poisoned-the-welfare-state/

Shennan, V. (1980) *Our Concern: The Story of the National Association for Mentally Handicapped Children and Adults*, London: National Association for Mentally Handicapped Children and Adults.

Simpkin, M. (1983) *Trapped Within Welfare: Surviving Social Work* (2nd edn), London: Macmillan.

Singh, G. (1994) 'Anti-racist social work: political correctness or political action!', *Social Work Education*, 13(1): 26–31.

Singh, G. (2002) 'The political challenge of anti-racism in health and social care', in D. Tomlinson and W. Trew (eds), *Equalising Opportunities, Minimising Oppression*, London: Routledge.

Singh, G. (2014) 'Rethinking anti-racist social work in a neoliberal age', in M. Lavalette and L. Penketh (eds) *Race, Racism and Social Work: Contemporary Issues and Debates*, Bristol: Policy Press, pp 17–33.

Singh, G. and Cowden, S. (2009) 'The social worker as intellectual', *European Journal of Social Work*, 12(4): 1369–1457.

Singh, G. and Cowden, S. (2013) 'The new radical social work professional', in J. Parker and M. Doel (eds), *Professional Social Work*, London: SAGE/Learning Matters.

Singh, G. and Cowden, S. (2015) 'The intensification of neoliberalism and the commodification of human need – a social work perspective', *Critical and Radical Social Work*, 3(3): 375–387.

Skeggs, B. (2014) 'Legitimising slow death', blog 17, 12 June, https://values.doc.gold.ac.uk/blog/17/

Slasberg, C. and Beresford P. (2014) 'Government guidance for the Care Act: undermining ambitions for change?', *Disability and Society*, 29(10): 1677–1682.

Slasberg, C. and Beresford, P. (2017) 'Strengths-based practice: social care's latest Elixir or the next false dawn?', *Disability and Society*, 32(2): 269–273.

Slate, N. (2012) 'The Dalit Panthers: race, caste, and Black Power in India', in N. Slate (ed), *Black Power beyond Borders*, Basingstoke: Palgrave Macmillan.

Smale, G., Tuson, G. and Statham, D. (2000) *Social Work and Social Problems: Working Towards Social Inclusion and Social Change*, Basingstoke: Macmillan.

Smith, A. (1776/1982) *An Inquiry into the Nature and Causes of the Wealth of Nations* (Vol 2), Harmondsworth: Penguin.

Smith, M. and Cree, V. (eds) (2018) *Social Work in a Changing Scotland*, London: Routledge.

Social Care Institute for Excellence (SCIE) (2010) *Personalisation Briefing: Implications for Social Workers in Adults' Services*, London: SCIE.

Social Care Institute for Excellence (SCIE) (2017) *Named Social Worker Learning Report*, London: SCIE, www.scie.org.uk/files/social-work/named-social-worker/nsw-learning-report.pdf

Social Work Action Network (SWAN) (2013) *In Defence of Social Work: Why Michael Gove Is Wrong*, London: SWAN.

Social Work Task Force (2009) *Building a Safe, Confident Future: The Final Report of the Social Work Task Force*, London: Department for Children, Schools and Families.

Sokoloff, N. and Dupont, I. (2005) 'Domestic violence at the intersections of race, class and gender', *Violence Against Women*, 11(1): 38–64.

Spektorowski, A. and Mizrachi, E. (2004) 'Eugenics and the welfare state in Sweden: the politics of social margins and the idea of a productive society', *Journal of Contemporary History*, 39(3): 333–352, http://www.jstor.org/stable/3180732

Stewart, M. (2016) *Cash Not Care: The Planned Demolition of the UK Welfare State*, London: New Generation Publishing.

Stiglitz, J. (2008) 'The end of neo-liberalism?', *Project Syndicate*, 7, n.p.

Sunker, H. and Otto, H-U. (eds) (1997) *Education and Fascism: Political Identity and Social Education in Nazi Germany*, London: Taylor and Francis.

Tax Justice UK (2018) 'Tax Justice UK submission to parliamentary inquiry into tax avoidance and evasion', 13 June, www.taxjustice.uk/blog/tax-justice-uk-submission-to-parliamentary-inquiry-into-tax-avoidance-and-evasion

Taylor-Gooby, P. (2012) 'Root and branch restructuring to achieve major cuts: the social policy programme of the 2010 UK coalition government', *Social Policy & Administration*, 46(1): 61–82.

Thomas, C. (2007) *Sociologies of Disability and Illness: Contested Ideas in Disability Studies and Medical Sociology*, Basingstoke: Palgrave Macmillan.

Thompson, N. (2011) *Promoting Equality*, London: Palgrave Macmillan.

Thomson, M. (1998) *The Problem of Mental Deficiency: Eugenics, Democracy and Social Policy in Britain c.1870–1959*, Oxford: Oxford University Press.

Tilley, E. (2006) 'The voluntary sector', in J. Welshman and J. Walmsley (eds), *Community Care in Perspective: Care, Control and Citizenship*, London: Palgrave Macmillan, pp 219–232.

Titmuss, R. (1963) *Essays on the Welfare State*, London: Allen and Unwin.

Tobis, D. (2013) *From Pariahs to Partners: How Parents and their Allies Changed New York City's Child Welfare System*, Oxford: Oxford University Press.

Tombs, A. and Tombs, M. (2005) 'A life of campaigning', in S. Rolph, D. Atkinson, M. Nind and J. Welshman (eds), *Witnesses to Change: Families, Learning Difficulties and History*, Kidderminster: BILD, pp 277–286.

Toye, R. (2013) 'From "consensus" to "common ground": the rhetoric of the postwar settlement and its collapse', *Journal of Contemporary History*, 48(1): 3–23.

Toynbee, P. and Walker, D. (2017) *Dismembered: How the Attack on the State Harms Us All*, London: Guardian Books.

Trading Economics (2018) 'Country list government debt to GDP', https://tradingeconomics.com/country-list/government-debt-to-gdp

Trevithick, P. (2014) 'Humanising managerialism: reclaiming emotional reasoning, intuition, the relationship, and knowledge and skills in social work', *Journal of Social Work Practice*, 28(3): 287–311.

UNISON (2014) *Community and Voluntary Services in the Age of Austerity*, London: UNISON, www.unison.org.uk/content/uploads/2013/11/On-line-Catalogue219293.pdf

Wacquant, L. (2010) 'Crafting the neoliberal state: workfare, prisonfare and social insecurity', *Sociological Forum*, 25(2): 197–220.

Waggoner, M.R and Uller, T. (2015) 'Epigenetic determinism in science and society', *New Genetics and Society*, 34(2): 177–195.

Walker, H. (2002) *A Genealogy of Equality: The Curriculum for Social Work Education and Training*, London: Routledge.

Wallace, S., Nazroo, J. and Becares, L. (2016) 'Cumulative effect of racial discrimination on the mental health of ethnic minorities in the United Kingdom', *American Journal of Public Health*, 106(7): 1294–1300.

Walmsley, J. (1995) *Gender, Caring and Learning Disability*, unpublished PhD thesis, Milton Keynes: Open University.

Walmsley, J. (2000) 'Straddling boundaries: the changing role of the voluntary sector', in L. Brigham, D. Atkinson, M. Jackson, S. Rolph and J .Walmsley (eds), *Crossing Boundaries: Change and Continuity in the History of Learning Disability*, Kidderminster: BILD.

Walmsley, J., Rolph, S. and Atkinson, D. (1999) 'Community care and mental deficiency, 1913–1945' in P. Bartlett and D. Wright (eds), *Outside the Walls of the Asylum*, London: Athlone.

Walmsley, J., Tilley, E., Bardsley, J. and Dumbleton, S. (2017) 'The changing face of parent advocacy: a long view', *Disability & Society*, 32(9): 1366–1386.

Wanless, D. (2006) *Securing Good Care for Older People: Taking a Long-Term View*, London: King's Fund.

Ward, L. (1989) 'For better, for worse', in A. Brechin and J. Walmsley (eds), *Making Connections*, London: Hodder and Stoughton, pp 188–198.

Watkins, S. (2010) 'Shifting sands', *New Left Review*, 61, https://newleftreview.org/issues/II61/articles/susan-watkins-shifting-sands

Watt, N. (2013a) 'David Cameron makes leaner state a permanent goal', *The Guardian*, 12 November, www.theguardian.com/politics/2013/nov/11/david-cameron-policy-shift-leaner-efficient-state

Watt, N. (2013b) 'Boris Johnson invokes Thatcher spirit with greed is good speech', *The Guardian*, 27 November 2013, www.theguardian.com/politics/2013/nov/27/boris-johnson-thatcher-greed-good

Weinstein, J. (ed) (2014) *Mental Health*, Bristol: Policy Press.

Welshman, J. and Walmsley. J. (eds) (2006) *Care, Control and Citizenship*, London: Palgrave.

West, K. (2013) 'The grip of personalization in adult social care: between managerial domination and fantasy', *Critical Social Policy*, 33(4): 638–657.

White, V. (2009) 'Quiet challenges? Professional practice in modernised social work' in J. Harris and V. White (eds) (2009) *Modernising Social Work: Critical Considerations*, Bristol: Policy Press.

White, S.J. and Wastell, D. (2016) 'Epigenetics prematurely born(e): social work and the malleable gene', *British Journal of Social Work*, 47(8): 2256–2272.

Wilkinson, R. and Pickett, K. (2009) *The Spirit Level: Why More Equal Societies Always Do Better*, London: Penguin.

Wilkinson, R. and Pickett, K. (2010) *The Spirit Level: Why Equality is Better for Everyone*, London: Penguin.

Williams, R. (1975) *Keywords: A Vocabulary of Culture and Society*, London: Fontana.

Wilson, K., Ruch, G., Lymbery, M. and Cooper, A. (2011) *Social Work: An Introduction to Contemporary Practice* (2nd edn), Harlow: Pearson Education.

World Health Organisation (WHO) (2017) 'Depression', www.who.int/mediacentre/factsheets/fs369/en/

Wright, D. and Case, R. (2017) 'Living standards squeeze tightens despite pay rises and tax cuts', York: Joseph Rowntree Foundation, www.jrf.org.uk/press/living-standards-squeeze-tightens-despite-pay-rises-and-tax-cuts

Young, I.M. (2013) 'Five faces of oppression' in *The Community Development Reader*, London: Routledge, pp 346–355.

Index